JEWISH THEOLOGY FOR A POSTMODERN AGE

THE LITTMAN LIBRARY OF
JEWISH CIVILIZATION

Dedicated to the memory of
LOUIS THOMAS SIDNEY LITTMAN
*who founded the Littman Library for the love of God
and as an act of charity in memory of his father*
JOSEPH AARON LITTMAN
and to the memory of
ROBERT JOSEPH LITTMAN
who continued what his father Louis had begun

יהא זכרם ברוך

'Get wisdom, get understanding:
Forsake her not and she shall preserve thee'
PROV. 4: 5

*The Littman Library of Jewish Civilization is a registered UK charity
Registered charity no. 1000784*

JEWISH THEOLOGY FOR A POSTMODERN AGE

◆

MIRIAM FELDMANN KAYE

London

The Littman Library of Jewish Civilization
in association with Liverpool University Press

The Littman Library of Jewish Civilization
Registered office: 4th floor, 7–10 Chandos Street, London WIG 9DQ

in association with Liverpool University Press
4 Cambridge Street, Liverpool L69 7ZU, UK
www.liverpooluniversitypress.co.uk/littman

Managing Editor: Connie Webber

Distributed in North America by
Oxford University Press Inc., 198 Madison Avenue
New York, NY 10016, USA

First published in paperback 2022

Catalogue records for this book are available from the
British Library and the Library of Congress

ISBN 978–1–800856–23–3

Publishing co-ordinator: Janet Moth
Copy-editing: Ezra Margulies, Connie Webber, and Mark Newby
Proof-reading: Andrew Kirk
Index: Florian Ehrensperger
Designed and typeset by Pete Russell, Faringdon, Oxon.

Printed and bound by CPI Group (UK) Ltd, Croydon, CR0 4YY

I dedicate this book to Marc and our children

To Marc
*in reciprocation for his unwavering belief in my travails
and his perpetual support.*

To our children
*in gratitude for the enchanting perspective on life and truth with which they bless me.
I have the delightful privilege of watching their emergent philosophical minds develop.
I only apologize to them that there are no pictures in this book, notwithstanding their demands.
I would like to thank each child in turn:*

To Odeliya
a prodigy of insight, whose entire life has been interwoven with this project.

To Revaya
*source of pure energy, who at six weeks old accompanied me
to submit my doctoral proposal.*

To Be'eri
wellspring of joy, whom I held in my arms at my doctoral ceremony.

To Elisha
*maestro of creative play, whom I carried within me during the submission of this book.
May you bring blessing to your people and to the world around you.*

*I conclude with the blessing expressed on reaching a milestone,
which in this instance reflects the joy of publishing this book:*

ברוך שההחייינו וקיימנו והגיענו לזמן הזה

*Blessed be the One who has given us life, sustained us,
and brought us to this day.*

ACKNOWLEDGEMENTS

I AM GRATEFUL to the University of Haifa and the Israeli Ministry for Absorption for a generous grant and prize. I thank the Lady Davis Fellowship Trust and the Mexican Friends of the Hebrew University of Jerusalem for generous postdoctoral fellowships. I also thank the Department of Comparative Religion and the Department of Jewish Thought at the Hebrew University for housing my research and teaching. I am grateful to the Truman Research Institute for an associate postdoctoral fellowship at the Hebrew University. I deeply appreciate the rigorous training in theological studies I received at the Divinity Faculty of the University of Cambridge.

For providing warm and conducive study environments my thanks go to the Van Leer Jerusalem Institute. Thanks are also extended to the Institute for the Writings of Rav Shagar for allowing me access to little-known publications, transcripts, and forthcoming works. Words cannot express my thanks to Professor Tamar Ross for the learning, mentorship, and stalwart support I have received from her for many years. I am honoured to call myself her disciple.

I would like to thank Rabbi Lord Jonathan Sacks for helping me think through the concept at its inception and Professor David Ford for nurturing my initiation into the world of theology. I thank the following illustrious scholars who have at various points contributed to my thinking: Alan Brill, Menachem Fisch, Yehuda Gellman, Steven Kepnes, Peter Ochs, Naftali Rothenberg, and Laurie Zoloth. I hasten to add that not all of them agree with my premise that a postmodern reality should be accepted, let alone be amalgamated into Jewish thought. Nonetheless, I have gained much from their scholarship and critiques, which have been integrated into the book. In addition I thank my doctoral supervisors, Menachem Kellner, Moshe Lavee of the University of Haifa, and Hanoch Ben-Pazi of Bar-Ilan University, for their acumen, guidance, and patience. I am grateful to special friends and colleagues who have read the manuscript and made many helpful comments.

I thank my students in the Department of Jewish Thought at the Hebrew University of Jerusalem for their responses and ideas, all of which have served to hone my thinking. Their individual and collective theological crises, a consequence of the collapse of the notion of truth, are my primary motivation. I promised I would write down how I envisioned a way forward despite the popular conception that this collapse was linked to a breakdown of religious values. And so this book is aimed at them and their many contemporaries.

This publication has been made possible through the immense dedication of the Littman Library of Jewish Civilization. I would like to thank, in particular, Connie Webber for her extraordinary leadership on this project, spanning conceptual elements, painstaking editing, and comprehensive advice. I am indebted to Ezra Margulies for his scrupulous and remarkable editing, which went way beyond the call of duty. The work of Janet Moth, publishing co-ordinator, who ensured that everything progressed smoothly, has been crucial to this endeavour. I also thank Mark Newby for the final copy-edit and Pete Russell for his expert design of the book jacket and for the typesetting. In a broader sense, I recognize the pioneering commitment of Littman to exploring a Jewish theology of the future.

I cannot conjure up in words the thanks I owe to my parents, Elizabeth and Mark Feldmann, for the education which I was privileged to receive, and for the values of curiosity and discipline which were instrumental in bringing this project to fruition.

CONTENTS

NOTE ON TRANSLITERATION

THE TRANSLITERATION of Hebrew in this book reflects consideration of the type of book it is, in terms of its content, purpose, and readership. The system adopted therefore reflects a broad approach to transcription, rather than the narrower approaches found in the *Encyclopaedia Judaica* or other systems developed for text-based or linguistic studies. The aim has been to reflect the pronunciation prescribed for modern Hebrew, rather than the spelling or Hebrew word structure, and to do so using conventions that are generally familiar to the English-speaking reader.

In accordance with this approach, no attempt is made to indicate the distinctions between *alef* and *ayin*, *tet* and *taf*, *kaf* and *kuf*, *sin* and *samekh*, since these are not relevant to pronunciation; likewise, the *dagesh* is not indicated except where it affects pronunciation. Following the principle of using conventions familiar to the majority of readers, however, transcriptions that are well established have been retained even when they are not fully consistent with the transliteration system adopted. On similar grounds, the *tsadi* is rendered by 'tz' in such familiar words as barmitzvah. Likewise, the distinction between *ḥet* and *khaf* has been retained, using *ḥ* for the former and *kh* for the latter; the associated forms are generally familiar to readers, even if the distinction is not actually borne out in pronunciation, and for the same reason the final *heh* is indicated too. As in Hebrew, no capital letters are used, except that an initial capital has been retained in transliterating titles of published works (for example, *Shulḥan arukh*).

Since no distinction is made between *alef* and *ayin*, they are indicated by an apostrophe only in intervocalic positions where a failure to do so could lead an English-speaking reader to pronounce the vowel-cluster as a diphthong—as, for example, in *ha'ir*—or otherwise mispronounce the word. An apostrophe is also used, for the same reason, to disambiguate the pronunciation of other English vowel clusters, as for example in *mizbe'aḥ*.

The *sheva na* is indicated by an *e*—*perikat ol*, *reshut*—except, again, when established convention dictates otherwise.

The *yod* is represented by *i* when it occurs as a vowel (*bereshit*), by *y* when it occurs as a consonant (*yesodot*), and by *yi* when it occurs as both (*yisra'el*).

Names have generally been left in their familiar forms, even when this is inconsistent with the overall system.

INTRODUCTION

THE PURPOSE of this book is to put forward a compelling theology for the postmodern, relativist age. My aim is to confront the crisis of Jewish theology today, which is premised on a growing ambivalence towards the idea of absolute truth, perpetuated by postmodern cultural and philosophical critiques. It has become difficult, if not impossible, to argue in favour of one's own world-view or way of life as preferable to those of others. Why? A central principle of postmodernism is that culture and its linguistic parameters determine what is true and that therefore there can no longer be any objective truth. How, then, can one particular religious culture demonstrate its greater 'truthfulness' than that of others? Multiple aspects of contemporary Jewish life are plagued with these questions. A Jewish educator might ask: 'How can I teach Jewish values if all beliefs are of equal value?' A parent will ask: 'How can I teach my child right from wrong?' The religious leader might enquire: 'How can Jewish practice, belief, and ritual remain compelling for an entire generation raised on relativism?' Indeed, how can Judaism compete in the supermarket of ideas available today?

The new postmodern reality is often deeply problematic. However, I seek to turn this problem on its head and ask what postmodernism has to offer. Could it actually ward off the late modern malaise that stultified strong religious identity? Many scholars are addressing these issues in several areas of Jewish life, but I concern myself specifically with the theological implications of engaging positively with radical postmodern critiques. I use the term 'theological' to refer to discussions and explanations dealing with conceptions of God. Unlike social scientists, who speak of religion from the outside, theologians treat their subject from the inside—from the wellspring of religious belief. Theology concerns itself with experience: with the ethereal, the ephemeral, the conceptualization of the divine of yore through historical narrative and its implications for contemporary existence.

I explore the possibility of a theology that will enrich the heartland of religion through examining and building on the fruitful efforts of others. The questions that lie at the heart of this study are: What responses are possible to the onslaught of science on the quest for meaning and truth? How might they be conceptualized as a potential resource for rejuvenating this quest? What implications would this have for religion? What, then, could a postmodern Jewish theology look like? There is an urgent need to deal with these challenges, particularly for those believers whose world has been rocked to its foundations over recent years. This book is a gift to them.

Conceptual Backdrop: The Enigma of Postmodernism

The momentous events which shook the twentieth century—two horrific world wars, the Holocaust, Hiroshima and Nagasaki, postcolonialism, and the collapse of communism—thrust Western civilization into the postmodern age. Totalitarian regimes built on absolutist values have disintegrated, often giving way to genocide and large-scale destruction. Additional developments, such as globalization, the expansion of the free market economy, the increasing use of social media, and so on, offer an increased, pervasive, and radical exposure to alternative cultures and belief systems. In modern times, science claimed exclusive knowledge about the world. The role religion played was changing fast: science had called into question some of its central functions.

These phenomena carry great significance, as they raise doubts about the possibility of an ultimate truth and, in turn, about the wisdom of continued commitment to a particular religious belief system. As a result of these phenomena, the very notion of certainty came under severe attack from twentieth-century thinkers. The optimism of modernity was shattered, giving way to a philosophical mood which proclaimed the death of God, the end of metaphysics, and the impossibility of absolute knowledge. On this basis, many forecast the complete demise of faith.

Those predictions, however, have proved misguided. The charted rise of religion in the twenty-first century thwarted the theory of secularization.[1] The inability of religionists to justify their beliefs on rationalist grounds no longer constitutes an obstacle to continued religiosity.[2] Indeed, individual spirituality has become a legitimate means through which people can approach and make sense of the world. An unwillingness or inability to prove religious beliefs to be dependent on external criteria—empirically and con-

---

[1] Sociology has buttressed this theory, with new research attesting to the rise of religious affiliation in Western society whether it be to established religions or to new religious movements.

[2] Simultaneously a turn to fundamentalist belief has served as another conduit for rejecting rationalism as seen in the demographical rise in ultra-Orthodox affiliation, which now supersedes by far that of all other Jewish denominations.

ceptually—has led to a focus on religion as an internal spiritual mechanism. A classic anthropological expression of the appreciation of the 'internal' has come through a breakdown of the idea of 'structuralism' ('poststructuralism'), which in major respects has corresponded with the rise of postmodernism.[3] This new focus finds various forms of expression in the Jewish world, in both Israel and the diaspora. It includes the emergence of neo-hasidism; the growing popularity of meditation techniques, such as mindfulness, yoga, and retreats; and the appearance of a vast body of self-help literature published under the guise of Jewish thought. While some have criticized these phenomena as New Age nonsense, others treat them as important attempts to reconfigure their own faith, to fill the void once occupied by theology.

This realization concerns different people in different ways. I would even claim that those for whom such reflections do not initially resonate, who still find meaning in traditional Jewish theology, might do well to consider the serious implications of such trends and their intricate connections with postmodernism.

Objectives

Many illustrious scholars have explored the subject of modernism and Jewish theology from multiple perspectives. Yet there is little scholarly literature which deals with Judaism and postmodernism. This is often related to a repulsion from even the term 'postmodern' as synonymous with 'relativism'—the position that all truth-claims have equal value. It is also likely due to the verbose, obscure (often downright unintelligible), and radical nature of many foundational postmodern works. Their loquacious style, full of plays on words, convoluted double entendres, and seemingly irrelevant references, do them no favours in winning readers over. This style of writing, however, echoes one of the central claims of postmodernists: that logical and objective reasoning are human constructs and in no way express any truth about the way things are. This phenomenon of postmodernism has appealed to some religious thinkers, to a greater or lesser extent, and is generally presented as something of a paralysing conundrum.

[3] Claude Lévi-Strauss, one of the first structuralist anthropologists, travelled to Africa to observe the Nambikwara tribe. He wrote of their rituals and activities and compared their practices with those of the Western world, claiming that at the root of all communities and cultures lies a common core of activity and belief. This method was refuted by the 'poststructuralists'—Jacques Derrida, Gilles Deleuze, Michel Foucault, Georges Bataille, and Emmanuel Levinas—who argued that the concept of a single or universal set of features to which language refers was fundamentally mistaken and that there are no ways to generalize what is signified. The commonality between postmodernism and poststructuralism is that

In my view, Jewish scholars must engage with different models of post-modern literature if they wish to articulate compelling responses to relativism and counter the threat it poses to the transmission of Jewish values and beliefs. It is in this direction that I hope to take the discussion forward. For this purpose, I have attempted to submit Jewish theology to the critique of a broad range of postmodern philosophers (many of whom deride the term or are associated with other philosophical currents as well), from Martin Heidegger and Ludwig Wittgenstein to Jean-Luc Marion and Slavoj Žižek. I present these authors' main ideas, as well as their theological implications, in order to lay out some potential patterns of positive Jewish engagement with postmodernism. In some cases, I will examine certain aspects of late modernism, including existentialism and hermeneutics, but these will be considered only as a means to address the main issue.

I deal with this subject primarily from a philosophical perspective: this book is neither a sociological study of contemporary trends among young Jews nor an examination of those biblical or talmudic sources which somehow converge with certain features of postmodernism. Rather, I am interested in the philosophical core of contemporary Jewish thought. This is a methodological as well as personal decision. Philosophy is a discipline that has long engaged with the fundamental questions of our existence: How did we come to be here? Is there a purpose to life? What is that purpose? What is my role in the world? What is right and wrong? How do I access the categories of right and wrong? Is there a God? How should I live? And so on and so forth. This book addresses the possibility of a theological reconciliation between contemporary Jewish thought and postmodern ideas. To this effect, I seek out models of appropriation of complicated postmodern theories into an already well-developed hermeneutical and scholarly Jewish tradition. This in itself could form an important link in the analysis of the development of Jewish thought and in particular of the ways in which Jewish thinkers have tried to incorporate contemporaneous philosophical and cultural trends into their understanding of the Jewish tradition. I consider here Jewish theology as an evolving sociocultural set of beliefs that have incorporated, over the centuries, many 'foreign' influences. Accordingly, the integration of postmodernist discourse constitutes merely another challenge. These efforts can present us with an opportunity to redefine and reinforce Jewish theology, rather than to tear it asunder.

By focusing on philosophy, my aim is to bring current trends in the philosophy of religion to the forefront of contemporary Jewish discourse.

each culture functions on its own terms. Postmodernism takes this to be important in the case of the turn 'inwards' in contemporary religion. See e.g. Saussure, *Course in General Linguistics*.

As part of this, I offer translations of large excerpts of Israeli literature on Jewish theology previously unavailable in English. I hope that this will have stimulating and far-reaching consequences. I hope this book will ultimately help bring the different worlds of contemporary Jewish thought closer in order to expand and enrich our understanding of the subject.

On this note, for those who reject the premises of our postmodern age, I will state from the outset that it is not my objective to persuade them to accept postmodern ideas. This book is concerned with theological attempts to respond to postmodernism, rather than with a wholesale defence of post-modernist ideas. I do believe, however, that whether one takes postmod-ernism to be inherently problematic or merely inconsequential, this book offers the opportunity to rethink those assumptions. I believe that, while the terms used to describe postmodern ideas are often complicated, their mean-ings are nonetheless fathomable to those with enquiring minds. I therefore do not apologize for being too philosophical. In the process, I strive to pro-vide the necessary explanations for all complex terms and ideas in order to make this work accessible to interested non-specialists. Yet when these do become difficult, I implore the reader to battle on, as they are crucial in deter-mining the role of theology in contemporary Jewish thought.

Concepts and Terminology

The term 'postmodern' was popularized in 1979 with the publication of Jean-François Lyotard's essay, *La Condition postmoderne*. However, Lyotard was by no means the first person to make use of the term. Postmodernism refers to a complex web of ideas which developed in the twentieth and twenty-first cen-turies and express an innate dissatisfaction with the certainty of knowledge —or epistemology—claimed by modernists. One key target of postmodern thought is metaphysics—a branch of philosophy that originated in ancient Greece (and was discussed in depth by Aristotle) which describes the exis-tence of concepts, facts, or beings beyond the physical world (hence the appel-lation, 'meta-physics'). The notion that God possesses metaphysical existence —an identity and a reason to exist—is one prime example of the application of metaphysics to theology. The metaphysical God is a universal being, defined by presence, or essence.

Postmodernists typically reject grand narratives that purport to apply to all of humanity when in reality they describe the culture of one specific group. While there are in fact (at least) two different streams of con-temporary philosophy—'continental' (French and German) and 'analytic'

(American and British)[4]—both are characterized by many of the thought patterns mentioned above. As I pursue my argument, I will introduce some additional concepts, notably deconstructionism and the problem of language.

Postmodernists associate themselves with a mode of thought that can be characterized by the following philosophical assumptions:

- That ways of thinking once perceived to be 'logical' or 'rational' hold no superior qualities to other discursive methods.

- That the assumption that certain systems of thought can be objective is just one of a multitude of ways to conceive of knowledge.

- That what makes up the 'rules' of each language is not derived *a fortiori* from a universal source but rather from collective human agreement on terms and ideas (which they term a 'language game').

- That each culture is governed by its own 'metanarratives' (subjective versions of history), grounded in the ideologies which govern those perceptions, thus confounding from the outset the assumptions involved in making universal truth-claims.

- That in light of this mass of overlapping narratives which emerge from the negation of metanarratives, no single idea can be entertained as universally 'true'. On these grounds, the ideas associated with rationalism, metaphysical certainty, and an ability to prove epistemological assumptions are negated in favour of the particular, multiple voices that make up our reality.

The Encounter of Postmodernism with Theology

The postmodernist critique is broad and variegated, but one of its fundamental themes is the confounding of the notion of absolute truth and the possibility of knowing certain facts about the world altogether. These principles undermine certain core religious beliefs, including those of a 'provable' God and a 'revelation' to humankind. In a wider sense, a number of contentions put forward by postmodernists seem to pose a threat to theology, such as:

- The assertion that one particular ideology espoused by one specific group comprises a mere drop in an intellectual ocean of ideas. How can this ideology claim any form of superiority over the myriads of alternative ones?

---

[4] Furthermore, Americans tend to concentrate on pragmatism (William James, Charles Sanders Peirce) whereas the British concentrate on empiricism (Bertrand Russell).

- The assertion that religious language no longer holds the key to describe or access reality. How can a single language, that happens to be one's own, purport to convey universal or absolute truths?

- The assertion that the tools for empirical verification have been shattered: many postmodernists would assert that a logical thought system is no more valuable or trustworthy than any other. If this claim is viewed as persuasive, religion would no longer require logical justification.

As I stated earlier, these challenges prompted many 'post-liberals' to predict the end of religion in the postmodern era.

Yet harnessing and applying postmodern discourse to the theological realm immediately signals a need for caution. Should religious perceptions of God not assume an 'existence' defined by metaphysics? More specifically, should the textual and oral accounts of the Jewish versions of history not be held as 'true'? If not, then what of the foundational events of the religion, such as the biblical accounts of Creation and the Sinaitic revelation? How can a truth-claim based on the unique nature of its propositions be sustained in the face of a seemingly relativistic zeitgeist in which no single world-view is any 'truer' or 'better' than any other? The questions that arise from this application of postmodernism to Jewish theology are framed in this book as potentially competing systems of thought.

The appropriation of postmodernist elements in Jewish thought is made up of a multifarious fusion of conceptual, ideological, and political facets. While admitting this plethora of disciplines, this study will, where necessary, make links and important connections to social and cultural phenomena surrounding the encounter of traditional and often Orthodox thinking with postmodernism. Given the complexity of postmodernism, it will be difficult to offer clear distinctions between these strands.

Theology and Neo-Pragmatism

I take the view that Judaism depends upon a theology that propounds a set of ideas about God and the world.[5] This would include the 'existence of God' in some way and the involvement of this God in the world, manifested through the intermediary of the Jewish people. The nature of the divine–human relationship is witnessed by an unbroken chain of the written word, from the Torah given to Moses at Mount Sinai (Chapter 3) through centuries of rabbinic interpretation.[6] The Hebrew Bible is thus often viewed as heralding a

---

[5] See Caplan, *Orthodoxy in the New Times* (Heb.), 58–66.
[6] See e.g. N. Solomon, *Torah from Heaven*, 33–46.

unique message for a single religious collective. The legal permutations of adherence to biblical and talmudic principles, perceived to be at the root of a halakhic system perceived as authoritative, are sacrosanct.

Each generation has seen new and profound interpretations of these ideas.[7] More recently there has been a perceived dearth of empirical verification underpinning contemporary responses to theological categories (often associated with certain twentieth-century phenomena—theodicean questions posed in the aftermath of the Holocaust[8] or continental existentialism, which emphasized the role of personal 'experience' in religion).[9] Accordingly existentialism provides a convincing argument for religion, much as theology did in the pre-modern era. Praxis, therefore, some would claim, is a sufficient condition for sustaining Jewish religion in view of the epistemological shadow cast over metaphysical certainty.[10] I sense that a shift has been made towards a more pragmatic way of Jewish thought in the light of postmodern ideas. As a result of this theological vacuum, many believe that Judaism is primarily an ethical system and a model for textual analysis.[11] Some have come to argue that ethics itself is a form of theology. Such a position is asso-

[7] This is not to say that epistemological doubt never reared its head in the pre-modern era. It has been argued that the 'theological principles' of Jewish thought have always been in flux (see Shapiro, *The Limits of Orthodox Theology*; Kellner, *Must a Jew Believe Anything?*). However, even though this is not the place for a historical study of epistemology in Jewish thought, it would not be wrong to assert that features of radical postmodernism pose an epistemological problem more acute than earlier ones, as will be suggested in Chapter 2. Steven Kepnes's introduction to the subject of postmodernism and Judaism addresses the originality of the problems inherent in postmodern critique (Kepnes (ed.), *Interpreting Judaism in a Postmodern Age*).

[8] For an overview of late modern responses to the Holocaust, typified by non-theological arguments, see Braiterman, *(God) After Auschwitz*. However, raising the question of theodicy, and thus forcing an answer, offers a typically modern application of logical questions to the metaphysical realm which is debunked by late modern and postmodern thinkers (e.g. Paul Ricœur, Theodor Adorno, Emmanuel Levinas), and this call to think beyond theodicy is one theme they have in common (see Pinnock, *Beyond Theodicy*, 147–50).

[9] See W. E. Kaufman, *Contemporary Jewish Philosophies*, 25–94. Kaufman deals with European Jewish thinkers. Israeli Orthodox Jewish theological respondents are difficult to locate, since writings after the Holocaust are of a historical or sociological nature.

[10] In general philosophy, the move to focus on social theory as a definitive shift away from metaphysical thinking has also typified the late modern era. For example, Regina Ammicht-Quinn argues that a focus on society has absolved us from posing metaphysical questions—not least the unrelenting questions of theodicy—since Voltaire's *Candide* (1759) and injects life with ultimate meaning more than theorizing about what is 'out there' (see Ammicht-Quinn, *Von Lissabon bis Auschwitz*, 250–60).

[11] Objections to empirical verification and specifically the realism of theology have been raised by Martin Buber (I–Thou) and Emmanuel Levinas (the Other), who sought through ethical theory to liberate the metaphysical fixation and thus could in some senses be classified as the first modern Jewish pragmatists. Christians who took a similar turn were D. Z. Phillips (to whom Ross refers more than once), Jürgen Moltmann, and Johann Baptist Metz, among others.

ciated with the term 'neo-pragmatism'. Neo-pragmatism refers to more re-cent variations of pragmatism which integrate certain aspects of postmodern thought.[12] Pragmatism, which is often associated with modernism, is a philo-sophical approach that argues that practice represents the paradigmatic arbiter in contemporary life.[13] Jewish neo-pragmatists focus on practical issues: halakhah, Zionism or post-Zionism,[14] education,[15] gender, the role of women,[16] or the digital age.[17]

Neo-pragmatism is identified with post-liberalism,[18] in that it places an emphasis on practice because of the unreliable epistemological foundations of modernism.[19] I will employ the term 'neo-pragmatist'[20] to refer to an important trend in contemporary Jewish scholarship, associated with Peter Ochs and Hannah Hashkes, who define their position as post-liberal.[21] In order to understand this position more, I refer to the neo-pragmatist Jewish thinker Avi Sagi. Sagi acknowledges the theological alienation of modernity and the collapse, and consequent rejection, of metaphysics. He writes of an 'alternative Jewish philosophy': 'Its starting point is Jewish life rather than some imagined speculative theory . . . Jewish philosophy is Jewish philosoph-ical "doing".'[22] Sagi claims that theology is a metaphysical enterprise and

[12] I am not referring to the 'post-Christian' theology with which Don Cupitt is often associated (see Cupitt, *Above Us Only Sky* and *Taking Leave of God*). Cupitt calls this move 'taking leave of God'. So, too, with Marc C. Taylor's 'a/theology' (Taylor, *Erring*). The second strand suggests an integration of postmodernist discourse into theology (called the 'end of foundationalism' by Hyman) that actually opens up the way for the return of theology (Hyman, *The Predicament of Postmodern Theology*, 2).

[13] One oft-cited religious pragmatist is William James (see James, *Pragmatism*, 42–57).

[14] For an overview, see the Eretz Acheret website (accessed 24 Apr. 2018).

[15] See Shay, 'Research in Jewish Thought and the Postmodern Discourse' (Heb.).

[16] Barel, 'On Patriarchy and the Voices of Women' (Heb.); Fuchs, 'Her Own Voice and Torah Study' (Heb.).

[17] Cahana, 'The Internet as Metaphor' (Heb.); Gur-Zev, *Education in the Postmodern Age* (Heb.).

[18] For an expansion on this claim, see Rorty, 'Remarks on Deconstruction and Pragmatism'.

[19] In this sense pragmatists have strong links with the 'logical positivists' (otherwise known as analytic philosophers), who tend to claim that metaphysics has become meaningless and that in the light of this a formalist, scientific language of philosophy must be developed using other methods of evidence such as mathematical equations and science.

[20] Avinoam Rosenak discusses pragmatism 'in contrast to classical foundations in Jewish thought where there is no one absolute truth' (Rosenak, *Halakhah as an Agent of Change* (Heb.), 66). Rosenak also describes Ross as a pragmatist who was influenced by John Dewey and William James, but I do not concur, since, as I will demonstrate, her central interests lie in formulating a new theology rather than only resituating halakhic praxis. See also Sagi et al. (eds.), *Judaism Inside and Out* (Heb.).

[21] Christian theological trends, like their Jewish counterparts, have also seen a neo-pragmatic turn, which is now experiencing a theological backlash, notably by the Radical Orthodox movement, Richard Kearney's 'anatheism', and John Caputo's return to a messianic religion.   [22] Sagi, 'Toward a Jewish Philosophy', 407.

must therefore be relinquished as the primary focus of Jewish existence. Instead, a shift must be made towards placing praxis, and to a lesser extent theology, at the centre. This is probably due to doubts that theology will be able to withstand the challenges that postmodernism brings. The notion that theology should be pushed to the side because praxis is a sufficient condition for Jewish existence, in my view, signifies the demise of theology, which cannot exist without metaphysical properties. I resist neo-pragmatism in its favouring of praxis as a substitute for theology, which, as I have stated, must be addressed in tandem with other trends. To this end I shall now examine another couple of examples of scepticism regarding neo-pragmatic Jewish thought.

Critiques of Neo-Pragmatism

While it could be argued that an emphasis on praxis is characteristic of a postmodern approach (take, for example, Richard Rorty's concern with societal 'freedom' as opposed to what comprises 'truth'[23] or Jacques Derrida's objection to 'non-situated thinking'[24]), there are also plenty of theologians who have returned to the theological realm and found it untouched by the very postmodern theory which had initially influenced them away from it.[25] I would like to cite two examples of such thinkers. The first is Gili Zivan, and the second is Cass Fisher.

Gili Zivan has produced an excellent study in Hebrew of four scholars against a backdrop of fundamental postmodern ideas, notably language games and deconstructionism, critically analysing the potential for metaphysical theology in postmodernism's shadow. It is an important contribution in Israel to the very new subject of postmodernism and Judaism. I concur with her on many of the issues that postmodernism presents; at the same time I am of the opinion that (taking into account the substantial differences between their positions) those scholars she chose to study would likely have identified as neo-pragmatists: Yeshayahu Leibowitz, Eliezer Goldman,[26] David Hartman, and Joseph B. Soloveitchik.[27] Her work highlights the areas of concern of each of them, such as Jewish peoplehood, halakhic practice, Jewish education, ethics, and rabbinic authority. For Zivan's neo-pragmatists, the

---

[23] Rorty, *Philosophy as Cultural Politics*.   [24] See esp. Derrida, *Writing and Difference*, 317–51.

[25] See Marion, *On the Ego and on God*; Kearney, *The God Who May Be*.

[26] See Goldman, Statman, and Sagi, *Judaism without Illusions* (Heb.), esp. 352–60.

[27] For critiques of Zivan for choosing modern and not postmodern (as she claims) thinkers, which, according to some, might present an area to be developed, see Ross, 'Religious Belief in a Postmodern Age', 224; Seri-Levi, review of Zivan, *Religion without Illusions* (Heb.); Roth, 'Judaism in the Straits of Modernity and Postmodernity' (Heb.).

postmodern malaise justifies a rethinking of praxis and a reassertion of religious authority in the absence of a sense of absolute 'commanded-ness'.[28] A classic example of neo-pragmatism is the notion that halakhic praxis generates religious faith. In a sense, halakhic practice has become a choice (since divine authority cannot be proven empirically). It is undertaken as if it could be empirically justified, since it is perceived to perpetuate religious commitment.[29] Zivan is well aware of the difficulty of positing metaphysics and the consequent turn to praxis:

All four thinkers fail to deal with metaphysical and theological arguments and seeking proofs or facts about the reality of God. As people who recognize the boundaries of human thought, they recognize the need to emphasize halakhah, but not belief in God.[30]

A second critique of neo-pragmatic responses to the shift to postmodernism is that of the American scholar Cass Fisher, who claims that theories of religion without theology are mistaken:

I would like to draw attention to the kind of arguments that are commonly proffered against Jewish theology. That Jews in the ancient world did not adopt the Greek-derived word theology does not mean they were not invested in thinking about God. A more forceful argument is that theology is inherently systematic and dogmatic, and since Jewish thought about God does not generally exhibit these features, Judaism knows little or no theology. But why think that theology is necessarily systematic and dogmatic? . . . In my view, the most generous and honest way to account for problems like scholars' indifference to rabbinic theology . . . is to admit that our readings of classical Jewish texts are shaped by our own philosophical and theological prejudices.[31]

To conclude, he notes that 'for many, the demise of metaphysics also entails the collapse of theology, as if all theology is a species of metaphysics'.[32]

Fisher argues that the contemporary insistence on praxis at the expense of theology reflects, more than anything else, the equally contemporary disenchantment with regard to theology. Historical insight reveals, on the contrary, that the practice of theology, in many different forms, was widespread among Jews over the centuries, from biblical times to the advent of the modern period. I concur with Fisher that the claim that Judaism always expressed

[28] Zivan, *Religion without Illusions* (Heb.), 273.

[29] The central objectives of Zivan and her four thinkers are to seek out new ways of *avodat hashem* in a postmodern age (as opposed to a theology that might springboard over such attempts—which, I suggest, is the objective of Shagar and Ross).

[30] Zivan, *Religion without Illusions* (Heb.), 105.

[31] Fisher, 'Jewish Philosophy', 82–3.

[32] Ibid. 83.

greater concern for praxis rather than theology is in fact characteristic of a post-theological age. It therefore appears necessary to *restore* a Jewish non-metaphysical theology, for the sake of renewing the practice of theology in our times. Also, this is not a zero-sum game—ethics, as part of theology, must be integrated into a practical outcome of a compelling theology.

The Israel-based scholar Baruch Cahana, in a synopsis of contemporary neo-pragmatic theologians in Israel, argues that there are in fact only three thinkers who accept and integrate postmodern thought into theology.[33] They are Rav Shagar, Tamar Ross, and Daniel Shalit, of whom Shalit writes more from a secular perspective about Israeli society. I align myself with those who critique neo-pragmatism as a valuable approach but one that does not sufficiently apply postmodern thinking to core Jewish theology, and for this reason and others I devote this study to Tamar Ross (b. 1938) and Rabbi Shimon Gershon Rosenberg (1950–2007)—otherwise known by the acronym formed from his initials, Shagar—the two thinkers who provide models for accepting and integrating radical postmodern critique into the body of classical Jewish thought.

The Focus of This Book

My aim here is to delineate, through the writings of Ross and Shagar, two pioneering models of engagement with the notion of multiple truths. These writings represent parallel treatments of postmodern ideas in which the authors propound a return to theology after postmodernism, albeit on more tentative grounds.

Tamar Ross, professor emerita of Bar-Ilan University and lecturer at Midreshet Lindenbaum, was raised in Michigan to parents of hasidic ancestry. She received her Jewish education from her father, then rabbi of a Michigan Jewish community, and informal philosophical training from her husband Jacob Ross, now professor emeritus of philosophy at Tel Aviv University. Ross's numerous articles attest to her deep interest in *musar* (Jewish ethical teachings), kabbalah, hasidism, and the thought of Rabbi Abraham Isaac Kook. In the past decade, Ross's writings have focused on contemporary adaptations of Jewish thought to feminism and postmodernism, perhaps most notably in her book *Expanding the Palace of Torah: Orthodoxy and Feminism*.

Shimon Gershon Rosenberg was head of the Siah Yitshak yeshiva and, preceding that, a teacher at other major yeshivas of the religious Zionist community in Israel, including Yeshivat Hakotel, Mekor Hayim, and Beit Morasha. Born in Jerusalem and educated at Yeshivat Kerem Beyavneh, he

---

[33] Cahana, 'Where the Wind Blows' (Heb.).

spent years writing and lecturing on hasidism, focusing particularly on Rabbi Nahman of Bratslav and Shneur Zalman of Lyady. He dedicated the last ten years of his life to exploring the works of some of the most prominent postmodern thinkers (Louis Althusser, Jacques Derrida, Jean-François Lyotard, Fredric Jameson, Julia Kristeva, and Roland Barthes) and finding affinity between their ideas and the world of hasidic teachings.

The writings and sermons of Shagar have only recently caught the attention of the wider community of scholars of Jewish thought, resulting in several articles on specific aspects of his philosophy.[34] I cite several of his books and essays, most of which were published posthumously. His works on postmodernism, *Broken Vessels* and *Tablets and Broken Tablets*, inform my discussion most notably in the following pages. English translations of several of his articles and lectures are now available in *Faith Shattered and Restored*.[35] Numerous other excerpts from his writings and transcribed lectures appear here in English for the first time. Alan Brill has also spearheaded some online discussions on aspects of Shagar's thinking, which deal with aspects of his personal life, as well as of his students, which probably influenced his turn towards postmodern philosophy.[36]

Ross's work on feminism and Orthodoxy has received much attention; however, her thinking on postmodern epistemology and the philosophy of language has not raised a similar level of interest. In addition to her *Expanding the Palace of Torah*, two of her writings on postmodernism will stand out in this study: 'Religious Belief in a Postmodern Age' and 'The Cognitive Value of Religious Truth Statements'. Both focus on the challenge to epistemology, or knowledge, that the postmodern era brings. She predicts that:

The epistemological challenge posed by postmodernism and the struggle between the neo-pragmatists and those who strive to preserve the basis for some form of metaphysical claim will continue to occupy the attention of Jewish philosophers of the twenty-first century in one form or another. The most critical question will be whether a religious tradition bereft of all claims to transcendence can maintain the passion and fervour necessary for its continued existence.[37]

---

[34] To date the works that have been written about Shagar deal with the sociocultural aspects of his writing: religious–secular relations (Mevorakh, 'Secular Belief as Reification of the Infinite' (Heb.)), women's Torah study (Barel, 'On Patriarchy and the Voices of Women' (Heb.); Fuchs, 'Her Own Voice and Torah Study' (Heb.)); and existentialism (Tzur, 'The Deconstruction of Holiness' (Heb.)).

[35] *Broken Vessels: Torah and Religious Zionism in a Postmodern Environment* (Heb.); *Tablets and Broken Tablets: Jewish Thought in the Age of Postmodernism* (Heb.). *Faith Shattered and Restored*, edited by Zohar Maor, was published in 2017. I am grateful to have been allowed access to many of his unpublished manuscripts by the Institute for the Writings of Rav Shagar.

[36] See also Magid, 'The Settler Nakba and the Rise of Post-Modern Post-Zionist Religious Ideology'.　　　　　　　　　　[37] Ross, 'Overcoming the Epistemological Barrier', 388.

Ross substantiates this claim in 'Religious Belief in a Postmodern Age', in which she diagnoses various forms of the alienation of the younger generation from religion by referring to popular bloggers who express a sense of dissatisfaction with contemporary Jewish thought. She warns that religion— its beliefs and rituals—will lose its meaning in the contemporary era if no attempt is made to reconcile it to the postmodern critique. She anticipates the challenges and beneficial aspects of that critique for religious life. For the latter, her detailed analysis assists scholars in assessing the compatibility and divergences between postmodernism and traditional Jewish thought. Her ability to write in English and Hebrew also makes her works accessible to a wider circle than those of Shagar.

In this book, I demonstrate that the emphasis which Ross and Shagar place on theology is unique in the context of postmodern Orthodox thought. Indeed, the postmodern critique has to this day focused exclusively on aspects of Jewish life other than Jewish thought,[38] and, because of this lack of interest there have been no attempts to compare the output of these two thinkers either textually or conceptually. The shift from epistemological certainty to a focus on praxis has already received scholarly attention, and I therefore wish to focus on the specific issue of postmodern theology.

Reading Tamar Ross: Two Theological Principles

Feminism as a Secondary Issue

To consider Ross's pioneering work on the feminist critique of Orthodox theology as her primary contribution to Jewish philosophy is to miss the point. The social and communal relevance and popularity of the subject have undoubtedly bolstered the image of her scholarship on Orthodox Jewish feminism. *Expanding the Palace of Torah* is, as a result, often misconstrued as being paradigmatic of her profound and ongoing contribution to Jewish scholarship. While this assumption is not completely unfounded, Ross herself has stated that the epistemological implications of the postmodern approach to religion as a cultural construct lie at the root of her philosophy: 'I need to spell this out as many of my critics prefer to present my view as furthering a "feminist agenda" thus preventing themselves from having to deal with the issues I [raise].'[39] Her treatment of feminism is but one such

[38] This is also pertinent to the criticism of contemporary Jewish thought by Nehemia Stern: that scholars tend to deal either with theology or with anthropology. For this purpose a sociological introduction bears witness to the fact that, although this study is a theological one, its permutations occur within the anthropological, sociological, cultural, and cognitive realms of Jewish thought (see Stern, *Post-Orthodoxy*).

[39] Ross, 'A Premature Enthusiasm?' (Heb.), 179. Others mention the background of phil-

consequence of the question. There is no denying that the overlap between the subjects of language, culture, revelation, and epistemology, on the one hand, and feminism, on the other, is rather narrow. These themes only meet in her philosophy through her treatment of revelation and its epistemological expressions, both of which are founded on language. Ross even laments the fact that many ignore her writings on language and theology and seek out instead the more 'practical' implications of her thought, rather than her theology. Orthodox traditionalist critics regularly dismiss her work on language and culture entirely, simply because they assume its sole purpose is to serve the feminist cause:[40] 'Feminism has merely provided the critical cause célèbre on which to centre these thoughts.'[41] She explains further, in response to Finkelman's review of *Expanding the Palace of Torah*:

I really am not a political creature, have no agenda beyond the honest exchange of ideas, and have gone into this whole exercise mainly in order to clarify my own theological stance, without much thought of pushing this or that tangible consequence. I have sympathy for JOFA, Kolech and other such organizations dedicated to improving women's position in the halakhic community, but I am not a card-carrying member of any of these groups, and that is not where my primary interests lie.[42]

I therefore consider her treatment of the challenge of feminism to epistemology as peripheral (although not unimportant), and I will concentrate on her treatment of postmodern thought and leave experts on gender and feminism to focus on the prominent and invaluable theories, directions, and visions for Orthodox feminism today.

The Centrality of Mysticism

Ross's early research and academic career in Jewish thought focused on Jewish mysticism. Her undergraduate, master's, and doctoral theses dealt with the subject, and she thus acquired familiarity with different shades of mysticism under the tutelage of some of the greatest Israeli scholars of mysticism,

osophy of language but do not detail its import in her conclusions. Yoel Finkelman acknowledges that 'Orthodoxy must come to understand that all language is inherently bound to a particular time and cultural atmosphere' but does not expand on the philosophical underpinnings of this point—though that may not have been his aim (Finkelman, 'A Critique of *Expanding the Palace of Torah*').

[40] The widely publicized debate between Rabbi A. A. Frimer and Ross is a case in point. The content of Frimer's critique, which takes Ross to task over her interpretation of halakhah and feminism, attests precisely to Ross's point that her critics fail to engage with her scholarship on the philosophical level (see Frimer, 'Guarding the Treasure'; Ross, 'Guarding the Treasure and Guarding the Tongue').

[41] Ross, *Expanding the Palace of Torah*, p. xii.   [42] Ross, 'Response to Yoel Finkelman', 11.

including Isaiah Tishby and Joseph Dan. The work of R. Kook currently represents one of her most active interests. Ross finds in the philosophy of R. Kook a methodological model in which mysticism acts as an internal, regulating force through which contemporary challenges could be integrated into Jewish thought.[43] This area of scholarship therefore testifies to her desire to amalgamate mysticism and modernity. Her attitude to mysticism is central to her treatment of the linguistic issues raised by postmodernism:

I do believe that traditionalists, confronting the radical implications of contemporary scientific and moral insights and seeking to incorporate these into their religious way of life without forfeiting its credibility or normative force, will intuitively gravitate towards some of the more promising implications that the postmodern sensibility holds for traditional Jewish belief when informed by a mystic sensibility.[44]

For Ross, the inclusion of mysticism in the discussion of postmodern theology is fundamental:

Postmodernism is much closer to mysticism in being holistic, and postmodern theology is not simply a matter of exchanging one philosophical master for another, in striving to correlate religious belief with postmodern interests and concerns rather than modern ones. Finding a middle way between pretensions to absolute and objective truths and denial of truth altogether is not its only concern. . . . This is because postmodernism involves not only a new epistemology and understanding of language. *It also involves a different mindset and way of experiencing our everyday world and its relationship to another dimension that lies beyond it—one that is closer to mysticism than to philosophy.* Rather than suffice with the vision of a fragmented and atomized universe, the path of postmodernism leads to viewing reality in holistic terms, as composed of various inter-related parts.[45]

Ultimately, Ross acknowledges and affirms the turn to 'spirituality' that, according to many, has accompanied the revival of popular interest in mysticism: 'These [mystical] ideas have brought me personal religious magic until this very day in my experience.'[46]

---

[43] There are of course many who disagree with Ross's reading of R. Kook as having anticipated postmodernism and who place him firmly in the camp of 'modern Jewish thinkers' (see e.g. Shnerb, 'A Parable of a Wise Man Who Despairs of Reason' (Heb.)).

[44] Ross, 'Religious Belief in a Postmodern Age', 239.   [45] Ibid. (my emphasis).

[46] Ross, 'A Premature Enthusiasm?' (Heb.), 181. 'I suppose that I am no different than most people, often coming upon what you so eloquently describe as "the elemental power of faith" in the indisputably high points of life (giving birth to a child, singing with eyes closed and heart open to the soaring of one's soul, standing on a hilltop and sensing a unity with nature, driving to swim on a sun-filled early Jerusalem morning, sensing the power of holiness in some Jewish

Reading Shagar

Shagar, in a different sense, was strongly affiliated to mainstream religious Zionist institutions, and it is this context that makes his treatment of postmodernism unique. He sets forth his views in a collection of essays and lectures compiled under the title of *Broken Vessels*—a reference to the kabbalistic concept of breakage and renewal. These writings are infused with mysticism as a metaphor of renewal and healing in light of the shattering of modernist epistemology.[47] He speaks as a religious leader rather than an academic—his ideas were often conveyed orally. Hence much of his work comes from the transcribed texts of his lectures or from his own handwritten notes that were subsequently edited and published. As a result, his writings often lack footnotes or references—a shortcoming for which he has been criticized, and in consequence of which some of his students later took on the task of supplying missing bibliographical information.

Shagar's greater involvement with ordinary people put him in close, personal contact with those who felt alienated from institutionalized religion. He was therefore able to address them more directly and intimately about religious disenchantment and offer helpful suggestions about how to return to theology on postmodern terms.

Comparative Methodologies

Shagar and Ross have the same objectives, even though they come from completely different worlds. Their styles and audiences differ significantly. Though Shagar occasionally took part in dialogues with secular Jews, Ross, as an academic, addresses a broader range of people. These differences are relevant to their respective methods of instruction. For example, it might have been deemed inappropriate for Shagar to refer to the works of Foucault and Rorty, who challenge the very notion of 'truth', in his yeshiva; however, that is precisely what he did. Ross probably does not lament the lack of strong religious conviction among young Orthodox Jews while speaking in an academic setting. Their respective methodologies reflect their work environments, each with its own advantages and limitations.

Their similarities therefore frame the subject matter, while their differences stretch the boundaries of the discussion. They share a commitment to tradition as well as a common objective: to harness postmodernism in a way

weddings, witnessing simple and spontaneous acts of human kindness, shouting, "A-donai Hu ha-Elokim" at the top of my lungs with the rest of the congregation at the close of Yom Kippur)' (Ross, 'Response to Yoel Finkelman', 21).

[47] See e.g. Shagar, 'My Faith' (Heb.), 5.

that will redefine, and indeed reinforce, Jewish theology. It could be argued that they target the same audience of halakhically committed students.[48] On the one hand, religious practice 'will remain a lifeless shell if unaccompanied by . . . belief'; on the other, the abstract nature of belief, its disconnection from a cultural background, fails to 'preserve the intensity of feeling'[49] that distinguishes theology from philosophy. Their concerns are clear at the outset: Shagar's is 'cleaving' to Torah and God,[50] and Ross's is enriching the religious beliefs of the current and future generations,[51] in order to sustain the passion of halakhic observance.[52] It will be interesting to see how they differ in the extent to which they find postmodern theories instructive and how these differences bear witness to the malleability of their respective theological boundaries.

It may be asked whether the more radical character of Ross's work developed under the pressure of the intellectual elite which she addresses or whether Shagar's greater traditionalism bears the influence of the yeshiva world to which he belongs. Ross has indeed acquired a reputation as a highly respected scholar, and a strong interest, often hagiographical in nature, in Shagar is rapidly on the rise in religious circles in Israel and abroad. Both figures have certainly attracted many followers in academic and religious circles. When discussing their methodologies and conclusions, I will take into consideration the relative receptiveness of their respective environments to the amalgamation of postmodernism and Jewish thought.

Through an examination of these models, I hope to construct a path forward for a Jewish faith in a postmodern age.[53] My conviction is that the challenges of this age should actually serve to enrich theology by changing the rules of the game.[54]

---

[48] Shagar, *Broken Vessels* (Heb.), 42–3. On prescribing halakhic norms for yeshiva students, see Shagar and Dreyfus, *Beloved Friends* (Heb.), 120. A particular mode of religious practice is obligatory at the yeshiva, one which Shagar seeks to uphold when he views elements of it as having gone awry. See also Shagar, 'A Group of Friends with Yarmulkes go to the Pub' (Heb.); id., 'Similar Qualities of Postmodern Religious Identity' (Heb.).

[49] Ross, 'Religious Belief in a Postmodern Age', 218.

[50] Shagar, *Broken Vessels* (Heb.), 27–8.

[51] Ross remarks on the need for the 'fundamental metaphysical conviction that has always ignited the long-standing devotion and passion marking our identity as creatures of faith' ('Religious Belief in a Postmodern Age', 240), and talks of 'transmit[ting] the passion of its message to future generations' (ibid. 218).

[52] Ibid. 217–18.   [53] See also Sacks, *Crisis and Covenant*, 194–7.

[54] Some of the material discussed in 'Feminism as a Secondary Issue' (pp. 14–15 above) has been published in Feldmann Kaye, 'Playing the Language Game'.

ONE

CULTURE

Cultural Particularism

'Cultural particularism' is a central feature of postmodernism.[1] It refers to the position that claims that understanding and interaction with the world are contingent upon one's culture. According to radical cultural particularism, there is no objective reality whatsoever, only multiple different perspectives based on local perceptions and interpretations, each anchored in a specific cultural context. Furthermore, the notion of objectivity is a figment of one's philosophical imagination, itself conceived through the lenses of one's particular culture. An introduction to the concepts discussed in this chapter should start with the Austrian philosopher Ludwig Wittgenstein, who is widely considered the founder of several contemporary philosophical movements—notably analytic, post-liberal, and postmodern philosophy (at least according to his later works). Common threads run between these movements, most obviously the rejection of a universal, objective sphere. According to Wittgenstein, a set of given beliefs is meaningful only to the group which understands them from its particular perspective:

The ideal, as we think of it, is unshakable. You can never get outside it; you must always turn back. There is no outside; outside you cannot breathe—where does this idea come from? It is like a pair of glasses on our nose through which we see whatever we look at. It never occurs to us to take them off . . . we think we are perceiving a state of affairs of the highest generality.[2]

The 'pair of glasses' Wittgenstein describes tricks us into a false sense of knowledge, as they purport to provide an objective vision of reality. In line with this observation, postmodernists claim that much of modernist epistemology produces a false impression of objectivity and that reality is, as a matter of fact, only ever comprehended from within a specific cultural confine.[3]

---

[1] The central Hebrew-language writings on postmodernism are Gurvitz, *Postmodernism* (Heb.), and Ophir, 'Postmodernism' (Heb.).

[2] Wittgenstein, *Philosophical Investigations*, 45–6.

[3] Wittgenstein, *Lectures and Conversations*.

Wittgenstein's later writings were further developed by two broad movements, each taking his observations in a different direction. The first includes continental postmodern theorists, in particular Michel Foucault, Jean-François Lyotard, and Jacques Derrida; the second comprises Anglo-American constructivist philosophers, such as Richard Rorty and Hilary Putnam.[4] Both groups have dismissed the pre-eminence of the individual, proclaiming the collapse of the famous 'cogito' at the heart of Cartesian philosophy.[5] By acknowledging that knowledge is contingent on external factors and only ever partial,[6] cultural particularism has come to typify postmodern thought.[7] Michel Foucault, for example, takes as a given the individual's inescapable immersion in her conceptual surroundings. In his account of the 'death of men as subject', he explains that an individual cannot accurately comprehend a given object because she is determined by the influences of the society and culture to which she is inextricably linked.[8] He sees the notion of the self as arbiter of knowledge as a farce, a fantasy meant to flatter the human ego. Individuals possess no real 'freedom' of thought since their opinions are necessarily conditioned by their respective cultures. An individual's environment will therefore necessarily determine her value system. Other theorists in this group came to argue that cultural collectives possess accepted cultural-linguistic patterns —'language games' (Wittgenstein) or 'phrase regimens' (Lyotard)—which determine their outlook.

The term 'particularism' takes individual local cultures, including their understandings of history, narrative, ritual, language, and so on, as contexts

---

[4] For general literature on the second of these two groups, see Griffin et al. (eds.), *Founders of Constructive Postmodern Philosophy*.

[5] 'Perhaps this being, on which I depend, is not that which I call God, and I am created either by my parents or some other cause less perfect than God. This cannot be. . . . It is perfectly evident that there must be at least as much reality in the cause as in the effect: and thus, since I am a thinking thing, and possess an idea of God within me, whatever in the end be the cause assigned to my existence . . . it possesses the view of self-existence' (Descartes, *Meditations of First Philosophy*, 33). The notion of the self as having an essential quality of 'self-existence' that supposedly renders it, like a soul, inseparable from God or truth, was reworked through existentialist philosophy and then critiqued by postmodernists and phenomenologists (see e.g. Merleau-Ponty, *Phenomenology of Perception*, 468–70).

[6] For a critique of cultural particularism as having played too large a role after modernity, see Eagleton, *The Illusions of Postmodernism*.

[7] Additional examples include Louis Althusser, who relegated the idea of the self—which he believed had been falsely catapulted to the centre of the universe—to near-insignificance. For him this led to an 'epistemological break' that opened the way to postmodernism. Further, Julia Kristeva's 'signifying process' points to an eternal repositioning or stirring of the self, meaning that self-consciousness is never static and thereby able to hold a certain position on something. It is impossible to capture self-identity and bottle it as an ideology.

[8] Foucault, *Ethics*, 93–106.

that inform human collectives.[9] The 'particular', or the affirmation of singular and subjective truths, constitutes a rejection of the 'universal'—the search for universal or objective truth.[10] It implies that different epistemologies arise from particular understandings of the world, or, as Steven Kepnes puts it, 'a movement away from the modern ideal of a universal, rational culture and toward a multicultural reality that celebrates the value of the local and particular and attempts a new openness to premodern forms and motifs'.[11] Particularistic understandings of reality are based on cultural assumptions and interpretations, necessarily informed by one's family, upbringing, education, environment, and so on. Cultural particularism therefore renders explicit the individual's epistemological limitations. As a result, epistemological certainty is not and cannot be based on supposedly universal proofs, since these do not lend themselves to empirical verification.

Relativism and Pluralism

A variety of anti-postmodernists, including Jürgen Habermas[12] and Andreas Huyssens,[13] have attempted to dismiss cultural particularism as a recipe for moral relativism and ethical apathy.[14] The most prevalent concern voiced against postmodernism is how to justify a preference for one set of truth-values over another or, in other words, the threat of relativism. Relativism is the view that truth is relative to a certain group, time, language, religious tradition, conceptual framework, or ethnicity.[15] Relativist knowledge is 'local, bounded, culturally-relative and limited'.[16] This outlook explains the

[9] Foucault's writings, influential equally in the sociological and political spheres, were, somewhat inevitably, taken up by anthropologists, not least Clifford Geertz, who used his theories in describing and evaluating localized cultures—for example, studying religion and belief as cultural and social phenomena (see esp. Geertz, *The Interpretation of Cultures*). His 'priority of local knowledge' became a shared venture of certain contemporary strands of theology and anthropology.

[10] For a popular theory on how religion came to be verified according to scientific principles, see Popper, *Conjectures and Refutations*; on the scientific study of Judaism, see Rosenberg, *Torah and Science in New Jewish Thought* (Heb.).

[11] Kepnes (ed.), *Interpreting Judaism in a Postmodern Age*, 1.

[12] Habermas, *The Philosophical Discourse of Modernity*. Yet Habermas does not attempt to salvage the self as independent of its cultural surroundings. He focuses on the anti-rationalist methodology of postmodern thought that seeks to cancel out in advance any self-critique.

[13] Huyssens, *After the Great Divide*.

[14] See Benson and Stangroom, *Why Truth Matters*, 65–85.

[15] The concept of relative truth-values is prominent in several academic disciplines, such as bioethics, business ethics, education, and journalism. It has its roots in various historical strands of philosophy, such as Greek philosophy and, not least in the modern period, through Kant's 'Copernican revolution', after which no philosopher could speak of an idea without acknowledging its abject subjectivity (see P. J. J. Phillips, *The Challenge of Relativism*).

[16] Ibid. 2.

terminological shift away from 'ultimate truth' and towards 'discourses' and 'narratives'.

Often viewed in Western philosophy as a pronouncement on the subjectivity of belief, relativism has spiralled into a late modern philosophical phenomenon spanning multiple subject areas. Frits Staal describes epistemological relativism (which he then refutes in favour of absolute knowledge) in the following way:

Views held by human beings reflect their particular locale—country, civilisation, language area, or time or faith, genes or upbringing, conscious motivation, or mental or psychological make-up; and are not valid beyond these restrictions. Some relativists go further and claim that no view is better or worse than any other. According to most, there are no universal truths.[17]

Relativist perceptions are also said to be constituted according to 'predicates of personal tastes, normative expressions, conditionals, colour terms, and future contingents [that] possess truth-values only relative to epistemic and subjective properties of the speaker or of someone who assesses the discourse for truth'.[18] Relativism in postmodern times has been described as 'one of the most serious problems people face, now more than ever', since it exemplifies 'the problem of establishing common standards, whether of knowledge, of morality or of beauty'.[19]

Patrick J. J. Phillips describes relativism in the context of philosophy of religion as an 'epistemology of choice'.[20] If religious values are relative to specific temporal or cultural conditions, then ultimately people have the choice over which 'sets' of knowledge to accept.[21] As he sees it, these sets of 'choice' extend to five areas: truth, logic, ontology, epistemology, and rationality. Paul O'Grady argues that relativism differs from scepticism and pluralism in all these cases insofar as it distinguishes between knowledge and values as relative to specific groups.[22] Relativism is often perceived as concurrent with pluralism. It is assumed that individuals who recognize personal epistemological limitations will, as a result, tend to respect and consider the positions of others more seriously. Indeed, Phillips postulates that relativism should be embraced for its

---

[17] Staal, 'Beyond Relativism', 37.

[18] Brogaard, 'Centred Worlds and the Content of Perception', 58.

[19] Berleant, 'Leaving Relativism', 69. The issue of aesthetics in universal and relative epistemology is subject to the same criteria: that the 'truth' of what is beautiful has no 'objective' or universal criteria—it is defined by cultural taste which itself is influenced by civilization, temporality, culture, locale, technology, and so on. Aesthetic beauty in this sense is on a par with notions of knowledge or ethics in discussions of whether universal beauty can be found. See Murdoch, *The Sovereignty of Good*, 1–44; Adorno, *Aesthetic Theory*, 60–80.

[20] P. J. J. Phillips, *The Challenge of Relativism*, 2.

[21] See Bernstein, *Beyond Objectivism and Relativism*.   [22] O'Grady, *Relativism*.

'promot[ion of] cross-cultural tolerance and understanding'. Yet this argument presents critical weaknesses: absolutists may hold liberal views in a particular subject area, just as relativists may have limits to their ethical relativism. Phillips thus suggests that 'even those who propound relativism as a principle of tolerance are hard-pressed to accept cultural practices universally; consider, for example, the highly contentious issue of the morality (or immorality) of female circumcision, or the cutting off of hands as a punitive measure for the crime of petty theft'.[23]

It may seem reasonable to assume a negative correlation between conflicts over truth and the acceptance of epistemological relativism. Thus (in areas other than religion) relativism is generally considered a more ethical option than nationalist supremacy, ethical arrogance, gender hierarchy, political opposition, imperialism (ascribing a value judgement over other groups and their values), and so on.[24] Some, however, disagree with this positive approach to relativism, arguing that it leads to epistemological chaos—resembling a Nietzschean nihilism where no values, even ethical ones, can be upheld as truthful.[25] They justify their position by resorting to a *reductio ad absurdum* argument: if values cannot be weighed, then democracy or peace are no better than totalitarianism or warfare. Jonathan Sacks, for example, expresses this concern in his work on religious violence:

Moral relativism is no defence whatsoever against those currently waging war against the West and its freedoms. If relativism is true, then nothing can be said truly or absolutely to be wrong. As a matter of subjective belief I may regard the killing of civilians, the use of children as human shields and the enslavement of young girls as bad. However, I will then have to concede that you see things differently. You believe it is a sacred imperative undertaken for the greater glory of God. Our values are different because our worldviews are. . . . Such discourse . . . is utterly inadequate to the challenge today.[26]

Sacks categorically rejects the idea that all beliefs and behaviours ultimately hold equal value. In terms of religious belief, the choice therefore lies be-

[23] P. J. J. Phillips, *The Challenge of Relativism*, 17. Shagar begins *Broken Vessels* with an example of ethical relativism, *sati* in Hindu culture (*Broken Vessels* (Heb.), 3–5).

[24] For an account of Derridean and Foucauldian remarks on the anthropology of non-Western (or 'oriental') religion, see Almond, *The New Orientalists*; for a review and analysis of ideas of tolerance and freedom of religion in Islamic countries, see Gole, 'Contemporary Islamic Movements' (Heb.); for a review of religious pluralism in the Balkans, see Mahmutcehajic, 'The Bosnian Question' (Heb.); see also Feldmann Kaye and Coric, 'Interreligious "Reasoning" with Israelis and Palestinians, Bosniak Serbs and Croats'.

[25] See Heidegger, *Nietzsche*. Contradicting viewpoints have resisted an all-out nihilism in the wake of Nietzsche (see Gillespie, *Nihilism before Nietzsche*; Rosen, 'Nietzsche's Double Rhetoric'). [26] Sacks, *Not in God's Name*, 15–16.

tween, on the one hand, holding one's own value system as truthful (objectivist) and, on the other, a total negation of values (radical relativism). One must walk a tightrope in order to confront the issue of non-absolute truth according to postmodern criteria and succumb neither to nihilism nor objectivism. Can one claim the absolute validity of one's own position while negating absolute truth in general? This question is more acute in the present era than ever.[27]

Postmodernists, however, have insisted on acknowledging the anthropocentric character of the notion of universal truth and recognizing instead a multitude of particular meanings. According to a postmodern understanding, in the place of a universally perceived truth lies a plurality of interpretations, each determined by one's own cultural collective ('narratives'). Instead of 'metanarratives', such as universal accounts of history, culture, or society, postmodernists now refer to an infinite number of 'micronarratives' in constant flux.[28]

Deconstructionism

The conceptual opposition between objectivity and subjectivity was one of the numerous polarizations established by philosophers until the postmodern era. Among others, Plato distinguished between body and soul, Descartes between mind and matter, and Kant between phenomena and noumena. A reverse process started in the nineteenth century, which led phenomenologists and existentialists, most notably Heidegger, to dismantle the very distinction between subjective and objective altogether. One of the fundamental lines of congruity between existentialists and postmodernists is the acknowledgement that the notion of 'objectivity' is based on false assumptions.[29] This has led many towards the murky waters of relativism where, in the absence of objective knowledge, anything goes. Relativism has, in turn, been bolstered by deconstructionism—another typically postmodern enterprise most often associated with Derrida and Foucault.[30] Deconstruc-

[27] See Ravitzky, 'The Question of Tolerance in the Jewish Religious Tradition'.

[28] 'The postmodern would be that which, in the modern, puts forward the unpresentable in presentation itself; that which denies itself the solace of good forms, the consensus of a taste which would make it possible to share collectively the nostalgia for the unattainable; that which searches for new presentations, not in order to enjoy them, but in order to impart a stronger sense of the unpresentable' (Lyotard, *The Postmodern Condition*, 81).

[29] See e.g. Heidegger, *The Phenomenology of Religious Life*. Steven Earnshaw distinguishes between postmodernism and existentialism by selecting the rejection of the self as 'a fictional construct' as an outstanding feature that distinguishes the movements (see Earnshaw and Dowson (eds.), *Postmodern Subjects/Postmodern Texts*, 60).

[30] See esp. Derrida, *Writing and Difference*; id., *Dissemination*; Foucault, *Discourse and Truth*; id., *Madness and Civilisation*. Foucault was actually opposed to deconstructionism, stating that it

tionism strives to displace binary oppositions by exposing them as linguistic constructs rather than accurate reflections of an original essence existing outside or prior to language.[31] The classical opposition between nature and culture, for example, has recurred in philosophical arguments since the Graeco-Roman period. Deconstructionists endeavour to restructure how such binaries are conceived by demonstrating that what qualifies as 'natural' or 'cultural' is itself dependent on particular cultural constructs and therefore varies from one era or society to another. These polarities thus crumble once one realizes the pervading influence of language and culture on one's understanding of reality.[32]

Derrida's investigation into the opposition between speech and writing had the greatest impact in the area of hermeneutics. Philosophers formerly privileged the former, on the basis that they understood the meaning of words to be more fully accessible to the interlocutor when in the presence of the speaker. In the context of writing, the author's absence makes the meaning of words doubly remote. Derrida deconstructs this opposition to expose the fallacy of the logic which underlies it: he demonstrates that such a conception of language implies the existence of an idea prior to language, which an author seeks to convey through the medium of speech. To Derrida, linguistic meaning is actually determined not by a metaphysical presence but by the endless chain of contrasts between different words. Such an observation implies that texts can never describe a static state of affairs but, rather, that their meaning is in perpetual flux, constantly changing depending on reader and context. The efforts to uncover the underlying message the author presumably intended to convey are therefore effectively rendered void. By privileging the reader's experience over authorial intention, postmodernism expands the borders of textual interpretation. For that reason, it presents a viable and, for many, exciting methodology for reading and understanding texts.

It is worth noting that many contemporary Jewish thinkers have embraced deconstructionism. Some even suggest that it fits naturally with Jewish theology. Fisher attempts to explain this popularity by highlighting the

---

was too verbose. Apparently, Foucault and Derrida did not speak for ten years because of this disagreement.

[31] Derrida sought to 'deconstruct' the work of the phenomenologists, whom I have considered above as providing a framework for understanding religion as comprising multiple phenomena. Shagar and Ross seek to reformulate phenomenology taking into account deconstructive techniques, in a similar move to that of Jean-Luc Nancy.

[32] Derrida did not seek to destroy the myth of textual meaning but rather to deconstruct its epistemological presumptions and in its place 'to inscribe a new theory of language *ex nihilo*' (Burrus, '*Creatio ex Libidine*', 143).

fact that the Jewish tradition systematically applies deconstructivist techniques to its canonical texts:

The Hebrew Bible is, perhaps, the epitome of a multivoiced text. One need not accept the documentary hypothesis to see the truth in this. . . . As the rabbis model for us, all of this demands to be read together. Indeed, at every Shabbat we follow their exegetical procedure by juxtaposing Torah and Haftarah and looking for thematic connections to better understand the text and the insights that come from the sages' framing of our readings.[33]

In addition, many argue that Talmud study resembles the deconstructivist enterprise because of its incessant pursuit of novel interpretations.[34] Avinoam Rosenak suggests that the combination of deconstructionism and Jewish textual learning is refreshing:

Studies like these, of philosophers and literary theorists, of important postmodern thinkers, have prompted scholars in Jewish studies to reconsider elements of Jewish thought in postmodern terms. Derrida's concept of representation has been useful in explicating rabbinic and Hasidic exegetical doctrines. Talmudic, midrashic and Hasidic texts are now frequently described as open-ended and dialogic genres of literature.[35]

Such approaches have been propounded by Daniel Boyarin,[36] Susan Handelman,[37] Edith Wyschogrod,[38] Adi Ophir,[39] James Kugel,[40] and Marc-Alain Ouaknin[41] among others. In an important volume, published in 2015 in Israel, several Orthodox-affiliated religious leaders similarly grapple with questions of how to read conflicting texts.[42] Deconstructionism is thus, without any doubt, gaining popularity.

Cultural Particularism and Jewish Theology

Having introduced the concepts of cultural particularism, relativism, and deconstructivism and the challenges each of them presents to conceptions of universal values and the self, I now turn to their impact specifically on the

---

[33] Fisher, 'Jewish Philosophy'.

[34] Derrida, *Speech and Phenomena*, 129. [35] Rosenak, '"Pre-Postmodern"', 294.

[36] Boyarin's work perhaps best exemplifies postmodern readings of the Talmud, illustrating a congruence between the two literary approaches (see Boyarin, *Socrates and the Fat Rabbis*; id., *Intertextuality and the Reading of Midrash*, esp. 345–50).

[37] Handelman has suggested that talmudic layering and the coexistence of multiple readings bear a strong resemblance to contemporary literary theory (Handelman, *The Slayers of Moses*).

[38] Wyschogrod, *Saints and Postmodernism*.

[39] Ophir, 'Postmodernism' (Heb.). [40] Kugel, 'Two Introductions to Midrash'.

[41] Ouaknin, *The Burnt Book*, compares postmodern deconstructive literary theory and talmudic reasoning. [42] Brandes, Ganzel, and Deutsch (eds.), *Between God and Man* (Heb.).

realm of religion. Firstly, postmodern theology regards religion as a particularistic endeavour, fundamentally rooted in cultural idiosyncrasies. As a
result, it downplays the modernist quest for universal truth and objectivity
outside one's own culture. Secondly, truth-claims no longer purport to represent absolute, universal, and justifiable statements about the world. A radical
postmodernist world-view conceives of an individual's values and beliefs as a
drop in an ocean of culturally accepted norms. This shift in thinking carries
far-reaching implications for Jewish theology. Currently, most Jewish religious responses to the challenge of cultural particularism have come, perhaps inevitably, from a generation of thinkers who have found themselves in
a transitional period between modernity and postmodernism. Even though
philosophically they accept the notion of multiple truths, they still dread the
ethical and practical implications of relativism.

Avi Sagi, for example, writes that 'a future Jewish philosophy will be
unable to handle these questions through relativism or scepticism, which
deaden Jewish commitment. . . . Jewish philosophy must join the philosophical enterprise addressing weighty questions about the meaning of multicultural existence, including all its concomitant problems.'[43] Sagi acknowledges that a viable theological response to the issue of relativism is crucial.
This would be because—and many would agree with him—an acceptance of
relativism would condemn Judaism to extinction. His reasoning, I would
suggest, characterizes a neo-pragmatist response to the issue of relativism:
a strong awareness, and a turn to praxis. This feature is also evident in the
writings of Jonathan Sacks, who deems the nihilistic tendencies of relativism
more lamentable than existentialist nihilism: 'Now, in place of the revalu-
ation of values, we have their devaluation. We are surrounded by choices with
no reason to choose this rather than that.'[44]

Lenn Goodman suggests a separation between relativism and pluralism
in order to distance himself from the former while retaining a now unavoid-
able theological openness to other cultures. This is, I believe, a common move
among contemporary Jewish authors.[45] In making it, some have demonstrated that the challenges both concepts present, especially those of relativism,
are not unprecedented, either to prove a historical point or more likely to guide
others to solve the issue.[46] Raphael Jospe thus compiled a selection of writings

[43] Sagi, 'Toward a Jewish Philosophy', 407–8.

[44] Sacks, 'Nostalgia for the Numinous'.

[45] Goodman, In Defense of Truth; for Goodman's more recent exposition, see his 'Doing
Jewish Philosophy in America'.

[46] See e.g. Margalit, 'On Religious Pluralism'; Last-Stone, 'Tolerance Versus Pluralism in
Judaism' (Heb.).

by historical Jewish figures who espoused, in his view, early versions of relativism.[47] Goshen-Gottstein has written extensively about Jewish theological
approaches to other religions, citing and analysing historical precedents of
the acceptance or tolerance of multiple truths.[48] Dov Maimon similarly suggests that Abraham ben Maimon developed a religious pluralist theology of
dialogue with Islamic mystics in the medieval era,[49] while Zvi Zohar goes even
further to claim that 'from the period of the tana'im until the Enlightenment
there was an almost complete dialogue between the sages of the Torah and
the cultural-intellectual elite'.[50] Few scholars would currently admit to being
'relativists' even though they routinely deny the existence of absolute truth and
values. Such positions, though, are significant insofar as they represent new
attempts at generating context-based versions of truth, based on sources drawn
from the wellspring of the Jewish textual tradition.

It is also worth noting the prominence of kabbalah in the various attempts
at reconciling postmodernism and Jewish theology.[51] Kabbalah, insofar as it
represents a culturally particularistic Jewish tradition, converges with postmodernism.[52] It presents a framework, according to Sanford Drob, of 'multiple
narratives and loss of centre', rather than a rejection of absolutes: 'Is it possible for Judaism to embrace such relativism? And might relativism itself be
a condition for a new Jewish faith and theology?'[53] The kabbalistic ontological
system conceived of a single, holistic realm of existence, rather than a dual,
complementary system which separates the human from the divine. Jonathan
Herman therefore notes that mysticism allows for the perpetuation of values
within a communal framework: 'Mystical experience is contextually bound and
thus only intelligible contextually.'[54] It is worth considering, on this basis, that a
commitment to a set of epistemic truths is not necessarily upset by the recognition of these truths as language constructs, possessing only relative value.
A few, more sceptical, authors have pointed to various discrepancies in tracing
a consistent, uniform historical account of Jewish engagement with other
truths.[55] It is reasonable to assume, in any case, that the challenges of relativism

[47] Jospe, 'Pluralism out of the Sources of Judaism'.
[48] Goshen-Gottstein, 'Towards a Jewish Theology of World Religions'.
[49] Maimon, 'Tolerance Despite Disagreement in Medieval Egypt' (Heb.).
[50] Zohar, 'Something Dreadful in the City of Damascus' (Heb.). Zohar explicates the 'non-
exclusivist Jewish theologies' of Rabbi Isaac Perahi (b. 1782) and Rabbi Moses Galanti (b. 1842).
[51] See Penner, Mysticism and Religious Traditions, 89–116.
[52] Some have pointed out that ideas in Jewish thought have always been centred on a
multiple-truths perspective. See, for example, Moshe Hallamish on Maimonides' reasoning
against ta'amei hamitsvot (seeking reasons for divine commands) (Hallamish, An Introduction
to Kabbalah).
[53] Drob, Kabbalah and Postmodernism, 338.   [54] Herman, 'The Contextual Illusion', 97.
[55] e.g. Jospe, 'Pluralism out of the Sources of Judaism'.

have become more acute in light of recent cultural, sociological, and techno-logical developments—such as globalization and digitalization—which bring people of strikingly different cultures into contact (virtual and intellectual) with each other.[56]

How can Jewish theology absorb such a paradigm shift? Shagar and Ross both argue that Judaism has internal theological resources, particularly in the realm of mysticism, that help break down these conceptual barriers.[57] They allude to kabbalistic motifs in order to amalgamate postmodernism with Judaism. Both thinkers present views of faith rather than knowledge to con-struct a perspective-bound theology, minimizing absolutism or fundamen-talism and increasing the chances of openness to other faiths.

In the first section of this chapter I analyse the steps Ross and Shagar take in negotiating these postmodern refutations and the impact of their insights on their broader theologies. I consider Shagar's refutation of universal reality and consequent reconsideration of the theological notions on providence and destiny. In parallel I analyse Ross's position on the cultural particularism of beliefs and their positive impact on society. I then consider their treatment of the problem of multiple truths and relativism, showing how their argu-ments facilitate the acceptance of a multiplicity of truth-claims. I underscore a persistent refusal on their behalf to accept what they see as a 'collapse' into a relativism according to which one's own faith holds nothing truer than that of others.

I have put forward the case for a 'visionary theology' which does not rely on an ultimate and singular truth but posits instead that the notion of a multi-plicity of truths is compatible with Judaism. The implications are twofold: first, since faith does not lend itself to scientific verification, it becomes diffi-cult to justify a preference for one's own world-view or way of life; second, if such truths are perceived as culturally particular social constructs, their prime function is limited to defining communal boundaries. I illustrate in the fol-lowing pages how changing conceptions of truth affect Jewish theology and their implications for coping with relativism.

---

[56]   See Feldmann Kaye, 'The Effects of Globalization on Religious Leadership'.

[57]   Similarities between kabbalah and postmodern deconstructionism are referred to numer-ous times throughout this book. The comparison was already ripe in discussions between Levinas and Derrida, noted by Thomas Altizer: 'When I was introduced to Derrida by Hillis Miller, Hillis told the story of the last time he and Jacques had visited Levinas, and Levinas looked Jacques deep in his eyes, and said, "Jacques, you cannot deny that you are a contem-porary embodiment of Lurianic Kabbalism"' (cited in Drob, *Kabbalah and Postmodernism*, 19). Drob explores the connection further. These links notwithstanding, Ross was unaware of Derridean and other continental uses of kabbalah.

The Deconstruction of Universalism

The Self and Particularism

In his conception of cultural particularism, Shagar relies on a deconstruction of the notions of objectivity and subjectivity and a reconfiguration of the self. By referring successively to postmodernist scholarship and kabbalistic sources, he argues that the individual mistakenly believes that she possesses the qualities of real 'existence':

[The individual] is wholly dependent on the world around him. He cannot be an independent being. He is part of a broader existence. [Therefore], his sense of subjectivity is lost [because in] reality he is wholly intertwined with [the lives of] others . . . rather than a separate entity.[58]

The individual is dependent on the holistic reality which surrounds her, with its distinctive cultural and theological norms. The pervasive influence communal experience bears on the believer's world-view leaves no room, according to Shagar, for subjectivity. The notion of the self as the arbiter of values and commitments is therefore obliterated, and replaced with that of the community. In the case of one's conception of and attachment to the divine, for example, Shagar claims that 'intimacy with God, from a Jewish perspective, is achieved through a collective effort, rather than as an individual. . . . [Hence] the experience [of the individual believer is] a mere trace of the holy covenant of faith.'[59] On the more general level, he notes that 'religious experience creates and sustains the [Jewish] tradition, both [in terms of how] it defines itself, and how it identifies itself on its own terms'.[60] In other words, the experience of religious worship concerns the community as a whole, rather than individual participants. It is therefore in the hands of this collective that the prerogative of shaping and defining the Jewish tradition lies. Shagar reads this idea into classical Jewish sources:

The Torah is necessary for the very existence of this world and [therefore] was not given voluntarily. In order to guard the absolute pre-eminence of the Torah it must be [understood to have been] given under duress . . . [because] this compulsion, based on its coercive powers, is designed to prevent escape. The Torah is forced upon the Jew, and he has no choice but to accept his Jewish identity.[61]

[58] Shagar, *In the Shadow of Faith* (Heb.), 125.
[59] Ibid. 69.   [60] Shagar, *A Time of Freedom* (Heb.), 125–6.
[61] Shagar, *Chance and Providence*, 78–80. Shagar is referring to a story of supposed divine coercion to 'accept' the Torah at Mount Sinai: '"They stood at the foot of [lit. beneath] the mountain" (Exod. 19: 17). Rav Avdimi son of Hama son of Hasa: "This teaches us that the Holy One held the mountain over them like a barrel. He said, 'If you accept the Torah, fine: if not, here will be your burial'"' (BT *Shab.* 88a; see Shagar, *Chance and Providence*, 77).

Jewishness is, according to Shagar, an inescapable facet of one's identity. The individual Jew is born into a particular Jewish community and necessarily develops its corresponding outlook. She is consequently only a tiny component of a cultural whole, and, however much she may wish to escape, she will never be able to succeed in substituting alternative constructs for her childhood ones. Ultimately, it is the collective that determines the individual's place in the world. In Shagar's words, society engineers 'the construct of the "individual"' in a way that prevents the self from ever finding expression.[62]

It is in this vein that Shagar comments on the status of the non-identifying Jew, be it the assimilated, the non-affiliated, or the apostate.[63] His understanding of the pervasive and inescapable influence of culture prompts him to deny the rationality of the choice such individuals make to cut off their communal ties, arguing that 'in a postmodern world the believer is absolved of the need to validate his belief and practice of *mitsvot* [as part of] an essentialist, rationalist decision-making [process]'.[64] In other words, one can lead the life of an observant Jew merely out of choice, without having to constantly justify it in rational terms. In Shagar's view, a secular lifestyle ultimately makes no more sense than a religious one. He adds that 'in my view, faith is a private language',[65] and one's decision to believe requires no further validation.

Shagar displaces the notion of subjectivity by shifting the locus of religious experience from the individual to the collective. This also influenced his understanding of objectivity. Someone who engages in a critique of her tradition, according to him, effectively places herself 'already outside it'.[66] His depiction of such a scenario presents two different worlds standing side by side: the internal communal context and the critical outsider's discourse. Someone who adopts

[62] Shagar, *On His Torah He Meditates* (Heb.), 185.

[63] Many who chart the effects of postmodernism and religious commitment refer to a rise in religious affiliation, which, it is often claimed, is prompted by a desire for a sense of community, a clear set of ethical standards, and the sense of certainty that religion affords (see e.g. Urian, 'Baalei Teshuvah'). However, even while this may be the case, both thinkers, Shagar in particular, speak of Orthodox Israeli Jews who are abandoning the tight-knit community under the influence of postmodern thought which calls into question the possibility of belief.

[64] Shagar, *On His Torah He Meditates* (Heb.), 185.   [65] Shagar, 'My Faith' (Heb.) 1.

[66] This is a reference to the idea that each Jew should perceive herself as an inseparable part of the collective of *am yisra'el* and not as an individual. Thus there can be no universal consensus or 'justice' insofar as the Arab–Israeli conflict is concerned since each *am* or collective functions according to its own narrative. The conflict has no ultimate truthful or providential outcome but is contingent and sustained by conflict between narratives. See Shagar, *Man to Woman, a Jew to His Land* (Heb.), 159–70. This state of affairs mirrors the dynamics between men and women and humanity and God through perpetual feelings of unrequited love and consummation of the relationship. For the contention that Shagar (and Menahem Froman), among other religious Zionist rabbis, presented novel methods of conflict resolution, see Sheleg, 'How Do You Like Your Halakha?'

an objective or critical standpoint can no longer aspire to contribute to the collective's religious experience, since she no longer engages with the language game of that particular culture.

Shagar's conception of cultural particularism relies on a forceful alienation and negation of the self, which leads to an awareness of the all-encompassing influence of one's surroundings. He acknowledges the strong parallels between postmodernism and hasidic introspection:

It is only through the self that truth can be known. It is when someone has nothing to lose anymore, and they [find themselves] in darkness, that this knowledge comes to light and it can be grasped. What is pure truth? It is my ability to live according to who I am, to how I understand reality.[67]

With the self utterly nullified, the individual is no longer subject to delusions. She can look into herself as if she were a perfectly limpid vessel and finally appreciate who she actually is and, indeed, the extent to which her identity and character are the result of a host of conditioning factors. In short, 'pure truth' is found when she fully grasps, acknowledges, and accepts, inter alia, the fact that her experience of the world is contingent upon culture. These two aspects of Shagar's conception of cultural particularism—the attack on the self and retreat in the collective—find certain parallels among contemporary Jewish thinkers. Several similarly stress, for example, the inescapability of one's Jewishness. Jonathan Sacks uses the notion of the covenant (berit) as a starting point to discuss the commitment of each individual to the community and refute the notion that faith is connected to empirical truth: 'Judaism . . . is not an abstract moral system grounded in reason, but rather a revealed moral tradition grounded in covenantal relationships and the historic experience of powerlessness and suffering.'[68] Similarly, Yehuda Gellman finds that the postmodern attraction towards Eastern religions (most strikingly, Buddhism) and the contemporary appeal of hasidism are rooted in one and the same phenomenon: the strong emphasis both traditions place on self-nullification and the internality of religion.[69]

Chosenness

Like Sacks, Shagar draws on the symbol of the berit, arguing that Jewish life is founded on an 'awareness of the covenant as inherited [through the tradition]'. Both thinkers balance an affirmation of individual choice with the claim that the Jewish people is involved in an indissoluble 'relationship' with God. Yet this sort of language leads them to discuss another pair of values set by philosophers

---

[67] Shagar, *Thy Face I Shall Seek* (Heb.), 63.
[68] Sacks, *Crisis and Covenant*, 265.   [69] Gellman, 'Judaism and Buddhism', 314.

as binary opposites: particularism and universalism. This question relates to the status of other world religions in the Jewish tradition.[70] For Jews especially, the concept of chosenness which transpires throughout the biblical narrative of divine revelation is difficult to reconcile with a willingness to engage in a dialogue with members of other religions. Goshen-Gottstein admits that this constitutes a 'hermeneutical and theological challenge': 'How . . . can one reconcile the pluralistic view of multiple relations coexisting with the prophecy that acknowledges something unique that Israel has to share with the rest of humanity?' The solution he brings forward to alleviate these tensions builds on the relational ontology suggested in the concept of chosenness:

Understanding revelation as constituting a people rather than as revealing a truth enables openness to the Other, as long as such openness does not affect the faithfulness mandated by the covenant. . . . Revelation thus establishes the framework from which we engage others in a dialogue of being, rather than limiting our interest in others as sole possessors of truth.[71]

According to Goshen-Gottstein, a reconsideration of the meaning of revelation in Scripture can accommodate chosenness without mandating a problematic hermeneutical absolutism. Yet, as Yehuda Gellman noted, there remain some 'potential dangers inherent' in the 'self-indulgence' of the notion of chosenness, particularly in an era which shuns egoism and embraces humility.

Shagar tackles this issue in a very different manner, by once again deconstructing the polarity of particularism and universalism. His alienation of the self implies a radical particularism, insofar as a Jew (even a secular one) inexorably finds herself enraptured by mystical 'cleavings' to the Torah. Ultimately, Jews inhabit in his mind a particular 'heterotopia' (a term he borrows from Foucault), a non-physical space created and sustained by a cultural group in which supplementary layers of meaning accumulate over otherwise ordinary features of reality.[72] In his words, 'the Torah is the physical heterotopia which Jews inhabit'.[73]

By rendering particularism as the necessary condition of human existence, Shagar highlights the impossibility of universalism. One might have thought, he observes, that a universalist outlook would encompass all possible

[70] Goshen-Gottstein, 'Towards a Jewish Theology of World Religions'.   [71] Ibid. 28.
[72] For both Foucault and Shagar the heterotopia is not a material or 'natural' space—'heterotopia [is] without geographical coordinates'—but rather an arena of thought, completely determined by the 'synchrony of the culture in which it is found' (Foucault, *Aesthetics, Method and Epistemology*, 180). The Shagarian heterotopic Jew 'alienates himself from the world which depends on nature (materialism) . . . and through this transforms himself into the other and the different' (Shagar, *In the Shadow of Faith* (Heb.), 126).
[73] Shagar, *In the Shadow of Faith* (Heb.), 126–7.

components. Yet the fact is, to take one example, that Jewish nationalism does not conform to that of other nations. Jews operate in a self-contained reality and thereby set themselves apart in a way that prevents their inclusion in the tapestry of universalism:

Postmodern thinkers offer new descriptions for universalism. This is a universalism which does not purport to include absolutely everything into its world view, and especially not those things which are different. . . . Indeed not everything can be subsumed by a singular world view, not even, for example, a national world view. . . . [One example of this is that of the *she'erit*.] What is the *she'erit*? It is the piece that has no place in the puzzle [of universalism]. Mathematically it is designed to fit into the whole, and [yet] it has no place.[74]

The idea of *she'erit* ('remnant') conveys the state of alienation which characterizes the Jewish people's place in the world order. The concept problematizes universalism by highlighting the fact that different nations and cultures do not necessarily conform to common norms or live in acceptance of one another. Shagar's main point is that the universal by definition comprises contradictory elements, and that, ultimately, nothing can truly be whole or single-faceted. The *she'erit* enables Shagar to reaffirm the doctrine of chosenness, while at the same time emphasizing its dependence on an awareness of and sensitivity towards the nations of the world which stems from the Jewish experiences of bondage in Egypt and exile. While it seems that the Jewish remnant benefit from a privileged relation with the divine, their interactions with others outside the circle of believers actually proves equally important. Like Goshen-Gottstein, he deduces from the biblical account of revelation a theory of divine–human relations which mandates a more inclusive attitude towards alternative truth-claims. This comparison may set the stage for developing models of a Jewish theology, the features of which are relational rather than empirical and based on the mutuality of covenant.

[74] Shagar, *In the Shadow of Faith* (Heb.), 125–6. Shagar's view of Israeli nationalism as culturally particularist allows him to generate a religious-Zionist political narrative from a theological perspective. In the context of international relations, therefore, he did view Israel as culturally particularist, which evidently allowed him to sustain a theologically based patriotism. In a lecture delivered on Israeli Independence Day in 1991, he linked Israeli statehood to the biblical harvest season through human dependence on the land as bringing closeness to God: see Shagar, 'Father God, Mother Land' (Heb.), 149–58; see also 'The Land is a Body' (Heb.), his discussion on innate holiness in the materialism of the Garden of Eden. On the basis of a set of cultural Jewish narratives, Shagar claims that Jewish nationalism is a world unto itself—an argument he strangely bases on a citation from Slavoj Žižek: '[The Jews] have no place in the order of nations.' In his view it represents the *she'erit*—a particularist, not universalist, case of attachment to the land, sovereignty, and patriotism (see Shagar, *In the Shadow of Faith* (Heb.), 126). On the disengagement from Gaza in 2005, see id., *We Walk in Fervour* (Heb.), 337–52.

Are Goshen-Gottstein or Jonathan Sacks postmodern thinkers, or are they in fact responding to disturbing features of postmodernism? They certainly possess elements of both. On the one hand, their positions are culturally particular, and they oppose the grounding of faith in reason. To the extent that neither of them understands religion as dependent on a provable absolute truth, their theological observations do seem postmodern. On the other hand, their resistance to relativism, which I have considered above, prevents them from embracing postmodernism unequivocally.

Mysticism

There is a reliance upon mysticism among those contemporary theologians who lend credence to cultural particularism in its postmodern form. Ross uses the mystical kabbalistic idea of *tsimtsum* to reiterate ontological singularity. The concept of *tsimtsum* refers to an act of divine constriction at the time of Creation, interpreted by Jewish sages both physically and allegorically.[75] It is famously attributed to the sixteenth-century kabbalist Isaac Luria, according to whom God had to constrict himself in order to make space for the finite world. Yet certain traces of God's wisdom remained in the material world following this act of *tsimtsum*. The idea was subsequently interpreted in various ways. The Vilna Gaon and Habad hasidic thinkers, for example, did not take the concept literally but, rather, related it to another mystical concept, that of *tikun*—healing of the world. Ross, however, understood the main question to be whether *tsimtsum* ought to be interpreted empirically or allegorically:[76]

One consequence of the allegorical understanding of *Tzimtzum* is the recognition that God's reality must be spoken of in terms of at least two differing perspectives: (a) how we, as perceiving creatures, see God's relationship to the world from *our* point of view—*mitzidenu*; (b) how we, as perceiving creatures, imagine that God relates to the world from *His* point of view—*mitzido* . . . such talk of God's *mitzido* is also not a pure reflection of the way things are, because in conceptualizing God's

[75] Drob notes that even though kabbalah presents itself as a metaphysical system for understanding the world, it 'resists specific or specifiable meaning and totalisation. Rather than producing a totalistic metaphysics or final analysis', it presents 'that which is beyond the horizon of ordinary discourse and experience' (Drob, *Kabbalah and Postmodernism*, 57). For a brief history of the development of the idea of *tsimtsum* in this context, see ibid. 65–6.

[76] My distinction between empirical and allegorical is used to illustrate a shift Ross makes from understanding kabbalah as a historical empirical system to an allegorical one. Yet this distinction should not be read without ambivalence, for many postmodernists call for a deconstruction of the possibility of understanding anything 'empirically' (as there is no hard and fast knowledge) and that all writing be understood as a poetic (and not an empirical) enterprise. Drob recalls that Wittgenstein proclaimed that 'philosophy ought to be written as poetic composition' (*Kabbalah and Postmodernism*, 57).

reality in his terms, as it were, we must still begin our formulation *mitzidenu*— referring to Him as distinct from the world, even as we come paradoxically to deny this distinction. But over and above these two levels of perception is an absolute unity which is ultimately all that there is, and as such, defies definition; even the attribute 'God' as applied here would be inadequate, as this would imply comparison with something else. At this stage, the distinctions between object and subject, ontology and perception (or reality and its linguistic expression), are superfluous and equally meaningless, for all these are one and the same.[77]

One implication of hasidic allegorical interpretations of *tsimtsum*, as opposed to mitnagdic empirical understandings, is that theology enters the realm of imagination. No empirical evidence could ever contribute to a greater understanding of the divine; any attempt to do so could only be subjective, *mitsideinu*. Yet behind the idea of *tsimtsum* lies a pantheistic world-view, wherein the entire realm of human existence is, in itself, divine.[78] The kabbalistic representation of the cosmic order envisions a single rather than dual sphere of reality.[79] God appears as a singular, monolithic, undifferentiated unity, making all notions of difference or distinction perceived by human beings illusory, as Ross explains:

If there is a basis for comparison between the Kabbala and Kant, it is because both views assert that all our perceptions are somehow limited, based as they are on how things appear to us, after having been filtered through the apparatus of human categories (for Kant) or the structure of the Sefirot (for Kabbala), rather than confronted in raw and unmediated experience.

Although R. Kook is perhaps unique in explicitly making this connection between the neo-Platonic and the Kantian view, he certainly was not the first Jewish traditionalist to have merged the older Kabbalistic grounding for the limited understanding of the human point of view in understanding reality with more modern varieties of epistemological modesty. This amalgam already appears in the writings of all the allegorical interpreters of the Lurianic doctrine of Zimzum who distinguish between God's point of view . . . and our human point of view.[80]

This Kantian, and more recently neo-Kantian, distinction between that which is known—the phenomenal—and that which truly is—the noumenal—

[77] Ross, 'Religious Belief in a Postmodern Age', 232.

[78] For a recent discussion of the issues surrounding hasidism as panentheism, see T. Kaufman, *In All Your Ways Know Him*, 27–43; for a comparative reading of theistic, pantheistic, and panentheistic themes in kabbalah, see Ben-Shlomo, 'Gershom Scholem on Pantheism in the Kabbalah'.   [79] See Elior, *The Paradoxical Ascent to God*, esp. 144.

[80] Ross, 'The Cognitive Value of Religious Truth Statements', 488. On postmodern aspects of R. Kook's philosophy, see Shatz, 'Rav Kook and Modern Orthodoxy'; Wurzburger, 'Rav Soloveitchik as a Posek of Postmodern Orthodoxy'.

marked a turning point in the history of Western philosophy.[81] The shift it triggered from absolutism towards epistemological scepticism continued in subsequent centuries, leading to the radical negation of objectivity and breakdown of polarities which postmodernists almost unanimously affirm. The result of this 250-year process in continental thought, however, was already anticipated in some respects among Lurianic kabbalists in the Land of Israel in the sixteenth century. Drob notes some striking parallels:

> God–world, subject–object, inside–outside, word–thing, good and evil, etc. are all things which break down in postmodern thought. . . . Many of these distinctions also break down in the Kabbalah and we might regard the Kabbalistic symbols as pointing to new concepts that are vehicles for overcoming the basic binary oppositions in western metaphysics.[82]

In the present era it has become evident that the distinction between that which is known and that which is imagined is illusory, since our own point of view is all that we have to work with. Yet the idea has far more ancient roots in Jewish mysticism, in the doctrine of *tsimtsum*:

> The act of *Tzimtzum*, then, refers merely to a hiding or a concealment of God's all-pervasive presence, in order to enable the establishment of a realm of appearance, thus affording the illusion of a boundary between subject and object, Creator and created being and the possibility of particularization and individuation of consciousness.[83]

That this 'realm of appearance' is a mere 'illusion' is a well-established claim in the mystical strand of Jewish thought. What lies behind it is the truth of God's absolute oneness, into which all of existence ultimately dissolves:

> In piercing the veil of illusion leading to our false perception of God's transcendence, we must strive to draw the *ahdut shava* (undifferentiated unity) that lies beyond *Tzimtzum* into the cosmic reality of this world, abolishing the dichotomy of spirit and matter, miracle and nature.[84]

Ross, like Shagar, dismisses the self as the frame of reference for determining reality. She reaches this conclusion by exploring the implications of a Kookian, hasidic conception of the divine as a singular unity, which converges with the postmodern breakdown of subjective and objective.

It is worth contrasting these two positions with a third one, that of

---

[81] On Kantianism and neo-Kantianism, subjectivity and intersubjectivity, see Makkreel and Luft (eds.), *Neo-Kantianism in Contemporary Philosophy*; Uebel, *Overcoming Logical Positivism from Within*; for Kant's original writings on the subject, see Kant, *Religion and Rational Theology*.   [82] Drob, *Kabbalah and Postmodernism*, 140.
[83] Ross, 'Religious Belief in a Postmodern Age', 231.   [84] Ibid. 234.

Jonathan Sacks, whose viewpoint is not necessarily rooted in mysticism and thus enjoys a broader appeal. He aims to formulate a contemporary Jewish theology that it is not dependent on scientific, rationalist enquiry. He shifts from objectivity as an overarching category towards a relational approach to the divine:

In the Bible, God refers to Himself as 'Eheyeh asher Eheyeh.' This was translated into Greek, Latin, and English as 'I am that I am', meaning, the Unmoved Mover, Necessary Being, or Ultimate Reality. That is the God of the philosophers, not the God of Abraham or the prophets. It is, of course, a complete and elementary mistranslation. The words mean, 'I will be whatever I will be.' It is a statement about the future, about choice and freewill and the unknowability in advance of how God will appear and when. It means, 'I am the future tense. I am the God of freedom, whose future can't be predicted by humans.' In other words, I am that Being who will never be fully known, mapped, charted in terms of scientific laws or philosophical constructions. This is the God of history, not ontology.[85]

The realm of 'scientific laws or philosophical constructions' was never meant to incorporate that of religion. Such a misconception stemmed from a mistranslation and confused the disciplines of religion and science. For Sacks, the concept of truth has been misapplied to religion: 'Almost none of the truths by which we live are provable, and the desire to prove them is based on a monumental confusion between explanation and interpretation. Explanations can be proved, interpretations cannot.'[86] I intend to delve further into his comments on the relation between religion and science in the Conclusion. Suffice it to note, for the time being, that his is an interesting alternative to the mystical narratives advanced by Shagar and Ross.

The Role of Truth-Claims

Having dismissed the individual, or self, as the frame of reference for determining reality, Ross expands her analysis to the formation of communal truth-claims. To her, any 'realistic' assessment of the contemporary relevance and value of religion must acknowledge as a starting point 'the fact that the subjective perception is all we will ever have to work with'.[87] She recommends abandoning the Platonic and Kantian distinctions between reality and subjective human perception, on the basis that the former is contingent from the outset on the latter and therefore necessarily subjective:

This involves abandoning the Kantian distinction between the 'thing in itself' and the 'phenomenal world' and rejecting the hope for achieving a vantage point

---

[85] Sacks, *Universalizing Particularity*, 115–16.   [86] Sacks, *The Great Partnership*, 32.
[87] Ross, 'The Cognitive Value of Religious Truth Statements', 489.

beyond this-worldly limitations. Instead of attempting to examine reality as it is, all that we are obligated to do is to relate to the world as it is perceived by us, seeking to understand it in the most satisfactory and coherent manner possible, all the while acknowledging that this is not necessarily all that there is.[88]

To conceive of universal values after the linguistic-cultural turn strikes her as delusional. One can only make sense of reality or truth from a particular perspective and through the filters of a specific cultural context: 'particular theological truth claims about reality or God are tied to perspective and historical location, and . . . all experiential data and criteria of judgment are paradigm-dependent'.[89] Ultimately, the religious community determines its own values and truth, based not on a source of revealed, objective knowledge but on external influences and other determining factors.

This realization effectively releases contemporary Jews from the yearning to grasp reality from an objective, empirical viewpoint. Exposing the fallacy at the root of this desire dismisses the dogmatic, absolutist sentiments Kant's insights engendered. Ross's comments on epistemology point in another direction, towards a non-foundationalist theology which draws much inspiration from kabbalistic ontology, generating powerful manifestations of religious experience without, however, requiring empirical validation or laying claim to absolute truth. The implications of such a position, which I will discuss at greater length in the next chapter, are actually liberating. Ross's aim is to find a meaningful purpose for religion even after the linguistic-cultural turn, one which can motivate contemporary generations to maintain their standards of observance even without believing that these somehow convey objective moral truths or sound knowledge of the divine. In short, she argues that religious discourse is not actually supposed to fulfil any descriptive purpose. Its aim is not to 'report about reality but rather to fashion and direct it in accordance with the guidelines unique to this discourse'.[90] Believers interpret reality through the filter of their religious world-view, as a result of which their daily existence is imbued with profound meaning. The value of religious truth-claims does not depend, therefore, on how accurately they correspond to reality, but simply on the degree to which they can illuminate or inspire one's being. In other words: 'the frame of reference and criterion of validity for its statements are *derived internally*'.[91] Only believers can testify to the efficiency of the claims they hold to be true.

Ross describes this postmodern religion as a 'self-contained universe of

---

[88] Ross, 'Religious Belief in a Postmodern Age', 235; see also Hefter, 'Is Belief in Revelation Possible in the Postmodern Age?'; Sacks, *The Dignity of Difference*.

[89] Ross, 'The Cognitive Value of Religious Truth Statements', 516.

[90] Ross, 'Religious Belief in a Postmodern Age', 205.   [91] Ibid. (my emphasis).

discourse'.[92] She concedes that her revised understanding of religious truth-claims leads to a 'second-order theology' that does not rest on empirical evidence.[93] In an age in which propositions gain acceptance only once they have been verified scientifically, her suggestions might strike the reader as unpersuasive. Yet it is precisely this systematic resort to scientific logic—a product of a modernist consciousness—which she, Sacks, and Shagar reject as wholly unsuitable for theological reflections.

Freedom and Destiny

In an essay entitled 'Holiness and Freedom', Shagar discusses the relationship between freedom and religiosity. He argues that truth and values are constructs subject to culture and that, as a result, each community has 'the liberty to create and formulate [its] truth and to enact it'.[94] The Israelites in the Bible, for example, did not conceive of freedom in the same way as later philosophers did. They accepted the Torah at Sinai only after the Exodus from Egypt, when they achieved collective freedom:[95]

Thus the 'freedom' given at Sinai, as recounted in the Hebrew Bible, is quite different from modern conceptions of freedom with which we are familiar today —the notion that a person controls his own destiny and plans out his life. . . . The Western concept of self-determination is distant from this one . . . it is not to create self from self, and it is not even existentialist freedom of just being what I am.[96]

The Israelites, instead, conceived of true freedom as a collective concept. To them, 'freedom was not expressed as an individual, but as a community, as a religion and as a family'.[97] In other words, the individual did not yet count as a subject entitled to freedom. Only the community of Israel as a whole could lay claim to it, and use it to devise its own truths.

Comparing aspects of self-negation in kabbalistic sources and in postmodern literature, Shagar guides his readers away from the existentialist idea of freedom as individual autonomy. He takes Jean-Paul Sartre to task by arguing that his understanding of the concept leads inevitably to nihilism or fatalism. Sartre's philosophy rests on the assumption that, for human beings, 'existence precedes essence'. He illustrated this idea by referring to an artisan who fashions a paper cutter according to a certain design, so that it may perform a predetermined function—hence the paper cutter's 'essence' (its purpose) precedes its 'existence'. According to Sartre's assertively atheistic stance, the

---

[92] Ross, 'Religious Belief in a Postmodern Age', 218.
[93] Ibid. 18.   [94] Shagar, *Broken Vessels* (Heb.), 51.
[95] On *na'aseh venishma*, see Shagar, *Thy Face I Shall Seek* (Heb.).
[96] Shagar, *Broken Vessels* (Heb.), 47.   [97] Ibid. 48.

opposite is true for human beings. Individuals come into the world with no essence and are therefore free (or more emphatically, 'condemned to be free') to imbue their lives with whatever meaning they choose. Human freedom is not contingent on external or internal circumstances, and one has no choice, therefore, but to define and live by one's own moral engagements.

Shagar takes exception to Sartre's understanding of the self. The latter lays the burden of freedom on the individual, placing on her shoulders the onus to choose her own essence and thereby devise the 'project' that is her existence. Sartre saw the self as the sole arbiter of values. Shagar, however, criticizes such a conception of freedom on the basis that it leads to anarchy, and proposes instead to shift the burden for formulating truth-claims onto the community.[98] Building on his negation of the self explained above, he puts forward a culturally particularistic understanding of truth as a realm of discourse unique to the community and therefore immune to external criticism.[99] It is an affirmation of internality, built on the idea that everything that exists is ultimately and necessarily relative: 'Freedom is a necessary condition for the infinity of truth. . . . Without this, truth would have to be limited [to] an inevitable, predetermined, and ultimately disappointing, materialism.'[100] To differentiate his understanding of the concept of freedom from the one which prevails in contemporary philosophical discourse, he qualifies his own version as 'mystical freedom', that is, an inspired freedom derived from 'the unity of the human and the divine' which enables the community of Israel to shape its own set of truths *ex nihilo* (or in mystical terms, as *yesh mi'ayin*).[101]

To reconcile this radical conception of 'mystical freedom', of a liberating ability to devise truth out of a void, with his acceptance of cultural determinism, that is, the pervasive and inescapable influence culture bears upon the individual's very reason and world-view,[102] Shagar refers to an aspect of psychoanalyst Jacques Lacan's thought and its subsequent critique by a contemporary postmodern cultural theorist, the Slovenian intellectual Slavoj Žižek.[103] Shagar draws on a metaphor used by Lacan: when an individual

[98] Some suggest that existentialists argue definitively against nihilism; others claim that existentialists, who deny essentialism, themselves put forward a nihilist position (much of this hinges on how Nietzsche's thinking is classified). Shagar seems to accept this latter claim. See also R. C. Solomon, *From Rationalism to Existentialism*, 111–30. For a parallel discussion on the Sanyata in Buddhism, see Nishitani, 'Religion and Nothingness', 77–118.

[99] On the effects of postmodern deconstruction on the study of religion and the methodologies at its disposal, given anthropological cultural relativism, see Patton and Ray (eds.), *A Magic Still Dwells.*   [100] Shagar, *Broken Vessels* (Heb.), 52–3.   [101] Ibid. 54.

[102] Maimonides was opposed to fatalism and thus upheld the notion of free will (see *Guide of the Perplexed*, iii. 48). On free will and determinism in Jewish thought, see Berger and Shatz (eds.), *Judaism, Science and Modern Responsibility.*   [103] Žižek, *Enjoy Your Symptom!*, 1.

posts a letter, she expects that it will reach its destination, the recipient. Lacan related this scenario to the individual's ability to determine the outcome of her actions. Moreover, the expectation that the recipient will read the letter and understand the intentions of the sender sheds light on how actions are interpreted. Psychoanalysts deduce from the claim that 'the letter always reaches its destination'[104] the mechanism of teleological illusion, which Žižek illustrated as follows:

> This illusion . . . could be rendered by paraphrasing a formula of Barbara Johnson: 'A letter always arrives at its destination *since its destination is wherever it arrives.*' Its underlying mechanism was elaborated by Pêcheux apropos of jokes of the type: 'Daddy was born in Manchester, Mummy in Bristol and I in London: strange that the three of us should have met!' In short, if we look at the process backward, from its (contingent) result, the fact that 'events took precisely this turn' couldn't but appear as uncanny, concealing some fateful meaning. . . . What if a letter does *not* reach its destination? . . . What would happen if my mother and father had not come across each other? All would go wrong, I would not exist. So far from implying any kind of teleological circle, 'a letter always arrives at its destination', exposes the very mechanism that brings about the amazement of 'Why me? Why was *I* chosen?' and thus sets in motion the search for a hidden fate that regulates my path.[105]

The individual's reaction when contemplating the result of contingent actions actually proves perfectly reasonable, when omitting (as people often do) their contingent nature. The same process of what Žižek terms 'imaginary mis/recognition' occurs when one views oneself either as the addressee of ideological interpellation or, in the domain of religious belief, of providential intervention.[106] In these scenarios, the metaphorical letter is not sent with any specific recipient in mind but to the symbolic Other who, by virtue of finding herself at the right place at the right time, will identify herself as its recipient. At that moment, the letter reaches its destination by simple virtue of the fact that the recipient discerns, retroactively, a reason for why she indeed received it.

The teleological illusion unfolds when a random, contingent occurrence of no intrinsic significance either occasions or awakens a momentous reaction. A simple scenario should suffice to illustrate this idea: a pregnant, religious woman passes a beggar without giving him any money. The beggar curses under his breath but just loudly enough for the woman to catch his words. Three days later she has a miscarriage. To anyone who believes in divine providence, the cause–effect connection between the events will seem readily apparent; indeed, it would take great courage not to interpret the

[104] Lacan, *Écrits*, 41; see Mehlman (ed.), *French Freud*, 39–72.
[105] Žižek, *Enjoy Your Symptom!*, 10–12.   [106] Ibid. 10.

pregnancy loss as a consequence of her failure to give charity. Of course, the way the recipient of the metaphorical letter interprets its content is highly subjective—it builds on the recipient's background, including her cultural baggage (be it a specific ideological background, a religious orientation, or some other influence). These factors affect the way in which she narrates to herself how and why the letter ended up in her hands and how she is supposed to act as a result. In his commentary on the Song of Songs, Shagar builds on all these observations when discussing Žižek's response to Lacan:

One becomes a recipient once the letter is sent; one becomes a recipient the moment the letter arrives. . . . It is like this with the meaning of the written word: if what is written is not meant for my reading, then what message can it possibly convey to me? . . . Meaning exists only in the context of purpose . . . your identity determines who you are. . . . Your identity . . . determines your destiny.[107]

In this essay Shagar develops a theology which maintains a strong belief in divine providence and predetermination. The figure of the 'recipient' emerges at two moments: when the letter is sent (in the author's intention) and when it arrives (in the recipient's imagination, the moment she recognizes herself in its content). The individual, Shagar posits, can never reach a vantage point through which the events of her life could make sense objectively. Only the way she narrates her life to herself and therefore interprets its unfolding actually bears any significance. He offers a personal anecdote to reinforce this position:

I once met a mature yeshiva student who, for reasons of life—worries about making a living and so on—began to work as well [as studying Torah]. I met him recently and he told me with excitement that because of an illness he retired early and began to learn in a *kolel* [a yeshiva for mature students]. What is the meaning of the events concerning the illness . . . ? Was it . . . his fate? . . . The true interpretation [of why he developed this disease] is in the hands of the receiver: the meaning of life is given to him and him alone; he should determine the content of the letter . . . in these instances one can find providence . . . and so the letter always reaches its destination.[108]

This argument emphasizes the individual's dependence on her environment; it debases, from a theological perspective, the notion of ultimate objectivity but also underscores the force and meaning carried by subjective truth. Consequently, the modern polarization of free will and determinism loses its potency as a theological problem once these nuances—of intention and imagination—are brought to light. In searching for alternative Jewish theological readings of the letter-recipient metaphor, a more recent interpretation has been made by Hanoch Ben-Pazi—that of the letter as representative of

---

[107] Shagar, *In the Shadow of Faith* (Heb.), 76–7.   [108] Ibid. 79–81.

'tradition'.[109] He has developed a Levinasian and Derridean exploration of the 'letter' or 'postcard'—a decidedly textual framing of the metaphor—as the tradition itself. The letter is sent—or passed down, as is tradition—it may or may not be 'received'. If it is received, then the notion of choice plays a significant role in how the contents of the letter are 'carried' and incessantly processed. The key question is how texts are interpreted by the recipient. Its delivery is in flux; it is open-ended and ongoing, referring to possibilities of interpretation in past, present, and future terms. This is an important reading of the metaphor, as it presents a strong contrast with the approach of Shagar, for whom its destination is comparatively fixed. The parallel reading brings into question his retention of determinism as a meaningful theological idea in a postmodern world, through propagating the belief that the divine plan determines the nature of humanity and the world and thus affects the purpose individuals ascribe to their own existence.

In other writings, Shagar adds to his explanations on providence and justifies a renewed religious excitement in contemporary times by offering an interpretation of a parable attributed to Rabbi Nahman of Bratslav.[110] Rabbi Nahman's teachings resonated with Shagar in the way in which they sought to bring the modernism of the growing Haskalah movement together with hasidic thought.[111] Rabbi Nahman combined esoteric and exoteric Torah study and achieved a scholarly rabbinic profile while at the same time immersing himself in kabbalistic contemplation.[112] It is not surprising that Shagar finds his synthetic aspirations very appealing.[113]

[109] See Ben-Pazi, 'The Immense House of Postcards'.

[110] The use of Bratslavian thinking in contemporary Jewish philosophy is beginning to receive significant attention from several angles, notably from Shaul Magid and Arthur Green (see Magid, *God's Voice from the Void*; Green, *Tormented Master*).

[111] See Miron, *The Waning of the Emancipation Era* (Heb.). Rabbi Nahman is thought to have reconciled Lithuanian and Volhynian hasidism upon his move to Tiberias at a time of friction between mitnagdic maskilim and hasidim. His efforts to link the two schools of thought were admired by Shagar and are mirrored in his scholarly efforts to combine modern and hasidic thinking in his *lamdanut*. On the social challenges R. Nahman perceived, see Mark, *Mysticism and Madness*; for internal Jewish theological illustrations of his attempts to amalgamate rabbinic and hasidic world-views, see Green, *Tormented Master*; Kaplan, *Rabbi Nachman's Wisdom*.

[112] Another hasidic master whose thought interested Shagar was the *rebbe* who took over the yeshiva of Shneur Zalman (incidentally, this was not one of Ross's keenest interests)—Reb Aharon Halevi. He is said to have introduced the significance of emotions in divine service, such as in prayer and Torah study. While this idea was contested in hasidism (for example, by the Mittler Rebbe, who emphasized the necessity of meaningful intentions in emotion), it still became and remains a characteristic element of hasidic Judaism. See M. Harris, *Faith without Fear*, 61–90.

[113] On the twentieth-century phenomenon of neo-hasidism with Bratslavian ideology at its core, see Garb, *The Chosen Will Become Herds*. Ross has also noted the rise of neo-hasidism among young Jewish Israelis from Orthodox communities. Shagar discusses the same phe-

Rabbi Nahman told the story of a king who, at night, left the isolation of his castle and descended into the town in order to observe the differences between his own world and that of ordinary people. Rabbi Nahman recounted that 'he used to stand behind the houses [of the village] to try to overhear the matters of ordinary folk'.[114] The king eventually came across a man who lived in a dilapidated house, who drank wine and played the harp, and who was 'completely happy, carefree, and worryless'. He asked the man how he earned a living, to which the man responded that he repaired broken objects. Thereafter, the king made several attempts, each with greater determination, to destroy the man's livelihood. Each time, however, the man found a way to overcome the difficulties. Shagar comments on the parable: 'Again and again, the hero . . . succeeds in creating new solutions which resolve the situation. . . . It turns out that this hero was none other than . . . the *tsadik* or messiah.'[115] He then presents his interpretation of the parable: 'Humanity is unable to create something from nothing [*yesh mi'ayin*] but must recreate reality using the . . . fragments . . . [that remain]. Man is unique in his ability . . . to revolutionize an idea and re-create it.'[116]

Reading more deeply into this parable, the destruction of the individual's wellbeing is necessary in order for a (supposedly) more positive situation to arise. As in the book of Job and other profound attempts to solve the problem of evil, the providential aspects of suffering for the purposes of creativity must be acknowledged. There is a direct analogy here with the formative idea in Jewish mystical thinking, especially in Lurianic kabbalah, of *shevirat ha-kelim*—'the destruction of the vessels'. This theory describes how God intentionally disappeared from the world and left behind a dark abyss, with the expectation, or hope, that humanity would rise up to imbue the world with holiness. God deliberately created a void, as it were, so that humanity could engage in creation. In Shagar's interpretation of R. Nahman's parable, the

nomenon (see *Broken Vessels* (Heb.) and 'New Age and Kabbalah' (Heb.)). While this is arguably a sociological development of kabbalah and hasidism in contemporary society (a trend that has been noted in other religions and societies as well), its significance for both Ross and Shagar is in the more widespread use of kabbalah in which strict halakhah is not observed. It presents for them strong undertones of their theories that merge kabbalah with postmodern thought. That the whole project might not be fully understood by their students (both note the difficulty of sustaining their postmodern Orthodox theories) and thus risked degenerating into more lax forms of religious observance was clearly an outcome that both attempted to avoid. Concurrent with the lax religious observance he witnessed in his students, Shagar would have agreed with Habad that 'happiness' may be acquired in various ways. For an overview of the historical and ideological background of Bratslavian and Habad hasidism, and especially the view of Habad leader Rabbi Menachem Mendel Schneerson on elitism versus individual autonomy (an idea put forward by maskilim at the time), see Assaf, *Untold Tales of the Hasidim*, 120–52.

[114] Shagar, *The Remnant of Faith* (Heb.), 38.   [115] Ibid. 36.   [116] Ibid.

individual who has been crushed must rise up. Shagar views contemporary philosophical developments such as deconstructionism as a divine challenge sent to undermine humanity's faith and see whether belief and commitment can withstand the absence of the divine. This reading demands an engagement in a creative theology. Shagar conveys, through R. Nahman's parable, the ideal response to philosophical adversity: resourcefulness.[117] The *tsadik*, according to Shagar, seizes the shards of destruction and refashions them into building blocks for reconstruction. Even though postmodernism may be perceived as a threat to religious values and beliefs, it also carries the potential for renewal. Shagar refuses to be confounded by postmodernism and instead harnesses it to generate something new.

A postmodern believer becomes a spiritual pioneer, a trailblazer in the process of religious regeneration. Shagar compares this individual to the protagonist of *The Matrix*. Released in 1999, *The Matrix* is a science fiction classic. Set in the twenty-second century, it tells the story of a hacker who discovers that his reality is in fact a sophisticated, cyber-generated illusion in which humanity in its entirety was trapped after powerful computers overtook the real world. He joins a group of underground rebels who appoint him as their champion (a messiah of sorts) to overcome the enemy. In order to do so, he needs to travel back and forth between the virtual reality he once inhabited and the real world, by plugging himself into and out of the system which generates the illusion.

Before commenting on Shagar's interpretation of *The Matrix* and the meaning it holds for contemporary believers, it is worth acknowledging Shagar's willingness to appeal to technology and popular media when discussing theology. He denies the view that rejection of technological developments in religious circles is based on fear: 'This would present a religiosity totally dependent upon a sense of fear, loss, and solitude. . . . I reject that interpretation.'[118] Furthermore, he dismisses any attempt at imbuing a new Jewish theology with a sense of anxiety concerning contemporary cultural developments, and ultimately turns the fear of postmodernism on its head by claiming that intellectual and technological advancements further, rather than weaken, traditional religious discourse:

[117] There is little doubt that Shagar was particularly influenced by the hardship that R. Nahman suffered: R. Nahman was born only four years after the Haidamak massacre of Uman in which thousands of Jews were killed, and he asked to be buried with them when he died some four decades later. He also suffered the deaths of close family members, including his wife and some of his children, and the destruction of his home by fire in 1810. Much of Shagar's existential thinking has been attributed to his suffering in the Yom Kippur War of 1973. His tank was attacked and overturned, and four of his friends were killed; he was the only one to escape.   [118] Shagar, *The Remnant of Faith* (Heb.), 35–6.

I actually think that existing in a technological age is designed to activate a return to religiosity: a return to the intimacy of the home and roots. . . . It is impossible to ignore the fact, which is demonstrated through science fiction movies—and through *The Matrix* in particular—that the virtual world, which is meant to be a computerized, cold, anaemic, simulated, and fictitious existence, is actually accompanied by a tremendously powerful, magical quality [fuelled by] human capability. . . . The virtual world itself has the ability to inspire a high level of spirituality.[119]

As to the film itself, Shagar probably finds the concept of multiple realities inspiring: cyberspace providing a conceptual illustration of how particular communities and cultures function. The idea is certainly reminiscent of the communal heterotopia explained above. In *The Matrix*, the virtual reality that humanity is trapped in conforms to the physical laws we are all accustomed to (such as gravity and velocity). In the context of the film, however, these laws are merely computer-generated codes. The protagonist, aware of this, develops the ability to bend or break these rules and thereby act within the simulated reality in ways that defy reason. Shagar was inspired by this idea. To him, the postmodern religious believer can take the role of the messianic hero by shaping her religious reality in such a way as to make it stand up to contemporary philosophical challenges:[120]

The hacker is the religious-messianic phenomenon of the postmodern age. He is a revolutionary, or more precisely, an explorer who is able to challenge [the status quo; however,] he is not a chess player, competing according to set rules; he is not confronted with [an absolute] 'reality', but a virtual reality, [and] even an absence of reality. The hacker is a lonely innovator. . . . The hacker changes reality.[121]

Communal religious experience requires little external validation. In Shagar's view, the religious community is compelling because it is the individual's and because her identity implicates her in its destiny. To him, an inspired insider can, through certain actions, reshape the rules which govern the communal heterotopia. His dual conviction—that the individual can never really defect from her community and that the rules that govern communal affiliation are malleable—allowed Shagar to address the problem he faced periodically as the head of a yeshiva, whenever one of his former students left the religious fold.[122]

---

[119] Ibid. 35.

[120] Derrida also experienced a revival of theological teleology in his later years, even considering a messianic age, which he described as 'waiting for the future'. Contemplating the messiah adds an imaginary layer of thinking to the physical reality with which we are surrounded. Sacks too has referred to the messianic era as a futuristic quality which retains its relevance even in our 'futuristic' age (Sacks, 'The Messianic Idea Today').

[121] Shagar, *The Remnant of Faith* (Heb.), 38–9.

[122] See also Shagar, 'A Group of Friends with Yarmulkes Go to the Pub' (Heb.); id., 'Similar Qualities of Postmodern Religious Identity' (Heb.).

He was acutely aware of the absence of a captivating theology which, combined with the ever-increasing progress witnessed in the secular world, acted as a motivating factor for disaffiliation.

Multiple Truths and the Perils of Relativism

Ross: 'Points of View' as 'Intersubjective'

Ross views local religious truths as valuable precisely because they are relative to a particular group. She uses this relativism to put forward a non-empirical, kabbalistic, metaphysical truth and, in so doing, endeavours to redeem relativism from its negative connotations. She affirms the relative nature of each religion and claims that such a conception of religious truth permeates the history of Jewish thought. In one instance, she quotes R. Kook to that effect:

Even the 'neo-Kantian' revival cannot match even the smallest part of Israel's strength. It is true, and we (Jews) have always known it—and we did not need Kant to reveal this secret to us—that all human cognitions are relative and subjective. This is the 'Kingdom' as a vessel that has no power of its own and the 'Synagogue' or 'Moon', that receives illumination. All our acts, our emotions, our prayers, our thoughts—everything is dependent on 'Zot', 'Bezot ani boteach'—in this will I be confident [Ps. 27: 3].[123]

Postmodernism, Ross argues, lays bare a belief, long held by Jewish mystics, in the subjective character of truth. She considers it a relief that the Jewish tradition championed centuries ago the notion that a truth is subjective to the group which holds it to be true. She quotes Eliyahu Eliezer Dessler in support of this view: 'What is the value of a relative perception? Its value lies in the fact that it is relative to us, in accordance with our situation in this world, the world of free will and worship, and therefore only this is the truth for us.'[124]

Having internalized the epistemological uncertainty characteristic of the postmodern critique, Ross seeks to establish solid ground for religious knowledge. She turns for that reason to non-foundationalism, a contemporary epistemological position that justifies truth-claims not on the basis of their purported grounding in some neutral or objective source of knowledge, but on the degree to which they cohere with other beliefs and opinions.[125] This

---

[123] Ross, 'The Cognitive Value of Religious Truth Statements', 487.

[124] Ross, 'Religious Belief in a Postmodern Age', 234. While there is currently no secondary literature on the usage of Dessler's writings as postmodern, the fact that both Ross and Shagar independently drew on his work to resituate the concept of truth is suggestive of the possibility of applying hasidic and kabbalistic writings to the postmodern enquiry.

[125] Ross, Expanding the Palace of Torah, 165–6.

attitude she contrasts favourably with the sort of radical postmodern relativism that turns the rejection of absolute truth into nihilism and anarchy on
the simplistic assessment that all truth-claims are of equal value. Instead of
establishing the truth-value of a proposition against the background of an
objective, metaphysical source, non-foundationalists simply rely on intersubjective agreement within the wider community:[126]

True, all religions have some truth to them, we might say, but these can still be
positioned hierarchically in terms of their relative worth, for some expressions are
more successful than others in leading to the ethical norms which are the common
ideal of all the great religious traditions. On this view, the more inclusive a religion
is of the truths of others, the greater its value and also its ability to co-exist with the
rest.[127]

Ross adopts a 'hierarchical approach', which she extrapolated from R. Kook's
thinking. What she finds most compelling is the way R. Kook managed to
establish truth while at the same time discarding its absolutist nature. This
provides a convenient bypass for Ross, one which demands neither relinquishing fundamental religious beliefs nor turning to radical relativism. The
hierarchical approach avoids the potential conflict between the two, thereby
leading her to a similar conclusion to Shagar about multiple truths. For Ross,
belief is perpetuated by the community, and its theological worth is therefore
greater than the concept of absolute truth:

There is no clear-cut transition between the area of basic religious truths and relative
ones. There are many different levels of necessity and constraint between what is
absolutely true from an intersubjective point of view and totally underdetermined
beliefs. The lower down we go on the list of common denominators, the more
'objective' are the constraints, but as we advance upwards on the scale of parti-
cularization, we move in the direction of 'cognitive underdetermination'. The further
we enter into the specifics, the more there is room for conflict and difference
of opinion and an open-ended list of formulae that we could adopt as renderings of
reality in different societies in different times and places. This implies the notion
of degrees of ontological commitment for human beings. There may be areas
where intersubjective constraints on religious truth claims are very strong indeed,
while there are other areas where the constraints are minimal.[128]

How is it possible to attain a consensus between different communities about
metaphysical truth? Could each community's truth-statements be judged

---

[126] The term 'intersubjective' is usually associated with the philosopher Donald Davidson;
however, it is unclear whether Ross was familiar with his writings.

[127] Ross, 'Reflections on the Possibilities of Interfaith Communication', 5–6.

[128] Ross, 'The Cognitive Value of Religious Truth Statements', 514.

on the basis of such a consensus? Who decides which communal truth-claims are more or less important? Ross calls these complex situations the 'middle level'. She refers to the truth-statements at the middle level as 'intersubjective' because they are neither totally 'other' nor immediately obvious to the members of her community. On such issues, Ross argues:

When dealing with the middle level of verbalized formulation, not all religious claims are equally valid; some contain only a grain of truth, and others are better because they contain more. But since, in absolute terms, all are equally off the mark, the justification for preferring one alternative over another must now be based on criteria for truth which are not primarily cognitive. . . . Some of these are still traditional and do not necessarily negate the presumption of agreement with reality.[129]

Truths are therefore valuable both because they belong to and because they are held by a certain group. So why is it that 'others are better because they contain more [truth]'? How, according to Ross, could the relative worth of religious truth-claims be measured? She answers this question by alluding to R. Kook, suggesting that what contributes to the progress of humanity can be considered truthful:

What R. Kook might be understood as saying here is that although no formulated belief can be equated, as is, with the object it seeks to depict, and for this reason can never be regarded as having more than relative ontological value, there are certain formulations of belief that bear constant and eternal validity—not because of their superior ontological grounding in an absolute scale, but because they are *universally bound to the nature of man, regardless of his particular moral state or cultural affinities. A person may therefore regard some of his belief claims as not merely subjective and personal, but as best for all other human beings as well, without yet being truly objective,* i.e. viewed, as it were, from God's non-anthropocentric vantage point. . . . Although this view does not deny the perspectival nature of all truth claims, it does limit the parameters of religious truth claims to a degree. As such R. Kook would be *avoiding a thoroughgoing relativism or nihilism* on grounds that are similar to Hilary Putnam's concept of 'objectivity for us.' So described, R. Kook's ontological claims would still remain very modest, indeed virtually insignificant. One does not know and cannot know God in Himself, but only God as we experience His effects from our point of view.[130]

In this sense, Ross attempts to reconfigure the either/or distinction between subjective and objective truth. She argues that the value inherent in truths does not only stem from their culturally particular subjectivity but also from the degree to which they contribute to society or humanity. This consideration is utilitarian in nature, a matter of 'the greatest good of the greatest

[129] Ross, 'The Cognitive Value of Religious Truth Statements', 494.
[130] Ibid. 514–15 (my emphasis).

number'.[131] In the hierarchical system Ross proposes, each truth is ranked according to the number of people who hold it to be true. While this may sound like a pragmatic espousal of truth-values as inherent in others' beliefs, she also makes it clear that such a viewpoint must receive theological backing:

Some people believe that another way is possible, if the representatives of various faiths simply agree to listen to each other empathetically out of a desire to understand the Other in his own terms. The contention . . . is that this is not enough when dealing with religions bearing claims to absolute truths, and that *the solution lies in a more subtle understanding of the theological import* of such claims.[132]

Neo-pragmatic ideology inclines towards pluralism, and its adherents regularly seek to establish cross-denominational or cross-confessional relations. Ross believes, however, that such efforts must be informed by a comprehensive theological argument in order to receive legitimacy. Such a claim distances her from neo-pragmatism. Adherents of such a theology ought to appreciate the relative—not relativistic—worth of their own world-view and way of life. They must recognize their affiliation to their own culturally particular truth-system, and thereby cognitively reckon with the force of those of others. Ross finds this approach in R. Kook's thought, identifying a form of 'cognitive pluralism' as a premise for acknowledging the similar claims of others. True monotheism, she argues, involves recognizing different truths.[133]

This position, Ross nonetheless acknowledges, does not provide that sense of firm certainty which past generations could rely on. A number of critics, such as Yoel Finkelman, have taken her to task for using human consensus as the criterion for determining truth-values and leaving no area of absolute certainty. Finkelman reads Ross as having done away with everything except for human consensus:

Other than my own conscience, what tools do I have to determine which new ideas are revelation to be embraced and which are heresies to be fought? . . . Are we willing to sacrifice our moral and religious conscience on the altar of communal consensus?

---

[131] Utilitarianism was a nineteenth-century British political theory in which Jeremy Bentham and John Stuart Mill suggested that society should be built on principles judged by the 'amount' of 'good' or benefit they bestowed on the greatest number of people possible. The theory assumes that only material pleasures or benefits are of relevance or value. See Mill, *Utilitarianism*.

[132] Ross, 'Reflections on the Possibilities of Interfaith Communication', 7–8 (my emphasis).

[133] Ross, 'The Cognitive Value of Religious Truth Statements', 525. The reference to monotheism here should be linked with 'scriptural reasoning', a movement of interreligious— Jewish, Christian, Muslim—joint textual study, developing broader and deeper theories of interpretation and treatment of the other often pertaining to postmodern qualities. See Feldmann Kaye, 'Interreligious Dialogue as a Postmodern Age (Heb.).

If not, what force is there to the claims that the communal narrative forms binding revelation? If post-modernism has taught us anything of value, it is that modernistic confidence in the morality of consensual human values is unfounded, to say the least.[134]

Finkelman questions the viability of the argument for 'communal consensus' on the basis that agreed-upon norms of right and wrong—what Jewish theology is and what it is not—are difficult to justify. How is one to know which revelations or truths should be accepted and which are heretical?

Ross, in her response, refers to R. Kook, according to whom there exists a level 'higher' than communal consensus which erases any potential for destructive influence:[135] '[R. Kook] believes that these constructions do not refer *merely* to people's own deepest convictions, values and visions.'[136] In rejecting Finkelman's critique, Ross signals her belief that communal consensus does not constitute the be-all and end-all of theology.

Shagar's Hierarchy of Truth

Numerous wars, according to Shagar, were waged over competing ideas of universal truth which contemporary thinkers no longer accept: 'We have given up hope for a great and absolute justice, which as we have said cannot be found, our expectations have decreased to weak localized "justices".'[137] Truth, he therefore argues, is particular to each culture, rather than universal:

The dilemma faced by the postmodern world is that it refuses to posit absolute values because according to [postmodernism] such values do not exist. There is no truth and there certainly is no 'Truth'. In today's world, truth is a cultural construct, and was described by Nietzsche as 'the politics of truth'.[138]

The focus has shifted from a universally applicable conception of truth to a culture-bound one. Despite some reservations, Shagar ultimately adopts a postmodern understanding of the fundamental role culture and community play for different religious groups aiming to imagine the divine. Under the influence of relativism, culturally particular thought systems must be able to coexist with, rather than compete against, one another. As Shagar argues in his interpretation of Richard Rorty:

The morals of justice [in postmodern times] . . . are different from traditional

---

[134] Finkelman, 'A Critique of *Expanding the Palace of Torah*', 8–9 (my emphasis).

[135] A cultural particularist reading of R. Kook has been criticized by Nadav Shnerb, who writes: 'Rabbi Kook has already written "in a place that I am not, God is not. And even more so you are not" (*Orot hakodesh* 3: 140)' (Shnerb, 'A Parable of a Wise Man Who Despairs of Reason' (Heb.), 210).   [136] Ross, 'The Cognitive Value of Religious Truth Statements', 516.

[137] Shagar, *Broken Vessels* (Heb.), 15.   [138] Ibid. 14.

[notions of] justice. Rorty, a contemporary American philosopher, argues that in discussing truths, we must reject the metaphor of what is revealed [as truthful] and work instead according to a metaphor of creativity on one's own [culturally] constructed terms. [This is because] metaphors of what [we believe to have been] revealed cause people to feel that they have discovered the truth and that [consequently] there is no room for other truths. In opposition to this, [the recognition of] our self-constructed, made-up metaphors encourages a view that each value is created within and by our [respective] societies, so that therefore they do not contradict the values of other societies. In fact, if restraint is exercised, it becomes possible to reach a state of harmony within the community and with the world outside.[139]

Multiple groups struggle over competing notions of truth, with the ultimate aim of triumphing over their opponents: in such circumstances, humanity can never 'reach a state of harmony'. Thus, while the search for universal truth supplies a strong sense of that which is right and wrong, it does not lead to the creation of a world in which different people with different value systems and lifestyles can truly coexist. Ross also discusses this theme in an article which outlines possibilities for interfaith relations.[140] Having moved away from a monolithic conception of truth, one can welcome 'conflicting revelations'. The different truths that Shagar is keen to recognize do not compete with each other. Rather, they appear as complementary, each originating from a different perspective.[141] Alan Jotkowitz provides an interesting comparison between the positions of Shagar and Sacks on the topic:

Both R. Shagar and R. Sacks recognize the difficulties of religion in the postmodern world in which 'no one creed has a monopoly on spiritual truth; no one civilization encompasses all the spiritual, ethical and artistic expressions of mankind.'

To this paradox, R. Shagar responds with silence and R. Sacks with conversation. But in reality they are addressing two different audiences. R. Shagar is concerned with the fact 'that we cannot prove our values and there is always an element of doubt' from the perspective of the individual, and to this he advocates silent acceptance. R. Sacks is concerned with the resolution of this dilemma from the public and societal perspective, and to this audience he recommends engagement and conversation.[142]

According to Jotkowitz, Shagar's response to relativism is personal: he views the challenges it presents as necessarily insoluble. Sacks's position, on the

---

[139] Ibid. 16.   [140] Ross, 'Reflections on the Possibilities of Interfaith Communication'.
[141] One consideration in reading Shagar is that he wrote for an Israeli audience, and Ross writes both for an Israeli and a diaspora readership.
[142] Jotkowitz, '"And Now the Child Will Ask"', 53–4 (my emphasis), quoting Sacks, *The Dignity of Difference*.

other hand, is similar to that of R. Kook (following Ross's interpretation, outlined above). It is one in which the value of truth is measured according to its ability to change society for the better:

Men kill because they believe they possess the truth while their opponents are in error. In that case, says God, throwing truth to the ground, let human beings live by a different standard of truth, one that is human and thus conscious of its limitations. Truth on the ground is multiple, partial. Fragments of it lie everywhere. Each person, culture and language has part of it; none has it all. Truth on earth is not, and nor can it aspire to be, the whole truth. It is limited, not comprehensive; particular, not universal. When two propositions conflict it is not necessarily because one is true and the other false.[143]

Fundamentalism flourishes when individuals lack the humility to recognize that truth can be partial and limited.

Is Mysticism Essential?

As mentioned earlier, Drob highlights commonalities between postmodernism and kabbalah:

Kabbalistic theosophy, which provides a mythical account of God, the elements of creation, humanity, and the purpose of existence, anticipates and is highly compatible with the relativistic, perspectivist, anti-foundational sensibility of postmodernism and . . . is able to adopt and integrate precisely those postmodernist ideas (multiculturalism, multi-perspectivism, non-foundationalism, philosophical relativism, and even *atheism*) that have traditionally been thought to be antithetical to a religious or theological world-view.[144]

The few authors who have addressed this issue need to further address the convergences between kabbalistic and postmodern discourses.[145] Ross stresses the need for a complete reconfiguration of the understanding of culture and the community in order to appropriately deal with postmodernism. In her view, such an outcome is only possible by reference to kabbalah:

I believe that theologians sometimes have the very important task of mediating between mysticism and empiricism, and that the non-foundational post-liberal may have something valuable to learn from the various theological positions that were developed in response to the latter-day Kabbalist understanding of the limits

[143] Sacks, *The Dignity of Difference*, 64–5; see also id., *Not in God's Name*.

[144] Drob, *Kabbalah and Postmodernism*, 16.

[145] For example, Pinhas Giller barely hints at a connection between postmodernism and kabbalah (Giller, 'Kabbalah and Contemporary Judaism'). On the unpopularity of kabbalah in the modern age as a result of specifically 'modernist' concerns and historical events, see Ariel, *Kabbalah*, 113–28.

of human perception and the possible forms of engagement between religious belief and metaphysics.[146]

Ross suggests that 'there is no clear-cut transition between the area of basic religious truth and relative ones', that these realms are not antithetical. Instead, she describes levels and degrees of truth perception, delineating an intersubjective outlook.[147] She justifies this position by arguing that cultural particularism involves neither a denial of a supreme God nor limitations to belief. Rather, it represents, in her hierarchy, the upper boundary. Since the 'specifics' of faith are so particular, the necessity for multifarious truths reflects, in her view, the texture of reality, involving 'different societies and different places'.

Conclusions

Relativism poses a threat to religion only when the latter makes an exclusivist claim to truth. Nadav Shnerb's warning exemplifies the suspicion with which religious leaders view radical postmodern ethics, which he claims represent 'an exaggerated form of doubtfulness, with mistaken terminology alongside useless jargon. . . . It leads to nihilism and dogmatism. . . . Do not take this path. It is not good. It is not true. It is also not original. It is just the latest fashion.'[148] Most of the postmodern thinkers mentioned so far tend to dismiss the terms 'relativism' and 'postmodernism'. Shagar at times expresses certain reservations about the view that truth is a human construct, probably in order to distance himself—like many other thinkers—from relativism.[149] He also rejects relativism in its most radical form: 'The values by which those in this type of society live lie in total contrast to the meaning of those who live in a postmodern world.'[150] This danger evaporates, however, when individuals start viewing truth as culture-bound. Many indeed, including Shagar and Ross (although they both avoid the term), accept in that respect the premises of both relativism and postmodernism. They consider the possibility that a plurality of truths such that particular sets of truth would not be presumed to apply universally could be beneficial for religion. Shagar's 'positive pluralism'[151] and Ross's 'cognitive pluralism' rely on a culturally particularistic conception of truth. Having 'closed the door on absolute truth', Shagar views many other possibilities for increased religiosity.[152] From what he terms a 'failure of the design of

---

[146] Ross, 'Religious Belief in a Postmodern Age', 232.
[147] Ross, 'The Cognitive Value of Religious Truth Statements', 514.
[148] Shnerb, 'A Parable of a Wise Man Who Despairs of Reason' (Heb.), 210.
[149] See his discussion on ethics (Shagar, *Broken Vessels* (Heb.), 1, 15–16).   [150] Ibid. esp. 16.
[151] Ibid. 21.   [152] Shagar, *Broken Vessels* (Heb.), 27.

the human condition [itself]', or the illusion of metaphysics, arises the 'possibility for a theology comprising exciting religious options'.[153]

Ross writes of the 'promise' that Shagar's position holds for the future of Jewish theology:

The epistemological modesty of non-foundationalism can help religious adherents move away from overly rigid definitions of doctrine and allow them to return to the pre-modern function of religion as providing a valuable universe of discourse and a compelling way of life. It can extricate them from a mindless and stultifying triumphalism and encourage the willingness to refine religious convictions by listening carefully to other points of view. Initial recognition of this promise has been articulated by the late Rabbi Shagar, an unconventional Religious Zionist Rosh Yeshiva in Israel. . . . But (as Shagar would have been the first to admit), if this unexpected expression of enchantment with postmodernism is to fulfill its promise, it must also be fortified by the discipline of immersion in the rich legacy of tradition and the rigorous cultural-linguistic construct that it provides for formulating our religious belief.[154]

For Shagar and Ross, it is preferable for a religious believer to reject absolute truth in favour of spiritual pluralism as long as this can be balanced with a definitive commitment to their own faith.[155] In order to explore alternative world-views, one must remain 'strong in oneself, standing in the world by not being swayed by absolutisms'.[156] The believer, according to Shagar, must be wary of a world in which 'anything goes'.[157]

Shagar appropriates cultural particularism by rendering truth subject to a cultural context. He offers his followers a blend of mysticism and postmodernism through which he redefines major philosophical concepts such as the self, freedom, providence, and destiny. He rejects the idea of a 'fixed, monolithic truth' as little more than an artificial, human construct.[158] The way he envisions the community 'playing' a sophisticated language game allows for a degree of freedom and human creativity rarely observed in traditional circles. Ross similarly takes R. Kook's innovative and non-traditional theology as an inspiring model. She describes him as 'wise to be suspicious of all claims to absolute truth, or to any direct and perfect correspondence between our perceptions and ontological reality'.[159] Indeed, she identifies with his scepticism and notes that such a feeling ultimately leads to 'a fundamental shift in the expectations surrounding traditional theological claims'.[160]

[153] Shagar, *Broken Vessels* (Heb.), 17.
[154] Ross, 'Religious Belief in a Postmodern Age', 239–40.
[155] Roth, 'Judaism in the Straits of Modernity and Postmodernity' (Heb.), 502–5.
[156] Shagar, *Broken Vessels* (Heb.), 27.   [157] Ibid. 28.   [158] Ibid.
[159] Ross, 'The Cognitive Value of Religious Truth Statements', 516.   [160] Ibid. 18–19.

As Jospe puts it, casting off the notion of absolutist truth should herald significant ethical improvements on the level of society:

I am guided by a twofold belief: on a theoretical level, that claims to 'one absolute truth' are inherently meaningless; and on a practical level, that such spiritual exclusivity constitutes an existential danger to the peace of the world, especially in the era of the 'global village' and increasingly widespread weapons of mass destruction. So long as religions continue to compete with each other in their exclusivistic claims, they will not be able to serve as an effective force for peace and cooperation, but rather will perpetuate their all too frequent desecration of God's name and affront to human dignity.[161]

Each of these positions reveals a deep concern over the concept of relativism, which pivots on how truth carries over into a postmodern age. The term 'relativism' often carries threatening overtones and has come to be associated with excessive permissiveness. I predict that this perception will fade away, but in order for this to happen, thinkers must search for a different phrase to replace the term 'relativism'—possibly 'intersubjectivity'.

Context plays an important role in determining beliefs and values, which implies that all reality is culture-bound and therefore in perpetual flux. The same applies to theology. Absolutist religion, as well as other forms of absolutism, necessarily involves the coerced imposition of one world-view or set of values on others. Its ethical shortcomings should be subject to the same critical examination as postmodern ethical relativism. Once an openness to different world-views develops—in a way that does not prevent individuals from adhering to their own value systems—the threat of relativism effectively loses its significance.

It would be misleading and counterintuitive at this point to continue to posit on the strictest of modern terms a single, motionless, lifeless truth. Postmodern subjection of belief to culture dissolves the modernist dichotomies between truth and falsity, or objectivity and subjectivity. The popular aspiration for absolute truth or knowledge—an artificial construct at the root of unspeakable acts of violence and bloodshed—effectively collapses upon this realization. It is obvious that the implications of this idea present an acute problem. Yet the benefits suggested above should dispel the concerns of those thinkers who decry the disastrous philosophical implications of relativism for ethics. We move, therefore, towards an exciting revivification of contemporary Judaism by recasting the religious believer as an innovator, a visionary in a changing reality. For this developing theological project, I propose the term 'visionary theology'.

---

[161] Jospe, 'Pluralism out of the Sources of Judaism'.

TWO

LANGUAGE

The Problem of Language

Before the advent of postmodernism, philosophers generally viewed language as concordant with reality. In other words, they assumed that words, phrases, and sentences corresponded to the objects in the world that they purported to describe. This assumption that a 'signifier' (most notably, in speech) necessarily relates to a specific 'signified' is known as 'correspondence theory'. Philosophers of language seek to investigate the nature of this relation. They consider, among other questions, whether and how language reflects reality. This is known as 'the problem of language'.

An outline of recent trends in the philosophy of language should begin with Ludwig Wittgenstein, whose works I also discussed at the beginning of the previous chapter. In particular, his *Philosophical Investigations* (in contrast to his earlier book, *Tractatus Logico-Philosophicus*) offers seminal philosophical reflections on language. A number of thinkers subsequently built upon his pioneering insights, attesting to new understandings of the nature, function, and use of language. The numerous implications of Wittgenstein's observations in fields as varied as semiotics, cognition, sociology, linguistics, and more testify to the acuteness of the problem of language for philosophy.[1]

Wittgenstein delved into the way language functions. In his later philosophical works, he abandoned the hope of constructing a linguistic system based on representation (one that could validate correspondence theory systematically). He recognized that the meanings of words cannot be derived solely from the objects they purport to describe (that is, from the world) but, rather,

[1] This does not mean that language did not concern philosophers prior to the postmodern age. James Harris has charted philosophical interest in language since Aristotle's writings on the meaning of propositions (*On Interpretation*), through and beyond medieval scholastics (Aquinas's *Summa Theologica*), preferring to refer to the postmodern preoccupation with language as the 'linguistic turn' in philosophy (as Rorty too has called it) (J. F. Harris, *Analytic Philosophy of Religion*, 2–5). Later Wittgensteinian thought was fastidiously developed in the 1920s through the 'logical positivism' of a group of philosophers known as the Vienna Circle, including Rudolf Carnap, Moritz Schlick, Herbert Feigl, and Friedrich Waismann, at the University of Vienna. This movement strongly influenced both British empiricism and American pragmatism and analytic philosophy of religion in general.

from the use we make of them in language. It is in this context that Wittgenstein coined the expressions 'language game' and 'form of life'. Following his
reasoning, the meaning of a particular word or phrase depends chiefly on the
language game in which it is used. The word 'game', to take one simple example, can appear in a host of different formulas and sentences with differing
meanings at each occurrence (board games, Olympic Games, mind games, and
so on). Concurrently, language games reflect different forms of life—the activities in which individuals engage on a daily basis. This realization carries far-
reaching implications. Its most basic ramification is that language should not
be understood to refer to anything beyond itself. Each language game operates
according to its own parameters and is governed by its own particular rules.[2]
Postmodernists thus note that meaning differs from one language to the next or
from one society to another—in other words, they refute correspondence theory
by conceiving of language as a product of culture. This is how their understanding of language challenges previously accepted notions.

Contemporary philosophers demonstrate that language does not describe
an objective state of affairs but, rather, reveals a particular perspective and world-
view, rooted in culture. Each community possesses its own semantic and interpretative universe, a world unto itself, or as Derrida put it, 'le jeu du monde'.[3]
The contours of a language game are recognizable only to those who have mas-
tered its usage and applicable only within the relevant form of life (in Heidegger's terminology, they are 'intraworldly'[4]). According to Lyotard, meaning is
contingent upon what is considered meaningful at a given time, in a particular
place, and according to a specific context.[5] Other thinkers, such as Rorty, have
claimed that language and hermeneutics serve the purpose of local collectives,[6]
while Habermas delved into how meaning arises in a particular cultural context.[7] These efforts all contribute to sharpening our understanding of the
mutual influences language and culture bear on each other.

[2] For the classic sources of the language game, see esp. Wittgenstein, *Philosophical Investigations*, 124; Derrida, *Of Grammatology*.

[3] This is a reference to Kant's 'freies Spiel', in which one signifier points to another, which
points to another in an unending game of signification. As a concept, 'le jeu du monde' is
comparable to the 'rhizome' and 'nomades' of Gilles Deleuze and Félix Guattari. The other oft-
cited quotation of Derrida is 'il n'ya pas de hors-texte': this is often translated as 'there is
nothing outside the text', but it has been argued that it should read 'nothing exists outside its
context'.   [4] Heidegger, *The Basic Problems of Phenomenology*, 169.

[5] See Lyotard, *The Postmodern Condition*.

[6] See Rorty, *Philosophy and the Mirror of Nature*. Though Rorty would not have situated
theological import in revelation and would have noted its social significance, his thinking on
this point does shine a light on Ross's 'cumulative revelation' through the assumption that
those within a particular language game propagate their own truths.

[7] In his Martin Buber Lecture at the Israel Academy of Sciences and Humanities in
Jerusalem (1 May 2012), Habermas noted that his project has not been to critique a Cartesian

Religious Language in a Postmodern Age

Language is composed of words, phrases, and sentences and is reinforced with intention, context, and meaning. It is used in different ways, in order to convey different ideas in different contexts. People in different environments employ language in different ways. In the realm of religion, they speak about shared concepts, namely community, rituals, values, history, beliefs, and experiences. In using language to describe these concepts, they presume that they will be understood by their interlocutors if they express themselves adequately.

If religious language is inextricably rooted in a particular culture, it necessarily appears limited in scope, perhaps even incapable of fully expressing religious beliefs. Prior to the cultural-linguistic turn, the idea that individuals could use language to describe, worship, or appeal to non-physical entities was widely accepted. This presumption extended to fundamental functions of religion, including the ability to communicate truths about God, the world, ethics, and so on. To some, most notably the logical positivists, the newfound awareness of the limitations of religious language put forward by Wittgenstein was even thought to represent a blanket refutation of religion. If language does not refer to anything beyond itself, it cannot be applied to the metaphysical realm—for the sake of prayer or to describe the divine. Such a realization, these thinkers argued, effectively disproved theism: if God cannot be spoken about, so the argument goes, then God does not exist. Yet such a position, as I show below, relies on an erroneous understanding of language propounded by modernity.

The postmodern recognition of the cultural-linguistic turn—the realization that language is determined by culture—therefore raises unprecedented challenges to the formulation of metaphysical ideas. If Jewish theology is to withstand these challenges, it must find a suitable response to the claim that Jewish beliefs and values are determined by culture and consequently reflect communal consensus rather than divine inspiration. Contemporary Jewish thinkers have to acknowledge that their religious principles are composed of a conglomeration of cultural constructs that have developed over the centuries, without undermining the power of religion altogether.

It is worth noting that the problem of religious language is not a recent one for philosophers. While I refer to the most recent developments in this area of philosophy, the fact remains that language bears significance in religious speech, prayer, study, and writing. It should not come as a surprise, therefore, that the issue of religious language has concerned philosophers of religion for

emphasis on the self (see Ch. 1 above) and a radical postmodern version where all is representation, but rather to rethink the role of language and the public sphere through dialectical philosophy (assessing both modern and postmodern ideas and forging a middle way).

centuries. With regard to the theological implications of the linguistic-cultural turn, the following questions should be considered. If language cannot describe anything beyond itself, how can any statement be 'true'? Do beliefs serve any purpose if they do not express something true about the world? How can one speak of God and religious beliefs if language is merely a human construct? Can religious language point, in any way, to the metaphysical realm? What does it mean for religion if theological discourse makes no claim to formulating factual statements about the world and aspires only to cultivate a particular mythology? Can Torah study retain ultimate value when understood as a social preoccupation rather than as a guide to the understanding of the forces that shape the world? When the problem of language is applied to theological discourse, does the very nature of theology demand redefinition?

In response to this crisis, language can be understood as a creative rather than a descriptive endeavour, one that does not merely represent reality but in fact generates an individual's conception of the world. The way an individual or a group employs language reveals more about themselves than it does about the objects they purport to describe. This radically innovative understanding of the problem of language therefore constitutes one of the fundamental challenges that postmodernism presents to religion.

I first wish to analyse Christian responses to these questions and assess whether they can provide instructive resources for Jewish theology. I will then explore the theological responses which Shagar and Ross formulate to the problem of language. Both thinkers acknowledge the premises of the linguistic-cultural turn, most notably the limited ability of language to represent anything beyond itself. This conception of language carries greater implications when applied alongside the notion of cultural particularism: it signifies that a particular community's understanding of truth may only be described in its own terms, through its own language. Ross, like many postmodern thinkers, deduces from Wittgenstein a negation of the metaphysical qualities of language. Shagar similarly describes language as a 'simulated' reality. Both thinkers effectively converge in postulating that language serves as an instrument through which cultural values are continuously generated. In other words, although the songs or prayers used by religious communities possess no intrinsic metaphysical value, they derive value from the fact that they feed into and invigorate the religious imagination. While acknowledging the tensions raised by postmodern philosophers of language, Ross and Shagar defend classical theological discourse by integrating Jewish mystical (kabbalistic and hasidic) ideas into their responses.

In contemporary Protestant theology, Richard Kearney suggests 'returning to God after God', thereby coining the term 'anatheism' (from the Greek *ana-theos*, literally, 'again-God').[8] The term implies that theism 'comes back again', albeit in a radically different form.[9] His purpose is to restate the fundamental inability to prove God and encourage engagement with a combination of deconstructionist and mystical perspectives. This return is based on a radically different conception of God, wherein God is plausible and potential, rather than actual:

My point is not to describe anatheism as some necessary historical dialectic—a pretentious temptation—but to indicate how certain bold minds of the twentieth century responded to spiritual questions of our age; namely, how might one speak of the sacred after the disappearance of God? Or how might one continue to have faith after the scientific enlightenment dispensed with superstition and submission and after two world wars exposed the fallacy of history as some Divine Plot? . . . This is what I mean by a return to God after God. God must die so that God might be reborn. Anatheistically.[10]

Kearney's starting point was the modernist 'death of God' narrative which posited the impossibility of epistemological certainty. God represents, in this light, a project of hermeneutic imagination and becomes as a result 'possible' through an 'agnostic' enquiry: 'Almost all of the great mystics and sages attested to a moment of agnostic abandonment as a crucial transition to deeper faith . . . a faith beyond faith in a God beyond God.'[11] This agnosticism comes with a mystical ingredient: 'Without some poetic release into a free variation, the return to a God beyond God is virtually impossible. But if faith is not reducible to fiction it is integral to metaphor. Metaphor involves a transportation (*metaphora*) between self and other. As such the metaphorical *as* contains within itself a mixed copula of *is/is not*.'[12] Kearney's 'God-who-may-be' allows theologians to imagine a non-empirical realm and thereby make room for the divine. His resort to imagination and creation, rather than description of that which is beyond the world, bears similarities with Ross's interest in language and Shagar's hermeneutics.

John Caputo, a postmodern Catholic theologian, makes similar observations. He too resists naming God so as to avoid stasis. God is a wish, a potential force, sought out through prayer. Caputo reconsiders the very meaning of the terms which refer to the divine:

[God] refers neither to an actual being or entity nor to being itself, but to an impulse or aspiration simmering within both the names of entities and the name of being, something that groans to be born, something that cannot be constricted

---

[8] Kearney, *Anatheism*.
[9] I should like to thank David Ford for this insight into the meaning of Kearney's term.
[10] Kearney, *Anatheism*, p. xvii.   [11] Ibid. 10.   [12] Ibid. 15.

to either the ontic or ontological order at all. Rightly understood, the event over-
flows any entity; it does not rest easily within the confines of the name of an entity,
but stirs relentlessly, endlessly, like an invitation or call, an invocation ('come') or a
provocation, a solicitation or a promise, a praise or benediction.[13]

The temporality involved in the act of name-giving always falls short of the
true nature of divinity which is, in Caputo's words, 'uncontainable'. This constitutes a move towards deconstructionism, away from the 'violence' Derrida
claims is inherent in naming, and placing temporal qualities onto God as a
force that may be neither accepted nor rejected, but whose possibility must
be considered. Caputo rejects the modernist stance of God being or not
being. His is a God of potency and potential, who must therefore be invoked
through mystical 'calls'. Rather than constituting a despised object of rejection, he is redressed as a magical appearance and reappearance, resisting the
'ontic or ontological order' altogether.

Another Catholic theologian who shares Caputo's contempt for the modernist approach to theology is the French academician Jean-Luc Marion. He
also affirms that religious truth statements were never designed to describe
God in a realistic manner. Only in the seventeenth century did theologians
start a 'metaphysical coup', using metaphysical language to refer to a real
state of affairs.[14] He undermines empiricist presumptions as wholly unsuitable to theology, since they persistently conceive of the divine in terms of
'being-in-the-world' and thereby reduce it to some concept (thus creating an
'idol' of God). As a way of distancing himself from this category mistake,
which still dominates modernist discourse, Marion raises an 'entirely different and opposing preliminary question' that 'might surprise and even dis-
turb'.[15] He casts God beyond human comprehension and proposes therefore
an understanding of religious language that is 'iconic' rather than 'idola-
trous'.[16] To him, theology should not concern itself with God's 'existence' or
'essence' but instead with the question: 'Do you love me?'[17] Such a question,

[13] Caputo, The Weakness of God, 5. 'Event' is one of Caputo's key terms, which he suggests is a
preferable description of the nature of God to 'naming'. Naming God (ascribing to God attributes
and characteristics) is merely a 'contingent privilege relative to the event' (ibid. 2). The temporality
of name-giving always falls short of the 'true' nature of divinity, which is 'uncontainable'.

[14] Marion believes the seventeenth century marked an age in which theology was 'no longer
the assumed goal of a journey toward [God]' (Marion, On the Ego and on God, 161). However, in
order to demonstrate the validity of the non-metaphysical conception of God, he cites a parallel
stream of seventeenth-century theologians who were not tempted to introduce scientific categorization where it was inappropriate. Certain theological ideas, in fact, remain to this day in
defiance of the objectification of God and have managed to remain in theological discourse,
such as the concept of 'transcendence'.   [15] Marion, The Visible and the Revealed, 49.

[16] See Carlson, 'Postmetaphysical Theology', 64.

[17] Marion, The Visible and the Revealed, 103.

he believes, 'liberates' God from the constrictions of metaphysics and brings theological discourse into the far more suitable arena of reciprocity and relationship. He therefore manoeuvres away from the notion of 'God as mathematician' and towards one of 'the God of love'.[18] According to Marion, God can only be approached through love and worship, not through the acrobatics of Cartesian rationalism. It is futile, therefore, to use religious language for the purpose of metaphysical enquiry. This strong stance puts a welcome end to the overly ambitious, if not pretentious, attempts by former generations of theologians to comprehend the divine, which in effect only succeeded in making an idol of God.

Shagar: Language, Semiotics, and Theology

The linguistic-cultural turn underscores the unreliability of language for the purposes of epistemic enquiry. According to Shagar, it can no longer be deemed appropriate to describe God or express personal beliefs. This conviction betrays the profound impact that late Wittgensteinian language theory had on his philosophical reflections. As a matter of fact, this can be appreciated just by glancing through Shagar's personal copy of *Philosophical Investigations* in which he left copious handwritten notes.

Shagar links the problem of language to a widespread misconception about truth. He states that 'there is no material with which we are able to discern truth' and eventually comes to the conclusion that truth does not exist, 'not because we have not found [the truth] but because there is no such thing'.[19] The purpose of religion was never to describe truth per se. Such a misunderstanding, he claims, stems from a perception that can be ascribed to the influence of modernity. In his view, language is, was, and always has been designed by God to be merely a tool to construe information. When discussing religious faith, Shagar notes the parallels between Wittgenstein's thought and certain insights from hasidism, particularly the reflections on language of Shneur Zalman of Lyady (also known, in traditional circles, as the Admor Hazaken). He thereby put forward his view of the role of language in religion:

Human existence depends on language. [For example] without the word 'stone', I could not describe that stone. . . . If I am unable to describe an object, then even the very word 'object' does not mean anything. 'What exists will return to its source through nothingness' (Admor Hazaken)—the word does not refer to [the thing that] I see; it *is* what I see.[20]

---

[18] Marion, *On the Ego and on God*, 164.   [19] Shagar, *Broken Vessels* (Heb.), 25, 96.

[20] Shagar, *We Walk in Fervour* (Heb.), 179.

Shagar claims that words are the physical objects we see around us. Elliot Wolfson's comments on the relationship between language and reality offer some interesting points of comparison. He connects the culturally particular character of the semiotic worlds we inhabit with the language we use:

The limits of the world are determined by the limits of semiosis to the extent that the structure of reality is mirrored in the structure of the language that gives shape to that reality; hence, the signs through which we interpret the world are the very signs through which the world is configured. . . . Language, therefore, is not principally a form of communication of what we know to be indubitably true but rather the socially conditioned means by which we approximate meaning for the sake of facilitating intersubjective commerce and exchange.[21]

Wolfson, like Shagar, argues that language represents an instrument through which people perpetuate an imagined reality rather than a means by which they can describe objective facts.

These observations establish a link between language and culture: individuals understand and employ language in specific cultural contexts. The language an individual uses not only reflects the world she inhabits; it frames the way she conceives reality. This is an idea Shagar puts forward in a forceful manner:

What is faith? It is speech, teaches the Admor Hazaken. . . . It is the realization and acceptance of the Presence who is present. This control over language, adds the Admor Hazaken, is developed by our tradition, [it is] a genetic ingredient of the Jew's identity. . . . Faith is not an abstract concept, nor must it require conscious effort; rather, [faith is] genetically inherited. Jewish people are simply born into it. In this sense, it is not individualist but rather a collective Jewish phenomenon, which embodies a certain way of life and, fundamentally, its own language.[22]

Since culture and language condition an individual's relation to the world, Shagar argues, someone who was born in a Jewish environment will never be able to escape the influence of the Jewish tradition. Keeping to his metaphor, religious belief is inscribed in that person's very DNA. Its influence will always remain.

When appealing to semiotics, however, Shagar steps beyond Wittgensteinian language theory and into the thought of Jean Baudrillard, a prominent postmodern semiotician. He alludes to Baudrillard in at least two of his works (*Broken Vessels* and *Luḥot veshivrei luḥot*) to initiate a discussion on the new nature of reality as simulation: 'a central feature of postmodernism is the notion of simulation . . . caused by technological sophistication in which

---

[21] Wolfson, 'Skepticism and Keeping Faith', 508.
[22] Shagar, *We Walk in Fervour* (Heb.), 177–8.

. . . there is no space left for prior [clear] distinctions between essence and external image'.[23] Shagar was apparently the first Orthodox Jewish thinker to express a genuine interest in Baudrillard's semiotics. It is worth considering why he found such an area of philosophy attractive and the extent to which he viewed it as relevant to his own attempts at merging postmodernism and Judaism.

Baudrillard is widely considered one of the sharpest critics of contemporary culture. I will therefore present his thought by referring to twenty-first-century Western society, which most readers will be familiar with. Semiotics is the study of signs. It relies on the fact that the individual's understanding of society comes through 'signification' (signs) which are referred to by language and in the media, but that do not exist in and of themselves. Hence language and cultural rituals symbolize, but do not embody, reality.[24] Today's world is full of 'signs'. Although the individual may not be fully aware of them, these signs surround her and effectively build up what Baudrillard terms a simulated 'hyper-reality'. Facebook and Twitter, for example, create an artificial, simulated social existence. Virtual exchanges in cyberspace—on smartphones and computers—allow individuals to bypass reality.[25] Advertisements saturate the world, each pretending to hold the perfect solution to any given problem. All the things that are believed to 'signify' reality are what semioticians refer to as 'signs'. The realities in which the individual operates are simulated by a variety of constantly changing signs. 'Simulation' therefore refers to an imagined situation, an imitation of reality, designed to encourage individuals to act in a certain way. It is crucial to recognize that a simulated reality is not a false reality. It means that the individual is aware of the factors that make her reality what it is. Just as people in every society live according to particular, distinct norms, so the realities they inhabit function according to different networks of 'signs'. In Baudrillard's semiotics, the simulated reality is in fact reality itself. There is no reality behind or beyond the signs. This implies a turning away from the former distinction between metaphysical reality and external image which pervades classical philosophy, and, concurrently, the levelling of the objective versus subjective opposition.

Shagar turns to Baudrillard to reconfigure the role of language in postmodern religion. His position is original on two accounts: it acknowledges the problem of language, and in response, re-envisages it as a network of

[23] Shagar, *Broken Vessels* (Heb.), 24.

[24] Baudrillard argues for the ultimate importance of the idea of reality as 'simulated': in the absence of 'pure' or 'natural' objects, nothing is outside the linguistic system (see Baudrillard, *Simulacres et simulation*, 10–14).

[25] On technology in and of itself as a marker of contemporary existence that deserves more attention in Jewish philosophy, see Tirosh-Samuelson, 'The Preciousness of Being Human'.

signs that help the religious community generate its own simulated reality.[26] To him, the language of the community serves to engender, rather than merely refer to, the religious values of its adherents. The way Shagar is able to accommodate these positions is by relying on the Jewish mystical tradition. He employs concepts drawn most notably from Lurianic kabbalah and Bratslavian hasidism to draw out a theological discourse that comprises both postmodern linguistic elements and traditional ones. *Broken Vessels*, for example, is replete with parallels between deconstructionism and kabbalah, such as: 'Postmodern deconstructionism smashes the vessels and argues that reality is nothing but a human construct. But the kabbalistic interpretation is that this breakage has a purifying purpose.'[27]

Shagar's use of kabbalah points to a way of positively relating to postmodernism. The convergence between both systems, noted in the previous chapter in connection with Drob, enables him to integrate contemporary understandings of language and knowledge into his theology while nonetheless appealing to terms and concepts already present within the Jewish textual tradition. In so doing, he offers engaging responses to the problematic rationalism of modernity. The four concepts he appropriates for this purpose are: *shetikah* (silence), *ḥalal panui* ('empty void'), Ein Sof ('the infinite'), and *tefilah* (prayer).

Shetikah: Silence

According to Shagar, silence is as powerful a linguistic tool in appealing to the divine as verbal expression: 'The [question of belief] cannot be qualified with the proclamation "I believe" but rather, silence plays an equal role to that of speech.'[28] This call for silence—apophaticism—betrays a deep disillusionment with metaphysical language. Shagar attempts to deflect the postmodern critique by emphasizing the role of silence in religious discourse, and to that end relies on mysticism:

The philosophers have refuted non-verbal proclamations of [religious knowledge]. Of course the Admor Hazaken differs on this matter. . . . *Essence is evident* [through] *pure religious action, independent of language, which thereby transcends language.* When considering [the nature of] speech, there is a disparity between words and

[26] The more scientific developments of semiotics seem to have been of far less interest to Shagar, who preferred to view simulated communities from poststructuralist, deconstructive, mystical perspectives. For example, he does not mention (at least in the writings published so far) the prominent semiotician Charles Sanders Peirce, who, rather than subscribing to the idiosyncratic versions of signing that are promulgated in poststructuralist semiotics, for example by Baudrillard and Derrida, argued that signs consist of mathematical philosophical deduction (see *Peirce on Signs*).

[27] Shagar, *Broken Vessels* (Heb.), 27.   [28] Shagar, *We Walk in Fervour* (Heb.), 174.

between what those words evoke; words have the capacity to conjure up their own, self-generating meanings, [and] thereby renew the meaning [of language] itself.[29]

Shagar forges a strong link between postmodern language theory and religious experience, which he develops by comparing and contrasting Wittgenstein's philosophy of language and the apophaticism of Rabbi Nahman of Bratslav:[30]

A postmodern reading of R. Nahman must take into account the fact that unconventional, metaphysical questions are beyond the capability of linguistic discourse. But contrary to postmodernism, R. Nahman concludes that such questions are meaningless and futile. This is similar to Wittgenstein in his shift towards [a pure focus on language]. . . . For R. Nahman, it becomes possible to believe.[31]

This is another illustration of Shagar's integrative technique.[32] He juxtaposes Wittgensteinian and Bratslavian observations on the way religious faith tests the boundaries of language.[33] To Wittgenstein, the fact that language cannot describe the metaphysical realm without causing conceptual confusion by no means implies its non-existence. Shagar relates this understanding of the limits of representation to R. Nahman's claim that religious language emanates from human prophecy, poetry, and conceptions of divinity: 'He knows, as far as it is possible to know, that an absolute statement crosses the boundaries of the multiple possibilities presented by language games. Actually, silence is . . . no [less significant] than language.'[34] He comments on the conception of *shetikah* put forward by R. Nahman:

R. Nahman proposes *shetikah*. He cites a *midrash* in which Moses asks God about the fate of Rabbi Akiva: 'This is Torah and this is its reward?' and is answered, 'Silence—this is what has been decreed!' [BT *Men.* 29b]. In our own words: the answers cannot be revealed through deep contemplation. They come through [an appropriate] response . . . through an original expression of human self-awareness

---

[29] Ibid. 179 (my emphasis).

[30] Shagar also interprets Maimonides' negative theology in the light of the problem of language and kabbalah, suggesting that 'for Rambam, the apophatic speech in the language of the mystic means that speech cancels out the self'. In an additional footnote on the subject Shagar writes: 'It seems Maimonides preferred silence, especially in prayer. . . . Speech in prayer is merely a relinquishing of true humanity. Without metaphysics, because metaphysics relies upon realist language, he was thus opposed to Wittgenstein' (Shagar, *We Walk in Fervour* (Heb.), 185; see Maimonides, *Guide of the Perplexed*, iii. 32). Through this, Shagar seeks to further his argument that as a result of the efforts of negative theology, positive speech and language actualize and reify an ontological sphere.   [31] Shagar, *Broken Vessels* (Heb.), 20.

[32] On Shagar's appropriation of the thought of R. Nahman, see Tzur, 'The Deconstruction of Holiness' (Heb.), 122–5.

[33] For Wittgenstein's refutation of correlation between a word and its meaning, see *Philosophical Investigations*, 32.   [34] Shagar, *Broken Vessels* (Heb.), 20.

of the world. The greatness of R. Nahman is his ability to transform difficulties [of belief] into *devekut* [attachment to God]. . . . There are questions which have no answers, and there is no need to [attempt answering]. This is faith, paradoxical as it is—and R. Nahman expressed paradoxes powerfully.[35]

Shagar quotes R. Nahman's interpretation of a midrashic passage in which the model for response to divine injustice is silence. He makes a somewhat tepid attempt at ridding silence of its passive connotations and depicting it as a natural human quality by linking it to the hasidic concept of *devekut*, or 'cleaving' to God. Bratslavian and postmodern theories of language converge to the extent that they recognize the artificial nature of linguistic systems. Postmodernists differ, however, on the power of silence. In the debate on the issue between Foucault and Derrida, it seems clear that Shagar sides with the latter.[36] In *Madness and Civilization*, Foucault critiques Western society's conception of the distinction between normality and madness (or hysteria, in his terminology) by demonstrating that it betrays a complete lack of awareness of the norms of other cultures. Derrida paraphrases Foucault in the following terms:

Madness is indeed, essentially and generally, silence, stifled speech, with a caesura and a wound that *open up* life as *historicity in general*. Not a determined silence, imposed at one given moment rather than at any other, but a silence essentially linked to an act of force and a prohibition that open history and speech.[37]

Silence, to Foucault, stands within a context and therefore reveals a structure of power relations: society first silenced the insane by removing them from its midst and then reflected about madness as an object contemplated from a distance. Derrida, in contrast, claims that silence stands beyond context; that every single piece of information that language provides is hidden when we remain silent. Our intonations, intentions, or cultural norms all find themselves concealed. If I do not speak, I am not heard, and my world-view is neither presented nor forced onto listeners. Derrida argues that silence can-

[35] Shagar, *Broken Vessels* (Heb.), 20.
[36] My intention here is not to argue, in the light of the stress he places on silence, that Derrida was a mystic. The connection between mystical silence and postmodern silence is that mystical silence provides the predicate (from traditional Orthodox Jewish thought) for Shagar's incorporation of postmodern silence, knowingly or not. Sanford Drob argues that, despite Derrida's arguments to the contrary, Derrida was indeed a 'mystic', claiming that 'there is much in Derrida that is Kabbalistic, and given Derrida's approving references to Kabbalistic ideas . . . it is hard to understand the force behind his disclaimer' (Drob, *Kabbalah and Postmodernism*, 20). If Drob's reading of Derrida is right, then my argument is further cemented through a more essentialist connection between a postmodern and kabbalistic meeting of ideas. However, I am inclined not to dismiss Derrida's own self-accounting: 'I am not mystical and there is nothing mystical in my work' (cited ibid.).   [37] Derrida, *Writing and Difference*, 54.

not be contextualized and therefore cannot be subject to a postmodern critique of history and speech. It is one of the only ways to completely seclude
oneself from one's surroundings and therefore to escape the violence he
associates with language, since naming or speaking of an object—a culture
or a set of values—involves violently forcing our own world-view upon it.
It is worth noting, tangentially, that postmodernists doubt for this reason the
possibility of passing value judgements on other cultures, since such judgements are made from an outsider's viewpoint.

The process of deconstructionism, of exposing the volatile and fleeting
nature of all truths, is endless. Yet in some cases, such as the appeal to justice
or the act of forgiving, even after having deconstructed the norms and values
which a society upholds, there remains, paradoxically, an irreducible, 'indeconstructible' urge which prompts the individual to reassess again and again
the mechanisms whereby justice translates into truth.[38] Since the two concepts can ultimately never perfectly cohere, justice becomes a force that is
sensed and longed for but never attained, something of a messianic expectation. For both Derrida and Shagar, silence is another example of an 'indeconstructible' force. John Caputo also appropriates the term when discussing
the 'indeconstructibility' of God: the divine cannot be grasped, it can only be
longed for. As he remarks, 'being loves to hide'.[39] He describes religious
experience as a 'messianic expectation, the hope', because it is only ever possible and never present, in both the temporal and essential meanings of the
word.[40]

By proclaiming the indeconstructibility of God, the theologian leaves
room to reflect critically on the idea of the divine while simultaneously com-
mitting to suspend such reflections when reaching a state of conflict with
God. Yet why should the idea of God not be given to deconstruction? Does
such a retreat signal a renouncement of the religious belief in the human
ability to grasp the divine? Is the notion of indeconstructibility a cowardly
attempt at fending off the postmodern critique?

Haḥalal hapanui: The Empty Void

We give names to objects and non-physical elements. In so doing, following
correspondence theory, we assume that the name ('signifier') relates to the
object ('signified'). We attempt to pin down the essence or most recognizable
constituent of that object. This practice was formerly performed unreflec-
tively. Postmodernists, however, have come to accentuate the violence
involved in it. To Derrida, the act of name-giving does not give enough recog-

---

[38] Derrida, *Acts of Religion*, 243.   [39] Caputo, *The Weakness of God*, 10.
[40] See Olthius (ed.), *Religion With/Out Religion*, 161.

nition to process, context, and temporality.[41] It is a superficial, arrogant, violent attempt at capturing meaning, rather than recognizing it as something that is in continual flux:

To name, to give names that it was on occasion forbidden to pronounce, such is the originary violence of language which consists of inscribing within a difference, in classifying, in suspending the vocative absolute. To think the unique *within* the system, to inscribe it there, such is the gesture of the arche-writing: of arche-violence: loss of the proper, loss of absolute proximity, of self-presence, in truth the loss of what has never taken place, of a self-presence which has never been given, but only dreamed of, and always already split, repeated, incapable of appearing to itself, except in its own disappearance.[42]

The formerly static conception of meaning has been overthrown. It is by use of violence that the namer attempts to impose a fixed meaning on an object based on its perceived characteristics. Yet this objective of name-giving—to capture the essence of an object—can never be achieved; it can only actually be 'dreamed of'. If anything, postmodernists argue, the act of naming reveals more about the person who names or the community that engages in the process of name-giving than about the object itself. Shagar connected this idea with the kabbalistic motif of the *ḥalal panui*, or 'empty void'. The sixteenth-century Safed kabbalist Isaac Luria intimated that the 'infinite light' of God (the Ein Sof) contracted itself and left the *ḥalal panui* in order to make room for the Creation:

When the light emerged from Intuition and radiated
Towards the six Directions below the first sphere to emerge was Knowledge
... Afterwards Grace emerged and shattered
And the vessel collapsed and fell
Meaning he was also unable to bear the light

    .   .   .   .

Since the amount of light was so brilliant
The base was not able to bear the light
And shattered like the others

    .   .   .   .

There were still sparks within all these vessels
They collapsed into broken shards
and from these were created the Shells or external energy
... there are still sparks of the sacred left within the vessels.[43]

---

[41] See Derrida, *Of Grammatology*, 107–17.
[42] Derrida, *Writing and Difference*, 112.　　　　[43] Klein, *Kabbalah of Creation*, 16–19.

This extract puts forward the classical kabbalistic paradox of the Creation: on the one hand, the infinite power of God constricted itself to make room, so to speak, to enable another entity to exist; on the other hand, the other entity remained imbued with divinity. Jewish thinkers throughout the Middle Ages and the modern period delved extensively into this apparent contradiction. Rabbi Nahman, for example, referred to it in his own meditations:

Only in the future will it be possible to understand the *tsimtsum* that brought the *halal panui* into being, because it presents two contradictions. . . . (1) the *halal panui* was created through the *tsimtsum*, where, as it were, he 'constricted' his Godliness . . . and so . . . in that empty place there is no Godliness. . . . [And yet] (2) . . . Godliness must nevertheless be present, because undoubtedly, nothing can exist outside God's creation.[44]

Shagar intuitively compares R. Nahman's interpretation of the *halal panui* to the postmodern argument for understanding language as devoid of essence. In his mind, the mystical motif supplies a helpful response for overcoming the problematic nature of postmodernist claims about the nature of language:

According to [Luria] the *halal panui* remains after the light of the Ein Sof has been destroyed in order to allow for the creation of the world. . . . The descriptive capabilities of language [despite this void] are possible through the destruction of this light. Since there is no 'signifier', God's presence rests in his absence.[45]

This passage is one of Shagar's most original and daring comments on the subject. To him, the *halal panui* parallels the Derridean 'disappearance' of meaning. Yet just as the kabbalistic paradox posits that the created world is nonetheless infused with holiness, so he maintains that language is, in itself, divine:

Our intuition instructs us [to think] that there is an essence or absolutism which we try to describe or represent with the help of language. . . . We could even say that language and its words put forward the case for divinity through which we understand reality. The capability of man to give names is actually linked to the image of God.[46]

According to Shagar, this absence of essence in the reality we try to describe is precisely a sign of its divinity. The paradox of the simultaneous presence and absence of God in the act of *tsimtsum* finds its parallel in language, where the lack of essence in meaning actually testifies to something higher. If the

---

[44] Nahman of Bratslav, *Likutei moharan*, i, §1: 61.
[45] Shagar, *We Walk in Fervour* (Heb.), 180–1.
[46] Shagar, *On His Torah He Meditates* (Heb.), 182.

act of name-giving is taken to originate from an interpretative-generative understanding of language (rather than an essentialist one), then the human tendency to give names, the necessity to fill the *halal panui* with meaning, is a creative endeavour—certainly one which bestows upon humanity the same role that God assumes in the Genesis account of Creation. It ultimately 'allow[s] the world to exist'.[47] The 'disappearance' of meaning which characterizes postmodern thought, however, highlights the fact that the *halal panui* still exists and generates some of the tension and despair that typify much of postmodern discourse: 'the postmodern contradiction is one of the difficulties to which R. Nahman believes there is no answer'.[48] Rabbi Nahman's interpretation of *halal panui* only goes so far in deflecting the postmodern critique. If reality ultimately defies linguistic codification, how can we believe in the divine character of language or in its ability to generate meaning? Does the truth that language purports to communicate somehow lie beyond language?

Ein Sof: Infinity

The third kabbalistic concept Shagar draws on is Ein Sof, the Infinite. As Drob points out, the 'loss of centre', the 'shattering of the foundations', the 'overcoming of binary oppositions', the 'role of negation', and the 'dissolution of God and self' are fundamental in kabbalistic and postmodern thinking.[49] Having silenced language and spoken of the all-encapsulating *halal panui* that defies empiricism, the kabbalistic notion of Ein Sof may be linked to postmodern refutations of God as having the property of 'existence'. If the empiric realm of 'existence' can be negated, then it lends itself neither to the discourse of proof nor to that of disproof. The ontological status of Ein Sof offers an opportune resolution to withdraw empiric qualities from the conceptualization of God.[50]

Edith Wyschogrod comments on these innate connections between kabbalah and postmodernism, suggesting that the role of Ein Sof 'renders possible the plunging of the individual soul into the abyssal apocalyptic non-

---

[47] Tzur, 'The Deconstruction of Holiness' (Heb.), 128.

[48] *Tablets and Broken Tablets* (Heb.), 74. Though one commentator has asked whether R. Nahman (and R. Kook—see Ross, 'The Cognitive Value of Religious Truth Statements') was anticipating a version of postmodern hasidism without even knowing it (Eldar, review of Horen, *Life as Longing* (Heb.)).   [49] Drob, *Kabbalah and Postmodernism*, 19–23.

[50] Even the oft-cited notion of 'transcendence', the idea that God transcends human existence and understanding, has been derided by Shagar as essentially a modernist argument, which still attributes empirical qualities to God and fails to engage in kabbalistic negation (or negative theology) without, of course, resorting to nihilism. The notion that God constricts himself through *tsimtsum* creates an absence, not a transcendental presence. See Shagar, *We Walk in Fervour* (Heb.), 173–84.

ground of the divine, nonground because the abyss cannot become an ontological foundation or anchorage'.[51] According to Wyschogrod, the 'nonground' (similar to Ross's non-foundationalism) turns on its head the
pre-eminence of epistemological certainty. In kabbalah, language is necessarily understood as generative and not descriptive.[52] In his discussion of the
Ein Sof and its postmodern interpretations, Wolfson distinguishes between
the writings of the Gaon of Vilna and Derrida:

The reality beyond the first book, according to R. Elijah Gaon, is the hidden concealment of *Ein-Sof*, which he calls by various Zoharic expressions including . . .
that [which] defies signification. All signification occurs within the textual boundaries of the first book, which is the book of concealment. The negative theology
implied by the Gaon of Vilna is not radically different from what is suggested by
the Derridean notion of the trace, for the origin to which the book of concealment
points is not an origin that can ever be known or demarcated. The *Ein-Sof* cannot
properly be referred to as a transcendental signified, for it forever eludes signification.[53]

The concept of Ein Sof is part and parcel of a radically acute theology of
negation, so far-reaching that it transcends the barriers of language and
imagination. According to Wolfson's account of Elijah Gaon, whereas 'all
signification occurs within the textual boundaries of the first book', the reality of Ein Sof actually resides 'beyond the first book'. Here again is the view
that the use of empirical language in theology constitutes a terrible category
mistake. Drob drew a similar conclusion in noting that postmodern deconstructionism retains distinct notions of polarity even while deconstructing
them (since they remain 'inferred' even when refuted).

Deconstruction nevertheless makes use of a dialectical method, in its constant
discovery of what is opposed, negated, and marginalized in all that is declared to be
true and whole. . . . Deconstruction provides us with a critique, but nothing
resembling a world-view or guide for life. For this reason, many have found
deconstruction unsatisfying, nihilistic and even immoral in its implications. The
Lurianic Kabbalah is, I believe, a system that can remain open in the deconstructive

---

[51] Wyschogrod, 'Hasidism, Hellenism, Holocaust', 312.

[52] Shimon Shokek concurs with this view of the nature of language in Lurianic kabbalah (see
Shokek, *Kabbalah and the Art of Being*, 24–37). Shokek claims that the infinite force of the Ein
Sof in kabbalistic thought would have been considered as overcoming competing 'truth-
claims'. The Ein Sof 'comprises a unity in which all opposites are equal and in which there is no
differentiation . . . the singular concealed unity who emanates multiplicity' (ibid. 24).

[53] Wolfson, 'From Sealed Book to Open Text', 153. The conclusion of Wolfson's distinction
between postmodern and kabbalistic negations lies, not coincidentally, in a Ricœurian phenomenological approach to understanding postmodernism through a kabbalistic lens.

sense without surrendering its efforts to provide (an albeit) tentative *weltanschauung*. It does so through its multiperspectivism.[54]

The postmodern tendency to view language merely as a cultural construct fails to provide the reader with inspiration or meaning, especially the sort which believers seek. If language cannot truly refer to anything, or if there is no ultimate truth, then there is nothing even resembling a cogent 'world-view or guide for life'. This is why Shagar developed an affinity for kabbalah, and also why he eventually extended his interests to semiotics and, parti-cularly, Žižek's scholarship on language.[55] The work of Žižek might be con-sidered a model for tempering total negation (mysticism) with linguistic nihilism. The problem of language, postulates Žižek, has been overdone by postmodernism to the extent that it has developed an ontology through its own self-negation. If this negation is to be justified, he says, then it must come through imagination of a 'symbolic order'.[56] Imagination as forming an ontological category is something that must have appealed to Shagar, due to its assumed positing of 'real' worlds through a negation. As Žižek puts it:

The main thing here is the opposition of the imaginary level between the experience of meaning and the meaningless signifier/signifying mechanism producing it. What lies beyond is not the symbolic order but a real kernel; a traumatic core.[57]

This Žižekian deconstruction of polarities is structured by the 'symbolic order': it offers a seminal motif for local 'truth'. It involves a linguistic dimen-sion: language encompasses symbolic and imaginary dimensions. In the midst of a 'fragile void', Žižek proposes an 'order' that fills that void, made up of symbols, and generated by its community. He speaks of 'bits of god' that fill gaps of emptiness between destroyed polarities, and it is this that is con-sidered to be 'Real' in a postmodern age. For Žižek:

The Real is the starting point of the Symbolic order: the Real is the fullness of the inert presence, positivity; nothing is lacking in the Real—that is, the lack is introduced only by the symbolisation; it is a signifier which introduces a void, an absence in the Real. But at the same time . . . the Real is in itself a hole, a gap, an opening in the middle of the symbolic order; it is the lack around which the Symbolic order is structured.[58]

Shagar compared the relevance of *ḥalal panui* in Jewish mysticism to Žižek's concept of the Real as ultimately a 'hole' or 'gap'. The Real can never be 'true' in an empiric sense. It raises the question: What fills the void after

---

[54] Drob, *Kabbalah and Postmodernism*, 19.

[55] Shagar possessed books by Žižek translated into Hebrew, which he annotated, and also refers to him in detail (Shagar, *In the Shadow of Faith* (Heb.), 66–81, 126–8).

[56] See Žižek, *On Belief*, 109–12; id., *The Parallax View*, 242–51.

[57] Žižek, *The Sublime Object of Ideology*, 132.   [58] Žižek, *Looking Awry*, 26.

tsimtsum? How can a divine absence actually equate with 'presence' or the essence that Heidegger saw fit to deconstruct? These are quite possibly the questions Shagar asks himself and thus seeks to answer through his reading of Žižek.

Tefilah: Prayer

Despite the problematic nature of language in relation to religious ritual, the theme of prayer has received a surprising amount of attention from post-modern thinkers in general, and Shagar in particular, as a way to compensate for the relinquishing of traditional notions of metaphysics. Interestingly, Sagi engages with the subject of prayer, albeit from a non-mystical perspective:

Prayer as an act of the subject is not necessarily conditioned by a positive response to the question of whether the prayer has an addressee. Prayer is an ontological characteristic of the individual and does not derive from any kind of metaphysics or theology. The believer addresses the prayer to God, and the nonbeliever does not necessarily address anyone in particular; but, through their prayers, both epitomise humans as beings who transcend their factual givenness. . . . This religiosity . . . conveys the human passion for transcendence.[59]

The fact that Sagi, a late modern neo-pragmatist, suggests that prayer transcends the limits of epistemology could imply an overall turn to prayer as one common feature of postmodern theology. Drob, coming from a different perspective, similarly argues that mystical language can be harnessed as an instrument to stimulate the religious imagination: 'There is, since Kant, a movement away from *mimesis*, a representational view of reality, to *poesis*, a creative view of reality; one in which the human subject is understood as constructing the very things it had once believed itself to be representing.'[60] The function of language in prayer truly fascinates Shagar. The act of prayer takes on a central role in his theology. In his words, 'prayer . . . completely symbolizes religious existence through its practice and intellectual activity [which creates] a powerful reality'.[61] This, I suggest, derives almost entirely from his integration of hasidic theosophy and radical postmodern philosophy in order to find a suitable way to fill the void left by the collapse of metaphysics. Prayer emerges in his thought as a powerful, creative theological practice due to the paradoxical fact that it captures the believer's imagination by employing religious language, and simultaneously denies language through apophatic silence.[62] His interest in the topic comes out most forcefully in an article in

[59] Sagi, 'Toward a Jewish Philosophy', 400–1.
[60] Drob, *Kabbalah and Postmodernism*, 45.
[61] Shagar, *The Remnant of Faith* (Heb.), 40–1.
[62] Shagar, *We Walk in Fervour* (Heb.), 176–7.

which he places late Wittgensteinian language theory alongside Shneur
Zalman of Lyady's comments on *tefilah*:

Contemporary discourse concerns itself with [the nature of] faith in the absence
of letters and words. It is to believe without justifying to oneself or to others that
I believe. . . . I [therefore] compare these numerous hasidic teachings [of Shneur
Zalman] with the philosophy of language of Wittgenstein.[63]

Shagar finds the innate resemblances between postmodern and hasidic discourses on the function of language particularly illuminating when reflect-
ing on prayer. This article also sheds light on his thought regarding the
development of character traits through language and prayer. To his mind,
the logic of rationalism and self-critique needs to be constricted in order for
true prayer to happen. Resorting to hasidic terminology, Shagar explains that
the individual must engage in self-nullification (*bitul hayesh*) through continual soul-searching (*ḥeshbon nefesh*). She must completely nullify her sense
of self in such a way as to consider herself an empty vessel. Only then can
prayer—the communal language of divinity—fulfil its role of filling the void
(*ḥalal*) and repairing the self (*tikun*). This way, prayer can change the individual as well as the community. The person of faith can 'create worlds' and
'enact change'.[64]

Language and prayer are underpinned by attachment to God and silence.
These concepts are fundamental to religious experience in hasidic thought,
and necessitate a sweeping denial of the self: they are incompatible with
pride in any shape or form. To Shagar, however, the resulting emptiness may
be overcome through emphasis on the surrounding community: 'The relin-
quishment and denial of each soul is a condition on which prayer is based.
[This is] because through this, both language and logic are liberated.'[65] By
appealing to hasidism, he comes up with a theology of community that does
not require external justification.

Prayer blurs the line between 'reality' and 'fiction'. Shagar suggests exor-
cising any form of rational thinking when discussing the topic. He sidelines
the ideas put forward literally in the liturgy and privileges the experience of
the encounter with the divine:

Prayer?! It is miraculous, because what happens in those moments is actualized.
External justification for prayer [is] not [required] . . . because it is experiential. The
lovingkindness [of God] is that [true] prayer becomes a possibility; a possibility
without promises.[66]

---

[63] Shagar, *We Walk in Fervour* (Heb.),   [64] Shagar, *The Remnant of Faith* (Heb.), 44.
[65] Shagar, *We Walk in Fervour* (Heb.), 181.   [66] Ibid. 178–90.

Shagar therefore constitutes a perfect example of the phenomenon Drob describes: he chooses *poesis* and aspires to generate, through prayer, a 'creative view of reality'. He hopes to enrich religious discourse by encouraging internal soul-searching rather than appealing to external reasoning.

Language and Hasidism

Hasidic concepts and terminology are ubiquitous in Shagar's treatment of the problem of language in the postmodern era. He mobilizes the *ḥalal panui* to deconstruct polarities; deflects critical scrutiny by falling into silence (*shetikah*); and places the divine beyond the grasp of human comprehension by recourse to Ein Sof. Shagar conceives of the religious ethos as a human product generated entirely by linguistic constructs. He reaches this conclusion after a lengthy reflection focusing on the potential of kabbalistic worship techniques in which he asks:

Is [God] really present? Is there no way of leaving the door open a little for the possibility of the presence of God himself? Is the possibility for faith now closed? Are these complex articulations of belief at all possible? Is it possible to believe without being able to explain to myself what it is that I believe in? Or even to tell myself that 'I believe' at all? What meaning is there to the statement 'God constricted himself' referring to the concept of constriction [*tsimtsum*]. . . . Can this [statement] be neither verbalized nor contextualized? . . . There is a definitive resemblance between earlier Wittgensteinian language theory and that of the Admor Hazaken— which is that . . . language does not aid religious belief; rather it is a prison in the hands of the believer . . . [and that therefore] it cannot be overcome.[67]

This string of questions shows how pervasive the problem of language appears to Shagar and the impact it has on his conception of Jewish theology. His answer places, as in a previous passage, Shneur Zalman alongside Ludwig Wittgenstein. He quotes *Tanya* (Shneur Zalman's magnum opus) to the effect that religious language can generate, in the adherent's mind, a certain kind of reality:

The ten utterances brought to life and into existence what had previously been static. [Consider the idea of] something created out of nothingness [in light of] the chaos which preceded the six days of Creation. . . . [And so] the inert nature of a stone is transformed and brought to life through the continual exchange of words and letters . . . and named . . . in the holy language. . . . This [idea] originates from the ten utterances in the Torah which have the capacity to create something from nothing.[68]

[67] Ibid. 188.   [68] Shneur Zalman, *Tanya*, 'Gate of Unity and Faith', ch. 1.

Shagar does not deny that the metaphysics that transpire in this extract and underpin the kabbalistic ontological discourse in its entirety are social-cultural constructs. To the believer who is sensitive to language's ability to generate a reality of its own and perpetuate the existence of a religious community, however, it is possible to accept the ideas put forward by Shneur Zalman as 'true'. There are therefore multiple methods of worship that successfully break through the barriers that language (or its limits) sets up to constrain religious epistemology: 'Language is understood as an embodiment of freedom, and so the world is exposed to a magical existence and from there receives its infinite value.'[69] And, indeed, one could even read divine intention into these possibilities.

Ross: Language and Imagination

I have shown that postmodern philosophy has led to profound changes in the understanding of language. Language is no longer thought to refer to anything beyond itself. It is construed as a reflection of its corresponding culture, rather than as a means to describe a metaphysical reality or state of affairs (realism):

Since . . . theology has traditionally operated out of realist epistemological assumptions, such a radical postmodernism which views language merely as a self-enclosed 'game', without some reference to a genuinely objective outside reality, would constitute a fundamental shift in the expectations surrounding traditional theological claims.[70]

Ross claims that the limitations of language do not necessarily spell disaster for religion. On the contrary, she notes that a release from literalism presents promising solutions to theological problems which had hitherto challenged the truth-value of certain religious claims:

Religious truth statements may indeed be regarded as false or nonsensical if we insist upon understanding them as literal or even figurative representations of an objective reality. But such statements can be validated when understood as guides to, or expressions of, a level of meaning extending beyond the empiric discussions of science.[71]

This release from literalism could be said to characterize Ross's presentation of the subject as a whole.

Literalism refers to the adherence to the explicit meaning of a word or

---

[69] Shagar, *We Walk in Fervour* (Heb.), 188.
[70] Ross, 'The Cognitive Value of Religious Truth Statements', 515–16.
[71] Ross, 'Religious Belief in a Postmodern Age', 194.

sentence. In most cases, we understand language literally, since the literal meaning of a word appropriately describes the object it purports to refer to. For example, everyone understands the meaning of the word 'table', since a table can be described objectively ('the table is rectangular and made of wood') and empirically verified. A typical philosophical problem arises, however, when language is used to describe something empirically unknown, such as a historically unverifiable event or a fictional being. The language that we use to describe a dragon, for example, does not refer to an empirically verifiable object. Therefore there can be no such thing as a literal description of a dragon.[72] The same philosophical problem occurs when we use language to refer to God. A literal understanding of language is inappropriate to describe God, since it is impossible to witness the object described. This problematizes the very notion of literality, and many continental postmodern thinkers underscore how a word or sentence of this sort can be interpreted in an infinite number of ways by different people, depending on their temporal, cultural, or social circumstances.

How do theologians respond to such a problem? If language can only literally correspond to a real state of affairs, then on what does the theological enterprise hinge? Ross imbues language with a divinity which informs, authorizes, and authenticates religious belief. She reveals a newfound function of language according to cultural-linguistic principles. In doing so, she develops a new understanding of how language is meant to function, reconfiguring it as a theological informant that was never supposed to impart metaphysical knowledge. Her reasoning follows two stages. The first states that religious language should not and should never have been understood literally. She roots this non-realistic approach to Scripture in what she perceives to be the hermeneutic tradition and stands convinced that her methodology is neither radical nor new. The main figure she relies on is R. Kook, who, in her view, held and bequeathed a non-realist outlook ensconced within Jewish orthodoxy. The second stage deals with the linguistic role of metaphor. It takes root in the doubts she expressed over the persuasiveness of non-realism and the need for 'firmer territory' in order to sustain religious adherence. It is not sufficient for language only to support the views of the community when it previously held, alongside text, an 'aura of objectivity'.[73]

---

[72] The notion of literalism has been critiqued by postmodernists, particularly by semioticians, who maintain that meanings are signified by events and occurrences numerous times and understood in a variety of ways. The field of semiotics concentrates on the meanings inferred from written and spoken signs and symbols in everyday life. Each event or sentence is to be interpreted in a certain way and its meanings communicated. Scholars of semiotics include Charles Sanders Peirce, Roman Jakobson (whose scholarship is the subject of one of Paul Ricœur's essays), and Umberto Eco. See Farber and Corrington, *Semiotics of Religion*.

[73] Ross, 'Religious Belief in a Postmodern Age', 216.

Indeed, her awareness of how a 'literal understanding of religious state-ments could lead to morally disastrous results' matches her acute realization that non-literalism could collapse into an anarchic state of affairs. At least some of this 'aura of objectivity' must therefore be preserved.

At first, then, Ross views language merely as a construct of human aspira-tions: theological claims are justifiable insofar as they present a certain amount of proof in order to appeal to ordinary people. Her approach is func-tionalist in giving pre-eminence to the notion of meaning inspired within the community. But ultimately she cannot go all the way in refuting all aspects of truth in biblical accounts, not least the formative narratives of miracles and revelation. The turning point for her is the way biblical metaphors inform religious language.

Renouncing Literalism and Realism

Referring to sacred texts, Ross claims that their truth-value does not lie in their literal accuracy but rather in the measure of meaning people ascribe to them[74] and the extent to which they strengthen religious belief: 'There is also no need to establish the sanctity of the Torah by seeking external evidence for the historical accuracy of the traditional account of the revelation at Sinai.'[75] According to Ross, it is the particular significance of the Sinaitic event that inspires religious belief within a community, and in this sense, the revelation at Sinai is truthful. Although I analyse the subject of revelation in greater depth in the next chapter, it is worth noting here how Ross's dismissal of lit-eralism, and more generally the changed significance of religious language following the cultural-linguistic turn, influence both her reading of Scripture and her attitude towards religious experience:

We may have no way of knowing whether or not the Red Sea did indeed split, whether the ancient Hebrews really did undergo some revelatory experience at Sinai, whether someday there actually will appear a Messiah who will inaugurate a new epoch in the history of mankind. Nonetheless . . . in the eyes of a construc-tionist the 'truth' of these accounts and their justification is not inferred from close testing of their accuracy. It is embodied in the spiritual attitudes which they en-gender, in the ways of reacting to and meeting situations which they inspire.[76]

The two passages quoted here converge in three ways. First, they both ex-press a sense of scepticism over scientific empiricism, rejecting the need to 'seek external evidence' or supply 'close testing of their accuracy'. Second,

---

[74] It is clear that Ross has relied upon interpretations of Rorty for an understanding of realism in epistemology. See Putnam, 'Rorty on Reality and Justification'.

[75] Ross, 'Religious Belief in a Postmodern Age', 194.   [76] Ibid. 220.

they stress the fact that the truth ascribed to a text is not necessarily dependent upon its empirical accuracy but can be justified by the value derived from
it by a particular group. Truth, Ross posits, is of subjective value. Third, and
as a result of the first two observations, both extracts come to emphasize the
cognition of the individual over and above the literalism of the text. Biblical
accounts of the formation of the Jewish people do not literally describe historical events, nor do they need to.

While Ross admits that taking leave of realism could appear difficult,
she insists that such a move also offers unexpected opportunities for Jewish
theology:

It is precisely because of the importance of everyday 'realist' assumptions in cemen-
ting religious commitment that so much effort is expended by religious conserva-
tives in cordoning off some religious beliefs as off-bounds to demythologizing or
re-interpretation. Because the notion of 'truth' and religious commitment are so
intimately connected in the human psyche, critical scrutiny of beliefs that appear
indispensable to the system is sometimes held back by upholding the remote
possibility that future investigation will overturn current impressions.[77]

But what of instances where it is precisely this brand of literalism which pur-
portedly serves as the foundational event of the Jewish religion? The main
challenge to Ross's departure from realism is the epistemological role played
by the biblical episode of God's revelation to the people of Israel on Mount
Sinai. She comments on the problematic aspects of such a belief in an act of
communication between the divine and humanity:

I am especially troubled by the very notion of divine revelation as verbal communication—given that language is a distinctly human activity, inevitably rooted in a
particular perspective and cultural bias. My solution is to regard belief in revelation as
an 'as if' statement, a useful fiction (or, in Maimonidian terminology, a 'necessary
truth') whose purpose is to represent and engender certain attitudes rather than to
describe an objective occurrence. I see this understanding as closely related to views
of religion as commitment to a range of doctrines and norms which serve as a cultural-
linguistic filter constructing the way we view the world, rather than as an objective
account of reality—metaphysical or otherwise.[78]

Hence language, according to Ross, serves as an instrument for 'constructing
the way we view the world, rather than as an objective account of reality'. Her
position is reminiscent of Wittgenstein's later philosophy, which construes
the meaning of language in relation to human activities, or 'forms of life'.
Each different form of life engenders a new language, and just as one could
identify an infinite and ever-evolving number of different forms of life, so

[77] Ibid. 217.   [78] See Brill, 'Prof. Tamar Ross Responds to the Comments'.

language continuously evolves according to historical and societal factors. According to Ross, 'justification is internal to the activity or "form of life" concerned'.[79] In other words, the value of a statement is determined by communal consensus and is manifested in the sociological and psychological behaviour of the group. This notion of communal consensus is taken by Ross to play out through collective understandings of revelation. Nevertheless, she keeps searching for some measure of assessment of its truth-value. Linguistic interpretation does not just come down to what makes sense for the community. There has to be, for Ross, some metaphysical element to the text if truth statements are to remain authoritative. The community cannot be the sole arbiter of truth:

Is there no connection between these human structures and the intrinsic nature of reality? If R. Kook were to take this track, and rely on universal consensus alone, without any ontological reference, one could hardly view him as a traditionalist theologian. Since . . . theology has traditionally operated out of realist epistemological assumptions, such a radical postmodernism which views language merely as a self-enclosed 'game', without some reference to a genuinely objective outside reality, would constitute a fundamental shift in the expectations surrounding traditional theological claims.[80]

Radical language theory undermines the ways in which we understand religious experience. Ross posits that the meaning of the text is both 'self-enclosed' and 'universal'—a necessary paradox. She is willing to accept that language cannot refer to anything beyond itself and yet seeks, like Shagar, to posit a metaphysical sphere. Language does not simply become a blur of multiple meanings continually disappearing into the ether: it must just be understood from a different, perhaps 'atheoretical' perspective. The function of religious language has altered: it acts as a lens through which the community visualizes, responds to, and behaves in the world. It is instrumentalist in binding together a community through self-expression of communal concerns and beliefs and is the guarantor of a temperament that remains inside the community.

So how does Ross treat those accounts which, often understood literally, constitute the foundations of religious belief? Her response hinges on metaphorical interpretations of biblical anthropomorphisms,[81] such as the idea of the outstretched arm.[82] With the objective of inscribing her own efforts with-

---

[79] Ross, 'Religious Belief in a Postmodern Age', 207.

[80] Ross, 'The Cognitive Value of Religious Truth Statements', 515–16.

[81] Postmodern theorists value anthropomorphisms to the extent that they are understood poetically and not realistically as metaphors and not credited with the anthropocentrism of what Derrida described as 'logocentrism' (see Hick, *Classical and Contemporary Readings in the Philosophy of Religion*; see also Derrida, *The Animal That Therefore I Am*).

[82] Ross, 'Religious Belief in a Postmodern Age', 215.

in a hallowed historical tradition, well established within Orthodox circles, Ross reinstates the use of allegorical interpretation:

In the case of descriptive statements open to critical scientific investigation (such as the age of the universe, the splitting of the Red Sea, the chronology of Biblical accounts), the sophisticated cultural-linguist will find the task of relating such statements to a presumed reality relatively easy, as there already exists a long history of naturalistic or allegorical interpretations within the religious tradition itself upon which he can draw.[83]

Her effort to read the biblical text in a non-literal manner rests on cultural particularism.[84] Language and text must be able to 'draw support from the interpretative tradition and prevailing communal sensibilities'.[85] Religious language therefore becomes valuable not only for its ability to transmit empirical information but also for its ability to decipher how people understand and attribute meaning to the world. Having taken leave of realism, Ross progresses to a theoretical plane where religious language can establish a meaningful connection with God, with no literalist expectations. Implicit in her reflection is an acknowledgement of the cultural-linguistic turn. Indeed, postmodern language theory forms the basis of her understanding of metaphors. It is worth examining Ross's insights into non-Jewish theology in order to gain a deeper understanding of her treatment of postmodern language theory.

Ross and Christian Theology of Language

Ross draws inspiration in her reaction to the cultural-linguistic turn from non-Jewish theologians. Her efforts to understand Christian theological responses to postmodern language theory make her stand out among Jewish thinkers.[86] The concepts she engages with sharpen her understanding of the challenges of postmodernism and of the differences between Christian and Jewish theologies.

One Christian theologian with whom Ross has engaged to a significant extent and found a certain level of common ground is George Lindbeck, who is widely associated with the 'post-liberal' camp (some have suggested that he and his theological circle coined the term in its relation to theology).[87] He develops in his works a religious response to the notion of cultural particularism, claiming that religious experience is actually anchored in culture and

---

[83] Ibid. 219–20.   [84] See Sagi, *Tradition vs. Traditionalism*, 5–14.
[85] Ross, 'Religious Belief in a Postmodern Age', 213.
[86] See ibid.; for her discussion of Phillips and others, see ibid. 216.
[87] For a broader consideration of the post-liberal strand of thinking in contemporary Jewish thought, see Hashkes, 'Towards a Post-Liberal Jewish Theology' (Heb.); see also Ochs, *Pragmatism and the Logic of Scripture*; id., *Another Reformation*.

manifests itself in a distinct way in each communal group: 'The sense of the holy or the sacred that is the identifying mark of religion for much of the experiential-expressive tradition is not a common quality, but a set of family resemblances.'[88] Ross makes explicit reference to Lindbeck's subjection of religious experience to cultural expression. Religious language, she notes, is an 'expression or exposure of a subjective experience of the divine dimension rather than . . . [a] description of an external state of affairs'.[89] Even though this point appears only in a footnote, it conveys her hopes in the formulation of a new conception of language, such that it may not refer to 'an external state of affairs' from an objective viewpoint, but can nonetheless communicate an 'experience of the divine dimension'.[90]

Another key philosopher of religion who examines the religious implications of language theory is Dewi Zephaniah Phillips. A neo-Wittgensteinian thinker, Phillips accepts the core claims of the cultural-linguistic turn—that each religious group comprises a distinct cultural-linguistic unit—and resists the effects of literalism on religion. He also claims that the distinction between religious language and other language games often put forward by post-liberals is over-simplistic. Individuals, in his view, operate simultaneously in parallel language games: 'The point of religious beliefs, why people *should* cherish them in the way they do, cannot be shown simply by *distinguishing between* religious beliefs and other features of human existence.'[91] Phillips maintains that the meaning of religious beliefs depends, in part, on their relation to other 'features of human existence'. It may not be possible to neatly distinguish language games from each other, since communities often intersect and interact. Ross agrees with this thesis, as it places the idiosyncrasies of religious groups within a larger framework. She quotes Phillips precisely to this end in 'Religious Belief in a Postmodern Age':

Approaching religious belief as an esoteric activity cut off from everything which is not formally religious, and without taking into account its relation to other modes of life, would amount to no more than conforming to 'a neat set of rules that could not be distinguished from sham worship . . . a charming game which provides a welcome contrast to the daily routine, but which has no relevance to anything outside the doors of the church. In fact, this is what religious practices often do become for those for whom they have lost their meaning: a charming game which

---

[88] Lindbeck, *The Nature of Doctrine*, 115. This is followed by Ross's interpretation of Sagi's efforts to broaden its reference with ultimately pragmatic outcomes, which she probably views as secondary to the post-liberal definition of language according to Lindbeck and others with whom she aligns herself.   [89] Ross, 'Religious Belief in a Postmodern Age', 192 n.

[90] Ross traces the linguistic developments of expressivism from existentialist Christian thinking in the writings of Paul Tillich to its post-liberal manifestations.

[91] D. Z. Phillips, 'Religious Beliefs and Language Games', 132.

provides a welcome contrast to the daily routine, but which has no relevance to anything outside the doors of the church.'[92]

According to both Phillips and Ross, the language game of religion maintains meaning and relevance in all areas of life. But it is necessary, in their view, to de-literalize religious language in order to enable its scope to extend beyond the religious community. Ross therefore understands religion as constituting one of many language games, yet one which carries ontological significance as a consequence of its mystical import. In light of Ross's inclusion of mysticism as a necessity in dealing with cultural-linguistic theories, it would be interesting to see how she might engage with the Christian theologians discussed at the beginning of this chapter, especially Kearney's mystical approach of 'anatheism'.[93]

Ross and Rorty: The Limitations of Neo-Pragmatism

I mentioned in the Introduction Ross's resistance to the exclusive emphasis on praxis put forward by Jewish neo-pragmatists. She maintains that religious observance must be informed by theology in order to remain meaningful. Yet many religious thinkers ultimately succumb to neo-pragmatism once they accept the premises of the linguistic-cultural turn: the fact that language reflects only the values of its corresponding culture undermines the possibility for ontological discourse. Hence while she initially expressed interest in the thought of Richard Rorty, she found that his conclusions fail to address the predicaments of religious belief in a postmodern age. Rorty accepts the notion of the language game and takes it to be indicative of how philosophy works as a whole:

Of course language can usefully be viewed for many purposes as a system of representations. . . . All that one has to do to make any of these approaches useful and productive is to take the vocabulary of the present historical period (or class or society or academy) for granted and to work within it. Once one is safely ensconced within this language game, questions about what correctly represents what, how we know that it does, and how it manages to do so will make admirable sense.[94]

Since individuals are immersed, and indeed trapped, within certain specific forms of life, they naturally take the rules of the corresponding language games for granted. This highlights the epistemological limitations of a conversation on ontology or theology: it is impossible to substantiate externally

---

[92] Ross, 'Religious Belief in a Postmodern Age', 217, quoting D. Z. Phillips, 'Religious Beliefs and Language Games', 134–5.   [93] See Kearney, *Anatheism*; Caputo, *On Religion*.
[94] Rorty, *Consequences of Pragmatism*, 104.

statements about the world or about the divine.[95] Rorty aligns himself, on this basis, with post-metaphysical theories of religion. Ross concurs, but only up to a certain point. Her understanding of what constitutes a community is different from Rorty's, for whom our knowledge of the world is dependent upon human experience: 'To accept the contingency of starting points is to accept our inheritance from, and our conversation with, our fellow-humans, as our only source of guidance. . . . We may gain a new sense of community.'[96]

While Ross may have benefited from Rorty's views in the development of her own reflections, she evidently feels that his conclusions fail on one crucial account: he does not provide an understanding of language that could either reinforce the believer's connection to religious faith or allow her to transcend the limitations of language and speak of the divine. In her view, neo-pragmatism undermines the credibility of theology and concedes too much ground to the cultural-linguistic critique:

It would be fair to say that a religious world view lacking any claims of attunement to a reality beyond its self-contained universe of discourse will never match traditional belief in its ability to preserve the intensity of feeling generated by its models and paradigms and to transmit the passion of its message to future generations.[97]

Jewish Mysticism as a Linguistic Model

Like Shagar, Ross believes that kabbalah has a crucial role to play in her efforts to resolve the problem of language. In her view, contemporary theology must take elements of kabbalistic thought into account:

What may appear to lay eyes here as abstruse metaphysical gymnastics are actually a serious attempt to overcome a tension even more extremely stated than in classical Kabbala, between two conflicting religious sensibilities (pantheism and theism), by developing a very intricate and finely tuned conceptual scheme, that will allow these two incompatible bedfellows to somehow lie peacefully together. For our purposes, however, the various theological constructs emerging from this effort can also point the way to a fruitful form of religious negotiation in a postmodern age.[98]

Ross strives to develop a 'conceptual scheme' through which she can construct a Jewish theology that responds to the issues of cultural particularism and the problem of language. This entails the integration of concepts that were previously conceived of as 'conflicting' and 'incompatible' theological 'sensibilities'—such as pantheism and theism. She notes, however, that the amalgamation of mysticism and postmodernism is not necessarily a task of great difficulty. Postmodernism, for one, is much closer to mysticism by

---

[95] See esp. Rorty, *Philosophy and the Mirror of Nature*.   [96] Rorty, *The Rorty Reader*, 115.
[97] Ross, 'Religious Belief in a Postmodern Age', 218 (my emphasis).   [98] Ibid. 238.

virtue of its emphasis on holism. Additionally, she notes that:

Postmodern theology is not simply a matter of exchanging one philosophical master for another, in striving to correlate religious belief with postmodern interests and concerns rather than modern ones. Finding a middle way between pretensions to absolute and objective truths and denial of truth altogether is not its only concern. Doing theology under the conditions of postmodernity also means that philosophy is no longer the exclusive determiner in setting the agenda for this type of activity. This is because postmodernism involves not only a new epistemology and under-standing of language. It also involves a different mindset and way of experiencing our everyday world and its relationship to another dimension that lies beyond it—one that is closer to mysticism than to philosophy. Rather than suffice with the vision of a fragmented and atomized universe, the path of postmodernism leads to viewing reality in holistic terms, as composed of various inter-related parts.[99]

Must the modern religious system be relinquished in favour of a postmodern alternative which incorporates mystical elements? The solution is not as straightforward, according to Ross. The process she envisages towards shap-ing a theology capable of addressing distinctly postmodern concerns will probably develop in a more organic fashion, as a greater number of tradition-alists progressively turn to kabbalah and language theory upon realizing that those disciplines may offer satisfactory answers to the questions of the time:

For a few rare intellectuals, grappling with the theoretical issues raised in this essay is a crucial element and direct expression of their yearning for the divine, and in this sense their unique method of worship. However, I fully realize that philosophy and theology are not everyone's preference, and certainly do not mean to imply that the wave of the future for all religious believers involves delving into language theory or the intricacies of Kabbalistic thought. But I do believe that traditionalists confronting the radical implications of contemporary scientific and moral insights, and seeking to incorporate these into their religious way of life without forfeiting its credibility or normative force, will intuitively gravitate towards some of the more promising implications that the postmodern sensibility holds for traditional Jewish belief when informed by a mystic sensibility. . . . *Postmodern language theory can redeem modern Orthodoxy from its counter-productive attachment to naive objectivism.* The epistemological modesty of non-foundationalism can help religious adherents move away from overly rigid definitions of doctrine and allow them to return to the pre-modern function of religion as providing a valuable universe of discourse and a compelling way of life.[100]

Mysticism represents a 'discourse', a 'mindset', or a 'sensibility' through which individuals may overcome the polarities and essentialisms of modernist

---

[99]   Ibid.   [100]   Ibid. 238–9 (my emphasis).

philosophy. Shagar and Ross both believe that kabbalistic insights, read with an awareness of postmodern language theory, allow a reconfiguration of religious language that ultimately dissolves many of the problems of the time.

Metaphors

Metaphors are figures of speech that operate through association, comparison, or resemblance. They appear as a prominent rhetorical device in all genres of literature, including, in numerous shapes and forms, the Bible and the talmudic canon, together with antithesis, hyperbole, metonymy, simile, and so on. The Greek etymology of the word 'metaphor' signifies a carrying over, a transfer of information between two separate conceptual spaces. According to Rorty, when a metaphor functions properly, it has no cognitive content: that is, it tells us nothing. This is because it uses words in a manner that remains outside conventional use. But while metaphors tell us nothing, they nevertheless can have a profound impact on the way in which we experience ourselves and the world. Metaphors, in this view, function not as a meaning but as a cause.

This notion is central to Ross's treatment of religious language after the cultural-linguistic turn. In her view, metaphors offer new opportunities for theological reflection in a religious discourse, a linguistic impetus for a new and creative point of view. She views them as persuasive tools for conceptualizing reality:

Metaphors have powerful existential value. The instrumentally successful model not only helps us to create a fuller or more multifarious reflection of the Divine from our point of view, but it also enables us to tease out of ourselves and our relationships more direct intimations of the Divine. Following this line of thought, it may be said that the religious believer may adopt certain symbols and theological visions for strictly instrumentalist reasons, but if he continues to live out these visions, he eventually will also have religious experiences which ground and affirm them. Thus R. Kook can tolerate an instrumentalist grounding for accepting Torah and Mitzvoth as a way of life (because of the beneficial effects upon national survival), but nevertheless be convinced that eventually this will lead to an inner conviction of their Divine nature. The more successful the religious model, the more it will allow us to experience the inter-connectedness of all beings, gradually diminishing the gap even between the human and the divine.[101]

Ross here undermines the neo-pragmatist's concessions to the problem of language. It does not suffice for her to suggest that language seals collective ties and points to communal aspirations. She comments that 'the alleged

---

[101] Ross, 'The Cognitive Value of Religious Truth Statements', 522–3.

"flight from metaphysics" attributed to modern continental thought and post-analytic philosophy may have been overdone; there may be room even in a constructivist position for a metaphysics that refers to something *beyond* the linguistic scheme'.[102] Although language must not purport to describe the metaphysical realm literally, it can still refer to it metaphorically.

Metaphors allow Ross to posit traditional metaphysics while at the same time responding to postmodern concerns: she explains that metaphors evade scientific or logical scrutiny and therefore perfectly suit a mystical discourse. By their very nature, they expand the boundaries of language, opening up new horizons for statements of religious truths:

Because the appropriation of metaphors is self-implicating, adopted metaphors can literally create worlds and determine their nature. . . . On this view, religious truths that were first justified instrumentally will eventually be confirmed by their ability to lead us to a level of experience which is recognizably beyond that which we have previously known not only on the existential and subjective level, but even in terms of the infinite possibilities capable of being realized in our external reality.[103]

Ross claims, in other words, that the function of a metaphor is to reframe reality within a culturally specific perspective. Since pre-existing beliefs and assumptions will always colour our understanding of the world, the believer can experience through the use of metaphors a sense of 'patent objectivity'— a poignant impression of objectivity that stands up even to the problem of language.[104] By virtue of their working within language, rather than beyond or against it, mystical metaphors can lead the individual to a closer contact with the divine as she envisions it. Literary devices, such as interpretative illustrations and allegorical exegesis, creatively convey otherwise incommunicable ideas about religious experience and successfully do so from within particular linguistic confines.

Some contemporary postmodern philosophers have expressed similar positions. According to Derrida metaphors can express truths with more power than any literal statement.[105] The phenomenologist Paul Ricœur similarly argues that metaphors succeed in salvaging language while simultaneously acknowledging its cultural linguistic boundaries.[106] He outlines a theory of

---

[102] Ross, 'Religious Belief in a Postmodern Age', 230.

[103] Ross 'The Cognitive Value of Religious Truth Statements', 524–5 (my emphasis).

[104] Ross, 'Religious Belief in a Postmodern Age', 222.   [105] Derrida, *On the Name*, 42.

[106] Phenomenology seeks to draw conclusions about religious subjectivism from a philosophical (not psychological) perspective. Edmund Husserl and his students in Germany (including Heidegger), France (mainly the existential branch developed by Emmanuel Levinas, Jean-Paul Sartre, and Maurice Merleau-Ponty, most of whom interested Shagar), and, later, the United States, have developed his claims of the nature of consciousness and reflection in

the metaphor which breaks down the distance between what is spoken and what is referred to—the signifier and the signified—by considering 'intentionality' or what prompted the individual to use a metaphor and what she meant when using it in a religious context.[107] In 'Metaphor and Reference', Ricœur claims that intentionality does have an effect on what is meant by what is said:

My whole aim is to do away with this restriction of reference to scientific statements. Therefore, a distinct discussion appropriate to the literary work is required. . . . Just as the metaphorical statement captures its sense as metaphorical amidst the ruins of the literal sense, it also achieves its reference upon the ruins of what might be called (in symmetrical fashion) its literal reference.[108]

This view echoes Ross's resistance to literalism. Ricœur suggests that the metaphor succeeds in conveying its message when scientific, literalist understandings of language are in 'ruins'.[109] Some have argued that Ricœur's engagement with biblical discourse can serve as the basis for a Jewish theology that pays closer attention to the forms of reason and experience that produce and support theological claims.[110] In such a light, it could be argued that the religious language of Torah never presumed to make scientific, logical statements, to be understood as doctrinal instructions, about what exists beyond the physical world.

Ricœur and Ross both harness the metaphor to guide the cultural linguist away from and beyond the Wittgensteinian trap of the language game. Ross's mystical theology of metaphor intimates that the language game does not adequately account for religion after the cultural-linguistic turn. One well-known application of this phenomenological understanding draws on the work of Iris Murdoch, who explores the role of metaphors in creating literary, poetic, aesthetic, and theological meaning:

The development of consciousness in human beings is inseparably connected with the use of metaphor. Metaphors are not merely peripheral decorations or even useful models, they are fundamental forms of our awareness of our condition: metaphors of space, metaphors of movement, metaphors of vision. . . . It seems to

the study of philosophy. For my purposes here I will use phenomenological writing to show that, in tandem with postmodernism, reflections on the intentionality and intuition (*noema* and *noesis*) of the thinker or individual play an important role in their subjective yet often ontological understandings of experiences and texts. On the phenomenology of religion (or 'phenomeno-theology'), see Cox, *A Guide to the Phenomenology of Religion*; on its connection to mysticism in different religious traditions, see Steinbock, *Phenomenology and Mysticism*.

[107] On Ricœur and theological language, see esp. Bourgeois, 'Ricœur and Lyotard in Postmodern Dialogue', 16.   [108] Ricœur, *The Rule of Metaphor*, 261.
[109] For an account of the Ricœurian connection between metaphorical language and metaphor in the text, see Klemm, 'Philosophy and Kerygma', 52.   [110] Fisher, 'Jewish Philosophy', 89.

me impossible to discuss certain kinds of concepts without resort to metaphor, since the concepts are themselves deeply metaphorical and cannot be analysed into non-metaphorical components without a loss of substance.[111]

The interpretation of metaphors by collectives is determined not only by cultural constructs, but also by context—in philosophical terms, 'intentionality' (what do they want to understand from it?) and 'temporality' (their mindset as they interpret it—are they tired? hopeful?). In line with Ricœurian phenomenology, Ross disregards analytical understandings of metaphor in favour of a theological approach which seeks to construct meaning. 'Intimations of the divine' are, in her view, necessarily communicated through 'symbols' and 'visions'. Indeed, she argues that her kabbalistic, metaphorical account of religion

seems to have a different and far stronger epistemological status than the previous one, employing what has come to be known as the eschatological test of truth claims. It has been pointed out by some philosophers that as metaphors are appropriated, lived and shared, they structure not only our subjectively felt experience of the reality they confront, but also that very reality itself. Because the appropriation of metaphors is self-implicating, adopted metaphors can literally create worlds and determine their nature. . . . *So long as there is some connection of belief with testable prediction, however tenuous, it is still possible to avoid the allegation that religious statements are absolutely unverifiable in principle, and therefore have no real ontological grounding.*[112]

A religious believer will therefore naturally, given her particular context, develop a religious world-view. Ross, in her account of the way religious language can 'create worlds and determine their nature', offers such an individual the tools to nurture such an outlook. She moves away from monolithic realism—the literal and the scientific—in her understanding of religious discourse and towards mysticism and poetry, symbolized by the metaphor. She therefore believes that mysticism offers the Jewish tradition an invaluable lexicon to describe the divine realm metaphorically, and offers some examples drawn from kabbalistic literature:

According to the original Lurianic image, the existence of a created world was first made possible by an act of withdrawal on the part of *Einsof* (the Infinite One) from the central point of His monolithic unity, contracting into Himself in order to make room within His absolute para-existence for a mode of being other than Himself. While this image (which provides an archetypal paradigm for the process of birth) is always accompanied by pious caveats of *kivyakhol* ('as it were'), *even a*

---

[111] Murdoch, *The Sovereignty of Good*, 75.
[112] Ross, 'The Cognitive Value of Religious Truth Statements', 524 (my emphasis).

metaphor must be a metaphor for something. . . . The main idea promoted by these later interpreters of Lurianic teachings is that the original image of divine contraction in order to make space for a finite world should not be understood literally, as an actual physical displacement and creation of a void, but as a metaphoric withdrawal.[113]

The kabbalists used this idea of withdrawal not only as a way to characterize God but also to comment on the role of humanity—God as having withdrawn from human comprehension and experience. For the metaphor to engender the desired emotion or behaviour, it must be formulated from within the community, in terms all adherents will understand. A language game, by definition, elicits a unique response from the communal body:

All our uses of language are 'language games' of one sort or another—meant sometimes to assert, sometimes to command, sometimes to engender empathy, sometimes to greet, and sometimes even to express our absolute commitment to an all-encompassing religious worldview. . . . None of this denies that many religious truth statements are by their nature dead serious, and almost the only sort that we might choose to live or die for.[114]

In this sense, the cultural prejudice inherent in human language becomes crucial for the religious believer:

The process of converting an unbeliever into a believer on this view resembles the teaching of a language, not because religion itself is a language, but because it functions as one, in helping us internalize views and acquire skills that have already been formulated and developed by others. . . . The final product of the religious learning process is not meant to be an authoritative list of religious dogmas or an ideal moral system, but rather implied or suggestive directives as to how to think about God and to conduct one's life in accordance with these thoughts. In a best case scenario, such directives become second nature, and fulfil an essential role in fashioning the life of the believer.[115]

Ross suggests that certain linguistic tools can still point to a metaphysical realm, just not on scientifically verifiable grounds. In a more general sense, language does not merely limit itself to describing that which exists; it also has a poetic element to it. The shared language of the community imbues certain metaphors with ontological significance. The idea of *tsimtsum*, for example, provides a model for absence that requires fulfilment. It represents an imaginative heuristic tool through which believers can grasp the nature of the divine, not a literalist statement expressing a metaphysical reality. Ross

[113]   Ross, 'Religious Belief in a Postmodern Age', 231 (my emphasis).
[114]   Ross, 'Response to Yoel Finkelman'.
[115]   Ross, 'Religious Belief in a Postmodern Age', 204.

proposes to alter the way we conceive of a major component of religion: epistemology. To accept the notion of language games, individuals must be willing to engage with contemporary philosophical insights into language and the way postmodernists have come to rethink its role in informing religious belief. Ross is clearly aware of the theological difficulties that a new understanding of language presents for twenty-first-century believers:

Is there still room in the world of the neo-pragmatist for a system of belief that relates somehow to metaphysics and to absolute standards, while at the same time taking seriously the radical nature of the postmodern sensibility and its revolutionary insights regarding the determining influence of context on the meaning of language, and the implications of this insight for the ontological status of religious truth claims and their justification?[116]

Theologians tend to cherish the conviction that language can describe and appeal to a metaphysical realm and, in that respect, often underestimate the impact of language-games theory on religion. Yet those, like Ross, who do fully acknowledge the cultural-linguistic turn have little choice but to seriously consider its implications when formulating theological claims. One can only wait and see how Ross develops these ideas in the future. From this quote, it seems obvious that she realizes that the modern phenomenon of Jewish neo-pragmatism will not disappear despite the fact that its proponents, who express the need for some measure of absolute, universal metaphysical conviction, do not fully appreciate the way cultural or social context influences their beliefs. Many feared that the refutation of literalist understandings of language would collapse into some form of hermeneutical anarchy. This prediction has manifestly proved to be inaccurate: contemporary phenomenological scholarship helps the reader acquire a nuanced grasp of Ross's 'perspectival' position, which takes into account the state of consciousness, the intentionality, and the intuition of the religious believer who uses her imagination to describe the divine. A sense of truth therefore remains even following a postmodern critique of language. In this respect, Ross's theology presents some highly innovative components. She nonetheless claims that one can retain a belief in revelation and find meaning in the performance of *mitsvot* even with a postmodern appreciation of the human character of language. This may be true for her personally, but it will probably not be the case for many others. Her attempt to relinquish literal interpretations of biblical texts will strike many Jews as wholly unorthodox. Her turn towards a Jewish theology infused with mysticism will also attract resistance, given the irrational—or anti-rationalist—stance this implies.

[116] Ibid. 201.

Perhaps, in the light of these anticipated objections, she too might end up turning away from radical postmodern theorists and repudiating the allegation that religion can survive merely on 'unverifiable' religious principles.[117] Ross does not claim to have the perfect answer to this issue. To the extent that she set out to incorporate postmodern linguistic theory into Jewish theology, she achieved her goal. By highlighting the widespread misuse of religious language among modern philosophers, she emphasized the shortcomings of modernist epistemology. In her mind, knowledge no longer comes as a static and absolute structure but rather as a network of linguistic and cultural interpretations of facts about the world. She successfully located the intersections between the two systems and came to realize that an appreciation of the context of beliefs actually strengthens, rather than weakens, religious commitment. The way in which she integrated feminism and Jewish theology exemplifies the perspectival character of her religious epistemology—it demonstrates that each individual's perspective engenders a new way of understanding religious truth-claims. Her reflections on the issue also delve into the problems which arise when taking the divine character of Scripture as the source of religious epistemology.

Conclusions

Sanford Drob notes striking similarities and conceptual compatibilities between postmodern and mystical ontological systems. He also sets out to dispel the common points of contention between philosophy and religion by suggesting that, since the time of Isaac Newton, widespread misuse of language has prompted people to conceive of theology in empirical terms. Kabbalistic ontology, he argues, concurs with the postmodern rejection of the empiricization of religion, because both seek to counter literalist misunderstandings of language:

With the symbol of the *Sefirot*, the Kabbalists articulate and seek to resolve the opposition between the simple unity of the Absolute and the apparent multiplicity of the world (the classical problem of 'the one' and 'the many'); in the symbol of the *Kellipot* (Husks) the Kabbalists articulate and attempt to resolve the antinomy between good and evil; in *Tzimtzum*, the chasm between being and nothingness; in *Adam Kadmon* (Primordial Man), the distance between God and man, and in the symbol of *Tikkun ha-Olam* (the Restoration of the World), the antinomy between theism (God created man) and atheism (man created God). Indeed, each of the Kabbalistic symbols can be understood as emerging dialectically, as a higher-order

---

[117] Ross, 'The Cognitive Value of Religious Truth Statements', 525.

sublation of a contradiction between traditional philosophical ideas, and, hence, as a 'resolution' to a traditional philosophical problem.[118]

Kabbalah, according to Drob, can be utilized to dispel mistaken understandings of language as empirical. It can serve to disrupt fabricated polarities that were propounded in modernist discourses (such as being/nothingness or God/humanity). Kabbalah can thus be seen as an ontological model for the perpetuation of postmodern deconstructions of language as corresponding to reality. In addition to the ontological model, Drob notes linguistic similarities between postmodernist and kabbalistic theories of deconstruction and creativity:

The question . . . is whether, with the demise of the distinction between words and things, there is any hope at all of attaining a consciousness or intuition of a 'real' that is somehow prior to, independent of, or beyond language. While the assumptions of postmodernism might immediately suggest that the answer to this question is 'no', we will see that the possibility of fulfilling such hope goes to the heart of the rational-mystical endeavor, and leads us to a Kabbalah that incorporates and yet transcends the challenges of postmodern philosophy.[119]

The kabbalistic and postmodern systems share a conviction of language's ability to generate a metaphorical mystical realm. To Drob, Lurianic kabbalah is and claims to be simultaneously creative and inventive but also a communal construct, a product of religious imagination:

Unlike other basic metaphors, the validity of the Lurianic theosophy is not undermined by the argument that it itself is a *historical narrative constructed* by humankind. This is because *constructing/creating* history, the world, God, and narratives about each of these is precisely what Lurianic Kabbalah is about! Collectively, the Lurianic symbols provide a narrative in which humanity, the world and divinity are in a continual process of creation, deconstruction, reconstruction and redemption. . . . Further, in opposition to dogmatic theology, the Lurianic Kabbalah recognises that both god and the world, like scripture, are subject to an indefinite if not infinite variety of interpretations, and that such infinite interpretability does not undermine, but rather provides the context for the world's redemption (*Tikkun*).[120]

Shagar and Ross both sense the congruence between this distinctive feature of the kabbalistic project and the radical refutation of empirical truth which characterizes postmodernism. The way they appropriate kabbalistic motifs in their respective theologies turns language into an instrument in the hands of the religious community for perpetually reimagining the divine. At the same time, both of them resist divesting language entirely of meaning and thereby

---

[118]   Drob, *Kabbalah and Postmodernism*, 7–8.   [119]   Ibid. 47.   [120]   Ibid. 11–12.

avoid the nihilism which many feared a postmodern theology might lead to. The linguistic problem of symbolism—in practice, whether a metaphor can actually refer to something beyond itself—therefore necessitates fresh consideration. Ross converges with Shagar when appealing to mysticism to reconfigure the role of language in response to the limits of representation. Yet where Shagar employs kabbalistic motifs to bolster religious commitment against the problem of language, Ross explores the feasibility of religious truth-statements in the framework of a non-foundationalist Jewish theology. Ross's thoughts on the subject might develop further in time. Still, her observations, as well as Shagar's, represent exciting, innovative progress in the area of Jewish theology. Both thinkers engage with the scholarship of contemporary philosophers and theologians—something highly unusual within Jewish thought—and therefore stand out as original attempts towards outlining a theology for the present and the future.

THREE

REVELATION

THIS CHAPTER brings together the ideas raised in the two previous chapters. Having internalized the postmodern critique of religion, my aim is to explore the potential for a new theology of revelation. I postulate that each collective is responsible for determining its own truth-claims. Each community is a world unto itself in which particular understandings and usages of language are perpetuated. I therefore integrate cultural particularism by maintaining the concept of revelation at the heart of Jewish theology, while recasting it as a non-metaphysical experience. I also tackle the problem of language through its textual manifestations. I explained in the previous chapter that postmodernists no longer understand language as referring to an objective truth. Linguistic functions or 'signifiers' reflect instead a communal reality. Those within the hermeneutical community are playing a game, and the meanings of the terms and expressions they use are dependent entirely on the context in which they are spoken. As such, language is used as an instrument to designate a variety of conflicting and complementary narratives rather than as a description of a metaphysical truth. The purpose of this chapter is to illustrate how this shift changes the very conception of revelation.[1]

Ross's non-realist application of mysticism to religious truth statements, together with Shagar's denial of language's ability to refer to anything beyond itself, allows for an instrumentalization of language. This bears heavily on a certain definition and perception of revelation and its relation to the Written and Oral Torahs. I claim that although language game theory should feature prominently in a postmodern theology, it must not completely define the way in which we understand revelation. My aim is to demonstrate that expressions of divinity can reach beyond particular cultural confines.

Torah min hashamayim through a Postmodern Lens

It is necessary to unpack the concept of *torah min hashamayim* in order to gain an appreciation of how Shagar and Ross reinterpret it in a way that

---

[1] On how philosophy of language has influenced European and North American Jewish philosophers, see Batnitzky, 'Revelation, Language and Commentary'.

bridges the gap between their traditional orientation and their interest in postmodernism. The biblical account of divine revelation on Mount Sinai is traditionally understood as an epistemological testimony of divine engagement with humanity in which God bequeathed the Torah to the people of Israel.[2] This characterization of the Torah as God-given appears in two common expressions: *torah min hashamayim* ('Torah from Heaven') and *torah misinai* ('Torah from Sinai'). Maimonides, in his introduction to chapter 10 of Mishnah *Sanhedrin*, argued that *torah min hashamayim* is a cardinal Jewish belief. His was the most famous attempt at rendering the doctrine into a dogma, one of the thirteen foundational creeds of Jewish theology.[3]

In order to examine this belief, I first need to define the term 'Torah'. I consider 'Torah' to comprise the 'Written Torah', which refers to the Hebrew Bible, and the 'Oral Torah', which includes all subsequent canonical sources expounding the biblical text, whether halakhic or aggadic (the Mishnah, the Jerusalem and Babylonian Talmuds, numerous midrashic collections, medieval scriptural and talmudic commentaries, and so on).[4] The Written and Oral Torahs are viewed as 'twin aspects of the same revelation'.[5] The debate over the concept of 'Torah from Heaven' does not solely focus on the content of revelation (that is, the precise meaning of 'Torah'). The term 'from'—denoting the way it occurred—has also been subject to a host of different historical and conceptual interpretations, ranging from verbatim dictation to more abstract inspiration. The traditional belief in a historical revelation conflicts with the contemporary consensus among academic Bible scholars, who view Scripture as a composite work comprising fragments written over centuries by various authors.[6] Norman Solomon, in his broad historical survey of Jewish interpretations of the motif of divine revelation from late antiquity to the modern period, has noted that the divinity of both the Written and the Oral Torahs *'was certainly intended by the rabbis as a factual, historical claim. It denotes an event firmly located in time and space, involving real people and identifi-*

---

[2] For Shalom Rosenberg the epistemological claim is twofold. Revelation involves the 'parallel revelations' of the godhead and of the information and commands as derivatives of that knowledge: 'Any discussion of revelation in the framework of Judaism requires us to concern ourselves not only with revelation whose content is the Torah, that is, with the revelation of some information about God, man or the world, but also with revelation whose content is religious commandments, namely a system of norms and laws. If we understand proposition in this broader sense, which includes commands, then the parallel is valid' (Rosenberg, 'Revelation', 815).   [3] See Kellner, *Must a Jew Believe Anything?*

[4] For a historical overview of how the canonization of texts played a role in later conceptions of what constituted 'Torah', see Solomon, *Torah from Heaven*, 19–37.

[5] Handelman, *The Slayers of Moses*, 31.

[6] I thank my undergraduate supervisor at Cambridge, Nicholas de Lange, for drawing my attention to the significance of proponents of divine revelation as what he termed a 'meteorite' that fell from the heavens.

able texts.'[7] He and Marc Shapiro have analysed why and how divinity was attributed to the text, as well as revisionist understandings of revelation post-Enlightenment.[8] They have offered precious insights into the historical development of the doctrine, illustrating the variety of ways in which it was interpreted among Jewish exegetes.

If the community is a self-contained unit, governed by its own language and values, can it maintain belief in revelation? Is it possible to hold that a truth transcends the community? The difficulty of retaining a metaphysical account of revelation constitutes one of postmodernism's primary challenges to religion. The cultural-linguistic turn prompts a re-evaluation of the metaphysical content of the biblical motif of Sinaitic revelation by revealing the cultural bias manifest in the scriptural account of the event. If there is no correspondence between language and reality, one would be forced to accept the view that all beliefs have been formulated, for centuries, through the repetition and reification of human language. A postmodern understanding of the concept of revelation, inspired by the notion of cultural particularism and insights into language, therefore denies metaphysics altogether. Levinas wrestled with how revelation can speak both internally to religious minds and also externally to critics. He has put the question most succinctly: 'The problem of revelation insistently arises and demands new conceptions. How are we to understand the "exteriority" particular to truths and revealed signs striking the human mind which, despite its "interiority", is a match for the world and is called "reason"?'[9] Similarly, the traditional conception of revelation is wholly dependent on the polarization of the human and the divine—a polarity subject to deconstructionist critique that cuts to the very heart of theology.[10] In the case of the Pentateuch, it challenges the divine origins or message presumed by many to lie at the heart of the text and therefore undermines the holiness and authority attributed to Scripture and its

---

[7] N. Solomon, *Torah from Heaven*, 36 (my emphasis). Solomon explains the Oral Law as follows: 'The sages of the talmudic period developed the concept of *torah min hashamayim* in such a way as to incorporate both Oral Torah and Written Torah. They elevated the Five Books of Moses above the rest of scripture as a criterion for all subsequent revelation, accorded these books the status of ultimate authority in all matters of halakhah, and absorbed both traditional and innovative teachings into them through the "Dual Torah" concept of an Oral and Written Torah, received together at Sinai, bound together through rules of exegesis, and faithfully transmitted to and through the sages themselves and their predecessors back to Moses' (ibid. 46).

[8] Shapiro, *Changing the Immutable*. For more on the divinity of the Pentateuch, from rabbinic to medieval to modern times and how its 'maculations' did not, until modern times, serve to render the Torah authoritatively defunct, see Halivni, *Revelation Restored*. For modern interpretations of *torah min hashamayim*, see Gillman, *Sacred Fragments*, 1–7, and Jacobs *We Have Reason to Believe*, 57–69; see also 'The Condition of Jewish Belief'.

[9] Levinas, *Beyond the Verse*, 131.

[10] See e.g. Kula, *Existential or Non-Essential?* (Heb.), 104–60.

commentaries. I mentioned, in Chapter 1, the rise of Jewish engagement with deconstructive hermeneutical techniques. One approach that seeks to explore the connection between deconstructionism and revelation was put forward by Steven Kepnes. He argues that the hermeneutic process constitutes in and of itself a manifestation of revelation. Kepnes, alongside Peter Ochs[11] and Robert Gibbs, points to the ahistoricity of reading texts, so that the very processes of reading and interpretation strongly resemble deconstructionism:[12]

All literature, whether it be rabbinic, philosophic, or poetic, exists in a long tradition of texts built upon texts that came before, and attempts to make significant textual innovations in that tradition so that texts in the future will refer to them. The literary term for this is 'intertextuality', and what this term means is that it is often the textual tradition in which, out of which, and to which the writers write that is more important than the 'original historical context' in which the writer lives. The primacy of intertextuality over historical context also means that problems and solutions that are formulated in one historical period by a thinker writing in and for his/her textual tradition, may very well be productive for a thinker writing in a very different historical period.[13]

The 'original historical context' of the Torah presents, for Kepnes, the starting point from which the learning process begins. It is not a fixed source of intentional meaning to be recovered by learning, but, rather, its multiple meanings are continually disseminated. This endless hermeneutic task he would probably refer to as 'continual revelation'. In comparison, Ross, whose theory of cumulative revelation I will explore below as a prime model of this view, writes that her 'openness to deconstruction of the classic dictation metaphor of revelation' provides new insights into the meaning of Torah study.[14] Deconstructionism provides new ways for understanding revelation that are both in line with traditional values and present novel ways of learning Torah. This learning is text-based, endless, compelling, jarring, engaging, multivocal, and multilayered. When considering the notion of revelation, my interest is how to retain the traditional terminology of revelation as divine, meaningful, instructive, holy, relational, while offering innovative ways of interpreting this terminology. Ross, who characterized her understanding of 'cumulative revelation' as divine to the extent that it enables manifestations of truth to unfold within different cultural

---

[11] For textual reading as constituting theology, see e.g. Ochs (ed.), *The Return to Scripture in Judaism and Christianity*, 3–52.

[12] For a full and concise explanation of the common conceptual strands between the two sensibilities of reading, see ibid. and Kepnes, Ochs, and Gibbs, *Reasoning After Revelation*.

[13] Kepnes, review of Hughes and Wolfson (eds.), *New Directions in Jewish Philosophy*; see also Kepnes, *The Text as Thou*.   [14] Ross, 'Overcoming the Epistemological Barrier', 388.

contexts, couches her original ideas in traditional language. As Norman
Solomon puts it, we witness a 'characterization of the attempts of theologians to
retain a stable vocabulary while assigning different meanings to it . . . rather
than endorsing the traditional reading'.[15]

Solomon and Shapiro adopt a literalist approach, drawing a historical
sketch of the doctrine of revelation and its place in Jewish theology. Their
investigations hold great value from a historian's point of view, but unfortu-
nately fail to account for religious experience. I therefore prefer the relational
approach promoted by Yehuda Gellman and Jonathan Sacks, both of whom
view revelation not as a one-off encounter but as something that manifests
itself in the Jewish historical experience and finds expression in the great
corpus of halakhic, aggadic, and mystical texts produced by Jews throughout
the ages.[16] Such an account of revelation does not limit the discussion to the
historicity and literality of a single event.

Jonathan Sacks, for example, has explored fundamental questions relating
to the clash between religion and science which have led to attempts to construe
Torah as a scientific manual.[17] In his presentation of 'new atheists', he denies
the allegation that contemporary scientific discoveries are inherently problematic to religion by denouncing the persistent polarization of religion and
science. One might use the same line of thought to confront the issue of higher
biblical criticism and the insurmountable problem it allegedly represents for
modern Judaism. Sacks has also charted some less well-known developments
in biblical criticism which concern themselves with phenomenological understandings of the Torah in communities.[18] In the light of these insights, Levinas's quandary of the internal and external meanings of revelation—a typically
modernist concern—finds relief in the conception of revelation as a non-
scientific, non-literal, theological concept and should be interpreted as such.

One final locus of contentious discussion concerns the relationship
between the divine and human input in revelation, on which Avi Sagi proposes
a helpful categorization, listing three models of understanding.[19] The first
model, which Sagi terms the 'realistic model', assumes that Torah is perfect
by virtue of its divinity and that halakhic decision-making represents a pro-
traction of the Sinaitic revelation. According to this model, the divine will
is actually manifested in the Written and the Oral Torahs. The role of the
halakhist is, therefore, to align himself with the divine will by locating within
these sources the appropriate interpretation for the community and applying it
to daily situations. This is a position in which 'options suggested by halakhic

<hr>

[15] N. Solomon, *Torah from Heaven*, 260.   [16] Gellman, *This Was from God*, 153–4.
[17] Sacks, *The Great Partnership*, 209–32.   [18] Sacks, 'Revelation'.
[19] Sagi, *The Open Canon*, 71–2; see also Silman, *The Voice is Heard at Sinai* (Heb.).

sages reflect real possibilities first set down at Sinai'. The differing opinions of individual sages are therefore of equal value.

In the second, the 'authoritative model', the sages' rulings represent socially constructed, often flawed attempts at making sense of divine utterances.[20] According to this model, the multiplicity of competing halakhic views is inevitable, since all these opinions represent partial human attempts at comprehending God's word. Halakhic rulings do not, therefore, represent a 'pure' reflection of the divine word.[21] This is a middle approach which undermines the competence and authority of the rabbis by emphasizing their fallibility, while at the same time stressing the potential for perfection inherent in Torah which can be achieved through the medium of human creativity.

The third model is the 'anthropological model', in which the human voice is understood as arbiter of the Oral (and sometimes the Written) Torah. Divine aspects of revelation are considered as theories of divinity constructed by individuals and propagated by communities. Accordingly, commandments are not necessarily translatable into halakhah, but rather into suggestions. A deconstructive critique of Torah would likely yield similar conclusions, emphasizing the human input over the divine one. Perhaps it is precisely for this reason that Shagar applies deconstructive hermeneutics to his scholarship on the Talmud, and not to that on the Pentateuch.[22]

Sagi goes on to construct a fourth approach, that of 'perennial revelation', which proposes that Torah was and continues to be communicated from God to humans: 'Perennial revelation, then, is the matching feature of text openness. As halakhic creativity is continuous, so is revelation, and vice-versa, as revelation is continuous, so does halakhic creativity grow and develop.'[23]

I believe that Sagi's second and third models give too much weight to the human element of Torah. His first, 'realist', position lends itself the most to the visionary, cultural, and creative understanding of revelation. I believe it is the most helpful for our purposes, and will now consider contemporary attempts at grappling with the notion of revelation by asking: How can we understand a 'realist' model of revelation in postmodern terms? How should individuals who espouse a postmodern outlook understand the concept of *torah min hasha-mayim*? What implications does multiple-truths theory have for

---

[20] Such an approach does not always imply a detraction from the Written Torah as divine writ. Rabbi Moshe Feinstein, for example, took this position to claim that 'halakhic truth' can differ from human halakhic rulings (Feinstein, *Igerot mosheh*, iii. 114–15).

[21] Sagi, *The Open Canon*, 80.

[22] For Shagar's deconstruction of talmudic comments on commandments for which it is halakhically preferable to be killed rather than to transgress (BT *San.* 73a) alongside discussions of Georges Bataille and Michel Foucault, see Shagar, *Loving You Unto Death* (Heb.), 18–20.   [23] Sagi, *The Open Canon*, 76.

understanding revelation? Some of the most developed theories to date are put forward by Shagar and Ross. I will explain what is meant here by postmodern positions on the phenomenology of religion and will then turn to Jewish approaches to revelation, analysing postmodern approaches to the impact of culture and language on the doctrine of *torah min hashamayim*.

Phenomenology of Religion

Phenomenology is the name for the philosophical articulation of human experience, the meaning experiences have for people, and how they affect their lives. Phenomenology is practised in many fields, notably anthropology and sociology, but these disciplines study human experience from a third-person point of view. In philosophy and theology, the person who "has" the experience is the one who decides what it means. Philosophical phenomenology is attributed to Edmund Husserl in the early twentieth century, and it was critiqued and further developed by later philosophers. Martin Heidegger, for example, put forward the case for phenomenological experience not being central to human existence but, rather, something that happens concurrently with it.

Phenomenology provides a different and more useful way of considering religious experience: from the believer's point of view, rather than as an anthropological study from the outside. Experience is a key component of how religious meaning and truth are understood. Religious phenomena include the sense of the miraculous, the encounter with a striking text, or the feeling of transcendence at a holy site. Two of the first phenomenologists to talk specifically about religion were Gerardus van de Leeuw and Brede Kristensen, who took seriously the experience of believers as a reflection of what religion truly can be: that is, the experience of the numinous, and the trepidation and bravery of the believer. The phenomenology of religion analyses the very root of religious consciousness.

Early phenomenology of religion assumed a core essence common to all religions. However, for postmodernists different religions are understood to be completely distinct cultural and linguistic systems, and this must be taken into account in considering religious experiences. This marks but one of the shifts in phenomenology in the postmodern era.

Culture and Revelation: The Role of the Community

The Jewish community upholds the belief in the divine character of the biblical text, and thereby forms a *phenomenological community*. Belief in the divine nature of Scripture unites the different members, forming a community.

According to Ross, the continued acceptance of Torah and its adaptation to temporal conditions is the central tenet upon which communal experience rests. She reconceives the concept of *torah min hashamayim* as 'cumulative revelation'. The divine character of the text manifests itself in its application to human society. Shagar identifies the method of exegetical interpretation developed by the community and enacted in traditional Torah study as its defining characteristic. He therefore reconfigures textual study, in its temporal conditions, as constituting a phenomenological religious experience.

Shagar: Text and Context

Lamdanut, intensive Torah study, has been understood in Orthodox circles as a divine commandment (for males at least) for generations. Shagar responds to the postmodern critique of religion by framing this act of collective engagement with sacred texts in culturally particular terms in order to imbue it with divinity: 'It is possible to "dress up" *lamdanut* in postmodern garb. . . . It is possible to present *lamdanut* as a language game, made up of all its own rules.'[24] His outline of this theory is hardly clear, and the fact that it is restricted to a very small collective undermines his efforts to resituate revelation in postmodern terms.

Shagar conceives of *lamdanut* as the communal act par excellence. Its culturally particular character, itself a necessary condition for *lamdanut*, hermetically seals it from the type of external critique I have set out in this book. It represents a world unto itself, an impenetrable bubble in which faith is effectively implicit and hence taken for granted: 'Religious discourse—like any discourse—is aligned to its own cycle of life, and from that it derives its meaning.' It is through the act of learning, rather than its content, that this meaning is derived:

Torah embodies its own way of seeing the world. It renews the world by restabilizing it through a new order, which bequeaths life meaning. [The idea of Torah] as offering an alternative awareness of the world presents a completely different type of discourse and erudition. Faith [thereby becomes] embedded in this world with the fixed meanings [which accompany it]. . . . [This meaning] is at the outset necessary and foundational [to Jewish belief]. The colour and tune of learning are more important than its content.[25]

The *lamdan* (learner), upon engaging in *lamdanut*, enters a unique framework. Its distinct 'colour' and 'tune' encompass the *lamdan* and set him in an alternative reality, with its own order and sense of meaning.[26] The *lamdan*'s faith

---

[24] Shagar, *On His Torah He Meditates* (Heb.), 188.   [25] Shagar, *Broken Vessels* (Heb.), 32.
[26] For a sociohistorical account of how and when textual study became popularized in Jewish

background informs his *lamdanut*. In Shagar's view, the *lamdan* breathes life into sacred texts when he studies them according to rabbinic hermeneutics. This practice therefore represents a distinct form of life which a *lamdan* engages in and which carries phenomenological significance:

The central methodology of *lamdanut* is phenomenological. . . . [The text is] explained and debated through its own internal explanations. Outside influences, such as critical research, should not affect *lamdanut*. This is because the phenomenon of *lamdanut* works according to its own laws. External influences would [be harmful] because they reduce faith by offering psychological or sociohistorical explanations: this is reductionism [and it] destroys the foundations of the principles of the believer. It presents nothing but a violent rewriting [of texts]. [This is because] it destroys understanding of the self through the force of external influences.[27]

Shagar purposefully employs a circular logic: the *lamdan* will find meaning in the text if he assumes that the text holds such meaning. Religious experience cannot be analysed, let alone grasped, from the distant viewpoint of an academic or an anthropologist. This sort of tautological reasoning is a cornerstone of postmodern theory.[28] It echoes a striking motif in Derridean thought: the notion of temporality—a set of inescapable conditions, such as space, time, and personality, which frame the individual's subjectivity. To Derrida, temporality invites, or perhaps even forces, the 'possible' (another Derridean term which, according to some scholars, approximates the idea of God).[29] In other words, future, expected events can only occur if the individual places herself in the temporal conditions that are suited to bringing forth this 'possible'.[30]

Following this line of reasoning, postmodernists understand knowledge acquired through texts as contingent on temporality. The following extract from correspondence between Derrida and a Christian scholar, Hugh S. Pyper,

practice, see Halbertal, *Interpretative Revolutions in the Making* (Heb.). 'Torah study', as Hannah Hashkes writes, 'is not merely a literary endeavour undertaken for the sake of religious functionality. Torah study . . . cannot be separated from any part of life's reality' (Hashkes, 'Studying Torah as a Reality Check', 153).

[27] Shagar, *Loving You Unto Death* (Heb.), 7.

[28] See, for example, Derrida's critique of the 'writing lesson' that anthropologists studying the lives of Africans sought to give the Nambikwara. The 'violence' Derrida ascribes to anthropology is a mere pretence at objectivity: those looking in from the outside seek to name that which does not have the 'presence' through which categorizations may even be formed. For this reason anthropology, or naming, is not only violent but impossible (Derrida, *Of Grammatology*, 101–40).   [29] See Kearney, 'Deconstruction, God and the Possible', 304–5.

[30] Some interesting comparisons can be made here to Ricœur's view of the text as opening up a variety of 'possible worlds', as well as to Gottfried Leibniz in the field of philosophy of mind, for whom possible worlds exist as ideas in the mind of God, arguing that the actual world must be 'the best of all possible worlds'. For a more recent development of this idea, see Lewis, *On the Plurality of Worlds*, 136–91.

conveys this idea quite succinctly. Pyper asked: 'Can I, as a non-Jew, a gentile, read, let alone, teach, the Hebrew Scriptures? . . . As a product of a Christian and post-Christian culture, can I read anything but the Old Testament?'[31] Derrida responded:

What would it be—to *have read* something? Some kind of act of memory, of enlarge-ment of the archive of your identity perhaps, but can one ever say that one has *read* something? There is always another reading—that is what iteration entails. . . . I shall be what I shall have read, perhaps, when yet another impossible condition is met.[32]

The text's meaning changes according to the reader's temporality: the parti-cular time, place, and mindset with which she approaches the text. This rea-soning informs Shagar's insistence on the conditions for *lamdanut*.[33]

Shagar's understanding of *lamdanut* relies on a unique understanding of Torah, one which sees the text as completely malleable:

According to the world-view of postmodernists . . . we could say the Torah is an absolute object, [whose ultimate meaning is] always absent, [and so] any attempt by the learner to define it is at the outset a linguistic error [and] can only ever be a description based on a presumption. The [meaning of the] Torah is continually in flux, rather than fixed: its content is created by connecting various representations. The existence—or essence—of the absolute object does not rest on the assumption of a foundation that creates meaning . . . [it is a] corollary of language games which come into play as part of the process of explanation. The 'essence of Torah' pur-ports to lead to a particular proclamation, or series of proclamations, through which [the Torah] appears as an addressee or an object of guidance. This interpret-ation is a claim which is outside the text itself and it should be approached accordingly.[34]

The Torah does not communicate a universally accessible message. Rather, its meaning is in constant flux, subject to the experience of the *lamdan*. The group of learners who engage in Torah study capture only their idiosyncratic experience of the text, but their perpetuation of the language of *lamdanut*

---

[31] Pyper, 'Other Eyes', 159.   [32] Ibid. 160.
[33] An insistence on temporal conditions typifies postmodern understandings of experience and reading. Richard Kearney has argued that Derrida's lack of interest in meta-theories such as 'truth' and 'God' is due to his placing a far greater value on the present moment. It is here, where an 'objective' justification of God becomes irrelevant, that Derrida, like Shagar, 'refrains from responding one way or another to any particular God-claim' (Kearney, 'Deconstruction, God and the Possible', 304).
[34] Shagar, *Broken Vessels* (Heb.), 34. These ideas are expanded on in detail throughout the chapter entitled 'Faith and Language according to the Admor Hazaken of Habad' from the perspective of Wittgenstein's philosophy of language (Shagar, *We Walk in Fervour*, (Heb.) 173–206).

through continued engagement with Scripture presents revelatory qualities.

Shagar sets rigorous conditions for *lamdanut*, involving the learner's temporality—including socialization, motivation, place, and textual methodology—which inform the way in which the text is absorbed and applied to daily life. Indeed, it is from context and temporality that the individual draws meaning: 'The role that context plays in a [particular] situation is the source of its power.'[35] Hence the use of a specific language game, an idiosyncratic textual methodology, is one of the essential features of the *lamdanut* experience. To Shagar, the experience of Torah study is also inseparable from the physical space of the *beit midrash* ('the house of study' designed for the performance of *lamdanut*). The setting in which study takes place affects the way the learner engages with the text. Where in a university one is driven to critique, in the *beit midrash* the *lamdan* adopts a different mentality, invoking the divine–human covenant, the *berit*:

[The *beit midrash*] can be described in a variety of ways: *devekut, berit*, and so on. But ultimately we are talking about an experience. It must be stated that this does not refer to a psychological event; it is not [even] an event as such. Its breadth [as an experience] is far broader than what is usually considered to be a psychological event, and therefore it should not be considered as such . . . in actuality, [*lamdanut*] is [made up of] . . . multiple experiences, all of which [are] understood by the learner as a religious experience of *berit* and *devekut*.[36]

Even prior to opening the Talmud, the act of leaving a modernist environment and entering a different setting intended for Torah study qualifies the whole enterprise from the outset. It lures the *lamdan* into a different mentality. The physical space of the *beit midrash* serves as an enclave in which, according to Shagar, *lamdanut* can take on an ontological dimension featuring revelatory qualities.

Another defining characteristic of *lamdanut* is its social nature. The fact that it is a group activity guarantees it a degree of enjoyment. Shagar illustrates this by alluding to the widespread appeal of the *daf yomi* among professionals: an increasing number of individuals taking the opportunity of their lunch break to study a page of Talmud. To Shagar, this exemplifies the rejection of autonomy in favour of a communal, collective, shared activity that is an essential feature of religious life:

What is the *daf yomi* learner seeking? . . . Is he searching for *halakhot* relevant to his office work? Obviously not . . . on the contrary! He is actually seeking a distinctive genre of study, an 'otherness' of learning, because this otherness is his contact . . . with holiness. The otherness, the difference from daily [activities], is [in fact] the

[35] Shagar, *Broken Vessels* (Heb.), 31.   [36] Shagar, *On His Torah He Meditates* (Heb.), 180.

Holy. . . . This learner is seeking the antithesis of critical learning . . . an enclave away from the chaos of modernity. This is the covenant of Torah.[37]

The phenomenon of *daf yomi* is intricately linked to the postmodern condition, in that the appeal of the experience of *lamdanut* represents a response to the contemporary world's social fragmentation. In Shagar's words: 'This renewal of *lamdanut* should not be understood as part of a revitalization of study, but rather as . . . an act of togetherness . . . of coming together and solidarity which is lacking in the world today . . . this is an overarching postmodern phenomenon.'[38]

In addition to the particular environment and modality of study which characterize *lamdanut*, Shagar singles out the *lamdan*'s motivation. The mindset with which he immerses himself in Torah study is also included in the notion of temporality:

Torah study goes beyond just reading and listening. The process through which I attempt to understand an idea in Torah constitutes a [religious] experience. Additionally [in the realm of] Torah, its language leads one to a profound experience of ideas for what they truly are. [Contemporary] use of [religious] language [allows for] the broken vessels [of religion] to be rejuvenated through new understandings, and to thus be renewed. The language of Torah remains intriguing, inspiring. It is the cycle of life.[39]

This state of mind, governed by 'the fear of Heaven',[40] allows the individual to overcome breakage. It directs the enterprise of *lamdanut* towards its desired goal, allowing the *lamdan* to witness first-hand the covenant and participate in its renewal: 'The root function of Torah study is the functioning of the covenant. We can present the study as "praxis" which comes to renew this covenant, and the whole "process" of Torah as saturated by it. Faith and involvement, fear of God and love of Torah are conditions for *lamdanut*.'[41] The learner who engages in this study views himself as involved in the covenant. The temporal conditions for *lamdanut*—be they physical space, social setting, or psychological mindset—allow for the experience of a revelatory moment.[42] Yet

---

[37] Shagar, *Broken Vessels* (Heb.), 31–2.   [38] Shagar, *On His Torah He Meditates* (Heb.), 181–2.
[39] Shagar, personal comment in response to a poem by Israeli author Sivan Harshefi (unpublished). I am grateful for access to this correspondence.
[40] Shagar, *Broken Vessels* (Heb.), 33.   [41] Shagar, *Loving You Unto Death* (Heb.), 6.
[42] Time is crucial to the experience of this revelation: it is continually in flux, where no single approach to how Torah is to be interpreted triumphs over another. The economy of *force et durée* (force and duration)—in other words, through a continual exchange of time—constitutes *lamdanut*. The nature of past events, the Orthodox perception of the Torah having been given at one moment at Sinai, is actually obscured by human understandings of time. 'Time', for Derrida and Shagar, does not stand still at moments in history, but rather is continuously mythologized and interpreted by communities. This idea is best represented in Derridean

Shagar's vision leaves us with numerous unanswered questions. What becomes of those who stand outside his community? Can individuals outside the circle of male students which he addresses experience revelation? Tangentially, one may ask, is Torah subjective? And if so, what does this imply?

Ross: Cumulative Revelation

Ross posits that a literal understanding of the biblical account of revelation is no longer possible. Additionally, ahistorical and non-literal readings inspired by modernity have become obsolete. She claims that *torah min hashamayim* cannot be a description of reality even in the figurative sense; instead, focus should be on the post-metaphysical sphere and the text's influence on the believer's internal experience. This approach to religious truths removes the necessity for Torah to provide empirical evidence for revelation. The role that revelation fulfils in the heart of the believer, and not necessarily the event itself, justifies religious belief. It is the particular significance of the Sinaitic event that inspires religious belief within the Jewish community, and, in this sense, the revelation at Sinai is truthful. The belief in the truth revealed at Sinai rests upon communal consensus.

How, then, is divine intent in the revelation of the Torah to be understood? Is the idea of divine interaction with the people of Israel merely a cultural construct, defined by communal consensus? 'How do we know when God is speaking to us, and how are we to be sure of what He is saying? . . . Such questions apply even to the original revelatory experience at Sinai. . . . [Even this] could be acknowledged as God's word only when filtered through the prism of past cultural symbols and traditions.'[43]

Historical consciousness—an awareness of the temporality of religious practices—plays an important part in Ross's reformulation of the concept of *torah min hashamayim*. It is through this capacity for perpetual growth, which enables the continued observance of Jewish law throughout the ages, that the will of God is revealed to Jews. Rorty underscores the fact that this

thought through his re-evaluation of 'gift theory' according to Claude Lévi-Strauss and Marcel Mauss. Derrida's contribution to anthropology and postcolonialism, especially through his post-structuralist critiques of Lévi-Strauss and Saussure, has been far-reaching, and relationships between language and gift have been at its centre (see esp. Derrida, *The Gift of Death*). Postmodern writing on time emphasizes spontaneity, intentionality, timing, force, reluctance, and so on as contingent factors that do not disrupt but actually define the nature of giving and receiving. Applying the revelation of Torah to this notion of temporality, the will, motivation, intention, and guilt, inherent at a particular time in the *lamdanut* community, defines its revelatory experience. This postmodern critique of structural linguistics has afforded Shagar and, as I shall show, Ross an intuitively broader understanding of the notion of the gift of God and the receipt of the community.

[43] Ross, *Expanding the Palace of Torah*, 217–18.

process, whereby interpretations change in accordance with historical context (especially the evolution of the language we use), occurs quite naturally
within faith communities. Ross postulates that the community is defined by
certain internally justified beliefs, all of which 'make admirable sense' when
considered from within.[44] It is the community which sets the parameters of
its own language game.

The divine character of Torah is testified to by its application to human
society. The perpetual adaptation of halakhah[45] to the needs of each generation constitutes 'cumulative revelation':

In the realm of halakhah there exists a whole literature of commentary, known as
'novellae' (*hidushim*),[46] in which . . . originality and creativity are not just acceptable; they are encouraged. This creativity is not viewed as threatening to tradition,
or as changing the Torah, but simply as elaborating upon its original meaning. . . .
The idea of accumulating revelation may be regarded as a natural outgrowth of this
traditional understanding of the nature of rabbinic interpretation and its relationship to the Written Torah.[47]

Ross's conception of cumulative revelation is comparable to that of Sagi's
'perennial revelation' in that it holds a 'moderate realism', conceptualizing
Torah as both divine and human. She elaborates further on this idea in a different piece:

[Religious truth formulations] do sometimes get outgrown. In a particularly poetic
metaphor, R. Kook likens the moral urge to a tiny sapling that begins to grow, and
every once in a while needs to be transplanted or its soil renurtured in order to
support and cultivate this new development. The need for such transplantations
arises whenever a discrepancy is revealed between the size of the plant and the
breadth of the soil on which it stands; i.e., when our authentic spiritual-moral urge
is no longer adequately expressed by our existing religious formulations.[48]

By appealing to R. Kook and adopting a cumulative conception of revelation,

---

[44] See Rorty, *Consequences of Pragmatism*, 104.

[45] Ross writes of the 'interpretative fluidity' of *peshat* (plain meaning), *derash* (applied meaning), *remez* (implied meaning), and *sod* (esoteric meaning) (Ross, *Expanding the Palace of Torah*,
199). She states: 'The line between interpretation and innovation is never clear-cut, such
methods [textual arguments based on 'context' and 'logical flow'] still leave considerable room
for legislative creativity under the guise of simple interpretation' (ibid. 50). For a full list of the
rules of de-literalized textual interpretation, including some that Ross, probably intentionally,
does not mention such as *kal vahomer* (the a fortiori argument), see N. Solomon, *Torah from
Heaven*, 41–2.

[46] 'Christian mystics attribute *devar hashem* in essence to Jesus, and we attribute it to
hidushei hatorah' (Ross, 'A Premature Enthusiasm?' (Heb.), 181).

[47] Ross, *Expanding the Palace of Torah*, 199.

[48] Ross, 'The Cognitive Value of Religious Truth Statements', 505.

Ross takes a step away from Rorty's neo-pragmatism. Rorty posits that our knowledge of the world is dependent upon human experience. He proves willing to invest exclusively in the humanness of language games and opts as a consequence for a 'post-metaphysical' religion, one which 'puts aside the attempt to connect religion with truth and so has no use for notions such as "symbolic" or "emotional" or "metaphorical" or "moral" truths'.[49] In a Jewish context, his position would rule out the possibility of a community being subject to successive revelations through the daily application of halakhic precepts.[50] Ross, as a theologian, finds this insufficient and departs from Rorty at this juncture. She discusses the role of the community through her interpretation of R. Kook's comparison of moral consciousness to a 'tiny sapling that begins to grow', emphasizing the crucial role communal consensus plays in her understanding of revelation:

the binding nature of this law (and that of the written Torah as well!) does not depend upon who gave it, but rather upon more internal considerations, such as the consensus of the nation to accept this law upon itself, the Divine importance invested in the nation, and its unique nature, which is evident throughout its history. . . . The binding nature of the oral and even the written Torah rests ultimately on popular consensus—the fact that the Jewish people voluntarily accepted this Torah upon itself as the ultimate authority.[51]

According to Ross's theory of cumulative revelation, each generation of Jews retroactively receives and re-accepts the Torah upon itself by embracing its precepts and values and employing them in daily life. Communal language about revelation—especially halakhah, the influence of which permeates daily Jewish life—sets the parameters of the conversation: 'The intellectual study of Torah and formal observance of the halakhah provide an ontological bond with the God that is beyond *Tzimtzum* even while operating within this-worldly perceptions.'[52]

Philosophically speaking, this concept depends upon an eternal dialectic between the human and the divine. Ross rejects the equation of her conception of cumulative revelation with the absolute relativism embraced

[49] Rorty, *An Ethics for Today*, 47. Rorty had read Gianni Vattimo's *After Christianity* and was apparently influenced by post-metaphysical versions of religion where absolute truth was recognized as an illusion (see Rorty, Vattimo, and Zabala, *The Future of Religion*).

[50] According to Michael Wallace, Rorty emphasizes what a community does with a certain truth, in contrast to Ricœur's interest in how a religious community perpetuates understood truths (Wallace, 'Ricœur, Rorty and the Question of Revelation'; see also Klemm, *Meanings in Text and Actions*, 275–91).

[51] Ross, 'The Cognitive Value of Religious Truth Statements', 503. The context of this section is Ross's elucidation of R. Kook's understanding of the superiority of halakhah as a moral system.   [52] Ross, 'Religious Belief in a Postmodern Age', 233–4.

by postmodernists: 'Such a view . . . should not be identified with a type of hermeneutic nihilism, asserting that anything can be taken to mean whatever we want so long as we want it enough.'[53] Refusing to place R. Kook in the same conceptual camp as Foucault, she speaks of a shared communal interest which binds all halakhic differences together. While she places an important stress on the influence of culture and language on revelation itself, she resists the traditionally expected collapse into relativism.[54] In her view, the notion that Torah is determined by culture is in fact fully in line with traditional conceptions of revelation, according to which the divine word continuously manifests itself in the history of the Jewish community.

In order to distance herself from a radical postmodern hermeneutics, Ross draws upon the ideas of two recent proponents of hermeneutic theory: Hans-Georg Gadamer and Stanley Fish. On the basis of their reasoning, she argues that the parameters of textual interpretation are necessarily subject to communal consensus. Since 'our perceptions are shaped by our previous conceptions, biases and interests . . . the simple act of observing already involves a significant amount of processing, on the basis of the hopes, fears, expectations, and "intellectual baggage" that we bring with us to the text'.[55] Hence the notion that halakhic decision-making could ever be based on the empirical, objective delineation of factual 'truth' appears dubious. The very act of interpretation being dependent on the reader's initial biases, it follows that 'the more laden these prejudices are, the fuller the interpretation'.[56] Moreover, she demonstrates that, in the context of halakhic discourse, communal consensus and social context also constrict the scope of options available to the halakhic decisor (posek):

The very way in which the observer approaches the object of his perception is always contextual and situated. The beliefs and practices to which he appeals are never merely his own, but are always shaped by the norms, traditions, and conventions of his surrounding society. . . . Admitting to the role of subjectivity in interpretation does not mean that the reader is free to interpret the text however he likes.[57]

Ross acknowledges the influence of culture and a priori conceptions on the reader's interpretation of the text, but turns away from 'utter relativism'.[58] In her view, the parameters of halakhic interpretation, which determine the validity of any given halakhic decision, are subject to and therefore limited by

---

[53] Ross, Expanding the Palace of Torah, 221.

[54] Ross's claim has also been contested by Yoel Finkelman, who argues that it is too tricky to sustain her metaphysical argument and retain Orthodox practice (Finkelman, 'A Critique of Expanding the Palace of Torah').

[55] Ross, Expanding the Palace of Torah, 169.   [56] Ibid.   [57] Ibid.   [58] Ibid. 170.

communal consensus. The individual inscribes her ruling within a historical tradition, which itself sets the boundaries for exegetical creativity.

Ross's theory therefore rests upon three assumptions, each of which already exists within the tradition:

- The revelation of the Torah is an ongoing, dynamic process.

- This revelation occurs through the intermediary of the *lamdan* or *posek*, either by means of divine inspiration (*ruah hakodesh*) or through pragmatic concerns—in other words, that the ideas that religious authorities put forward are 'essentially another form of ongoing revelation, a surrogate prophecy'[59] and that divine providence is witnessed throughout Jewish history.

- While successive relations may at times appear mutually exclusive, they never actually replace each other, but remain 'the primary cultural-linguistic filter' through which the subsequent statements are understood.

She discusses the impact such an understanding of revelation has on the individual's religious allegiance:

When this fluid approach to truth is limited to Torah, it fosters in the religious believer an attitude of respect toward every point of view, as the bearer of significant meaning on a theoretical level, yet still attaches great importance to which opinion is to be applied in practice, signifying the precise method of interaction between God's truth and a finite temporal reality.[60]

The will of God is recovered by religious leaders as part of the halakhic decision-making process. The authority of the rabbis is thus the elemental factor in determining where and how exactly divine truth manifests itself. Ross's position has much in common with that of Mikhail Bakhtin, for whom the group reading of texts reifies a world by bringing about divine revelation. According to Bakhtin, 'the event of the life of the text, that is, its true essence, always develops on the boundary between two consciousnesses, two subjects'.[61] The solicitation of the text within the language game makes up the 'life of the text'. The 'life' of the collective and that of the text form 'two consciousnesses'—the divine and the human—which generate an ever-changing revelation. Bakhtin's phenomenology casts a new light on understanding the way in which Ross approaches the postmodern language game. For her, certain postmodern aspects of revelation are sustained in the language game of halakhic interpretation, yet extend beyond those human aspects through the 'life of the text':

---

[59] Ibid. 198.   [60] Ibid. 150.   [61] Bakhtin, *Speech Genres*, 106.

Undoubtedly there is a significant difference, beyond semantics, between the claim that the received word of God contains infinite possibilities of interpretation and the postmodernist rejection of metaphysics and the notion of universal truth altogether. For the Rabbis, the grounding of various views in a common metaphysical source indicated that a point exists at which they are all ultimately reconcilable. In the words of the Talmud, conflicting opinions are all valid because 'all of them are given from one shepherd.' The postmodernist attitude, by contrast, tends to deflate the pretensions of any point of view's claim to truth. As I have indicated, the postmodernists would regard all choices as random selections from arbitrary collections of isolated and unconnected viewpoints, whose relative worth can be understood or assessed only from within their own partial terms.[62]

Language and Revelation: Mysticism and Deconstructionism

I now turn to language and the effort to reconcile deconstructionism and the notion of the Torah's divinity. Shagar achieves this by criticizing the values implicit in his generation's approach to the study of sacred texts and suggesting an alternative methodology based on kabbalistic sources. Ross, in contrast, demonstrates that ontological statements need not be expressed in realistic terms. Her approach, inspired by Ricœurian hermeneutics, aims to preserve the singular meaning of the traditional conception of an absolute revelation at Sinai, while at the same time acknowledging the inadequacies of language in communicating its content. Their respective efforts are based on a non-realist theological outlook which finds its roots in the mystical tradition, and on the understanding that believers can maintain the truth-value of Scripture while renouncing literalism. These two presuppositions, which underpin the rest of my argument, can also help the reader ease the tension that arises from apparent contradictions within canonical texts.

Shagar: Deconstructionism and the Divine Text

Shagar proves inconsistent with regard to the possibility of blending external criticism (including academic scholarship) or deconstructionism, on the one hand, and traditional Torah study on the other. At times, he emphasizes the fruitful outcome of such a partnership:

In a postmodern age the concept of halakhah is not determined at the outset; nor is it coherent; it comprises different viewpoints, which are impossible to understand without historical background. . . . The postmodern viewpoint allows us to better

[62] Ross, *Expanding the Palace of Torah*, 150.

grasp and disseminate the true understanding of the Torah, [which is] a broad discourse of different genres—not only of logical concepts—using different disciplines from various realms to put forward its message.[63]

There is undoubtedly an important strand in his thought which encourages readers to study canonical texts with a critical, methodological mind. While he acknowledges the fact that researchers and Torah scholars engage in very different discourses and pursue different objectives, he nonetheless believes that their approaches could be mutually beneficial:

In addition to aiding the critical-constructivist approach that brings integrated disciplines, external research is meant to shed light on, and even support, the concepts that have been assumed in *lamdanut*. This is without doing away with the linguistic and cultural distinctions and gaps between them.[64]

He considers here that the respective disciplines of scientific research and *lamdanut* are independent truth-systems, operating in distinct circles. The modernist problem of textual criticism clearly concerned him. He sought to deal with it by utilizing the science of the laboratory or the university to the benefit of the truths that appear to the *lamdan* but without compromising the vocabulary of divinity which he and his students affirmed:

From the different aims of *lamdanut* and research are carved out different disciplines and alternative truth-values. Torah truth is not obligated [to respond] to scientific historical truth. Concepts of truth and their different conditions of truth do not need to hide [from each other].[65]

Shagar turns to postmodernism as a get-out clause when addressing the application of critical scholarly tools to sacred texts. He suggests that each discipline represents a world unto itself, which need neither hide from nor respond to the truth-claims put forward elsewhere. By resorting to this relativist notion of overlapping truths and claiming that neither scientific nor traditional truths should be denied, he allows himself to evade the problem of contradictions within both worlds. There exists another strand in his thought, however, that conceives of the marriage between traditional Torah study and external, scientific disciplines in more confrontational terms. On occasion, he sees emerging from the violent clash between these partners the potential for renewal: 'The role of postmodern deconstructionism is to destroy the hermeneutic vessels and mould them in order to offer new possibilities for inspiration

---

[63] Shagar, *Broken Vessels* (Heb.), 43–4.
[64] Shagar, *Loving You Unto Death* (Heb.), 6.   [65] Ibid.

and awe.'[66] As I showed in Chapter 1, Shagar believes in the believer's ability to harness postmodernism's destructive potential for the purpose of religious renewal.

On yet another occasion, he recoils significantly while discussing the partnership between the 'cultural-linguistic worlds' of Torah study and scientific scholarship. He realizes that a lack of assiduity in religious observance would 'undermine the continuity and stability' of halakhah, presenting it merely as 'a set of options' and admits that the believer pays a heavy 'religious and emotional price' when no response can be found to challenges that arise from critical methods. Yet he finds a way to close this reflection on a more positive, if esoteric, comment:

The religious and even emotional price [of integrating a scientific world-view with Torah study] is too heavy. Integration of [these] disciplines must not be reduced to ultimatums—[the *lamdan*] could live with simplistic faith. But [actually this clash offers a] reflection of the internal situation in which we find ourselves. The union between Torah and science is a communication between parts of our soul.[67]

Shagar is certain that a synthesis between the two fields must not lead to compartmentalization. The ideas put forward in the areas of science and Torah 'must not be reduced to ultimatums', and the 'internal situation' must allow a cognitive balance in which the two elements of study can coexist.[68] The uncertainty of this equilibrium necessarily implies that there is no single truthful way of reading a text. How, then, can the *lamdan* cultivate this balance? Shagar resorts to deconstruction to answer this question:

[The quest for] objectivity is linked to the idea of [Torah] learning for its own sake that causes the learner to *fail* to reach true Torah. And it is the ego which introduces [talmudic and halakhic] dispute. Rabbi Israel [Salanter] discusses the individual character traits [that fuelled] the arguments of Hillel and Shammai and their stubborn persistence in their positions, and therefore he lends legitimacy to preventing this [egotistical approach] and [in light of this] *one must express personal subjectivity in study*.[69]

---

[66] Shagar, 'My Faith' (Heb.), 5.   [67] Shagar, *Loving You Unto Death* (Heb.), 7.

[68] Shagar discerned a resonance with Rabbenu Tam as a talmudic scholar (and liturgical poet) who, in his *Sefer hayashar*, sought to solve talmudic textual problems without resorting to emendations of the received text. He wrote of his 'historically negotiated sense-making' (*Loving You Unto Death* (Heb.), 10).

[69] Shagar, *On His Torah He Meditates* (Heb.), 66. The Brisker analytic method of *lamdanut* originated in mitnagdic yeshivas in Lithuania through Rabbi Hayim Soloveitchik of Brisk. This methodology continues to permeate the religious-Zionist central yeshivas in Israel and provided Shagar with an analytical and empirical mode of thinking about learning and halakhah. He believes himself to be drawing on this model and broadening it, in the light of Rabbi Joseph B. Soloveitchik's existentialist development of it, to one with a more interdisciplinary outlook,

What comes out here is Shagar's realization that a coherent theory of synthesis between Torah and science passes necessarily through pedagogy.
He expresses his conviction that the traditional methodology of Torah learning for its own sake (*torah lishmah*) inculcates an erroneous, selfish mindset.
The *lamdan* comes to view textual study in unequivocal terms, a zero-sum
game, on which his ego effectively rests. This approach prevents students from
cultivating the balance which would allow them to negotiate the internal
tensions produced by conflicting truths. Shagar therefore propounds an alternative learning method by advocating the nullification of the self alongside
a more dynamic understanding of hermeneutics, one which leaves room
for the acceptance that a text's meaning is in perpetual flux. He suggests, as
I demonstrated previously, turning away from the original or authentic intention behind the text and privileging instead the learner's imagination.[70]
To this end, he appeals to mystical sources, and particularly R. Nahman's
hermeneutics.[71]

It is worth noting that scholars of mysticism read R. Nahman very much
in the same way as Shagar does. Shaul Magid writes that R. Nahman's 'meta-
midrashic literary trope' is 'intended to train his reader to perfect his imagination, the final *tikun* [repair] before the advent of the Messianic Age'.[72]
Underpinning this argument is a kabbalistic hermeneutics:

It may be true that the Kabbalist constructs his myth from images and ideas
embedded in Scripture, but these scriptural and rabbinic referents are lifted out of
their context to become independent symbols, only to return later as a hypertext
used to uncover elements of Scripture heretofore concealed.[73]

In this picture of esoteric interpretative techniques, the kabbalist ultimately
overcomes textuality: scriptural details are pulled out of their original context
and given a life of their own. The reader can later read them back into different settings in order to uncover mystical secrets. The study of Torah is thus
not merely an interpretative game, but in a sense generates divinity.

Deconstructionism reveals that there is more at stake in Torah study than

which includes kabbalistic elements of contemplation. Ross outlines the impact of the Brisker
method of *lamdanut* on halakhic thinking and argues that its proponents do not sufficiently
apply it to their surrounding cultures and societies. The notion that it might be 'spiritually
meaningful' as a methodology or activity was sidelined, as it was judged and valued according
to its own yardstick of truth-attaining: the will of God through the halakhah. See Ross, *Expanding the Palace of Torah*, 66–70.

[70] Leora Batnitzky has argued that Franz Rosenzweig sought to emphasize linguistic rather
than essentialist versions of revelation by arguing that deconstruction of texts is a 'Jewish'
'theopractice' in and of itself (Batnitzky, 'Revelation, Language and Commentary', 300–23).

[71] Shagar reportedly visited his grave each year on the High Holidays to pray and meditate.

[72] Magid, *God's Voice from the Void*, 16.   [73] Ibid. 17.

halakhic minutiae. There is an experiential element in Shagar's *lamdanut* which actually bears divine import. Drob lays this bare when drawing parallels between deconstructionism and kabbalistic hermeneutics:

The conception of mysticism as a puncturing or rupture of one's received discourse, and hence the opening up of the possibilities of new meaning and experience, may actually accord quite well with the more traditional notion of mysticism as an experience of the transcendent, the real, or the divine. This is because, in each view, the 'mystical' is that which is beyond the horizon of ordinary discourse and experience.[74]

The mystical enterprise, like deconstructionism, opens the text up so as to discover in it additional layers of meaning, which further inspire the reader's connection with and experience of the divine.

Ross, Ricœur, and Conflicting Interpretations

Ross seeks to alter our perception of interpretations to place it in line with an awareness of cultural particularism and linguistic presumptions.[75] Her 'perspectivist' approach, introduced in Chapter 1 in the context of the debate about relativism, is actually implied by Ricœur, who also accepted the implications of the cultural-linguistic critique and the notion that language and text generate communal life. In *The Conflict of Interpretations*, he seeks to marginalize the 'problem of interpretation', which he understands to be the de-universalization of texts implied by the cultural bias inherent in the reader's subjectivity:

If exegesis raised a hermeneutic problem . . . it is because every reading of a text always takes place within a community, a tradition, or a living current of thought, all of which display presuppositions and exigencies. . . . Thus, based on philosophical principles in physics and in ethics, the reading of the Greek myths in the Stoic school implies a hermeneutics very different from the rabbinical interpretation of the Torah in the Halaka or the Hagadah. In its turn, the apostolic generation's interpretation of the Old Testament in the light of the Christic event gives quite another reading of the events, institutions, and personages of the Bible than the rabbinical interpretation. . . . More precisely if a text can have several meanings, such as a historical meaning and a spiritual meaning, we must appeal to a notion of signification that is much more complex than the system of so-called univocal signs required by the logic of argumentation. . . . A discursive statement is a grasp

---

[74] Drob, *Kabbalah and Postmodernism*, 40.

[75] Ross, *Two Commentaries on the Teaching of Tsimtsum* (Heb.). This book was based on Ross's doctoral thesis. While she had not yet engaged with postmodernist ideas, it highlights her prior interest in these thinkers, who then served to buttress her interpretative approach.

of the real by meaningful expressions, not a selection of so-called impressions coming from the things themselves.[76]

Ricœur delves into hermeneutics. To his mind, the text does not convey an 'impression' of reality; rather, its interpretation represents an 'expression', on behalf of an author or reader, of the world. It is also worth noting that he comments here on halakhic and rabbinic logic, and at no point suggests that rabbinic hermeneutics holds no ontological significance. Indeed, it represents the divine will as the rabbis understood it.

The conclusions that Ricœur reached through his phenomenological approach, Ross achieves by alluding to language theory. Her earlier scholarship focuses on two mystical masters: Shneur Zalman of Lyady and Hayim of Volozhin.[77] The latter, in his groundbreaking work *Nefesh haḥayim* ('The Living Soul'), established the foundations for Torah study on kabbalistic grounds. Ross's first published work addresses this idea.[78] She refers to it again in a later book while outlining a non-empirical and non-foundational understanding of Jewish theology that 'is rooted more profoundly in some modern formulations of older mystic traditions of Judaism'.[79] By supplementing halakhic and talmudic expertise with an appeal to kabbalistic terminology, she demonstrates that it is possible to read ontological descriptions of reality phrased by means of allegories, homilies, and metaphors without making empirical, realistic assumptions: 'The solution of the mystics is to recognize the metaphysical inadequacy of religious truth claims, acknowledging their partial or illusory nature as descriptions of reality.'[80] It is worth noting here that her investment in mysticism parallels, in a way that is hardly incidental, Shagar's interest in hasidism.

For Ross, a postmodern religion interprets religious truth-statements in a non-realistic fashion:

If literal meanings are problematic, we must reject the formulations, qualify them, or bring logical argument and empiric evidence in order to resolve the difficulties

---

[76] Ricœur and Ihde, *The Conflict of Interpretations*, 3–4. 'Things in themselves' refers to the Kantian *Ding an Sich*.

[77] See Shneur Zalman, *Ma'amarei admor hazaken* (5569); for a recent treatise on the later spiritual and interpretative impact of his writings in modern times, see Huss, Pasi, and von Stuckard (eds.), *Kabbalah and Modernity*. Shneur Zalman is said to have sought to intellectualize the teachings of the kabbalah, calling his hasidic movement Habad—*ḥokhmah, binah, da'at* (wisdom, understanding, knowledge). While knowledge of God was the objective, it had to be gained through use of various scientific disciplines, which he himself had encountered. He was a master of halakhah (*Shulḥan arukh harav*), kabbalah (*Tanya*), talmudic commentary, and liturgy (Habad prayer book). In light of this, it is little wonder that both Shagar and Ross have based themselves on his writings.

[78] Ross, *Two Commentaries on the Teaching of Tsimtsum* (Heb.).

[79] Ross, *Expanding the Palace of Torah*, 194.   [80] Ibid. 298 n. 30.

they raise. I suggest that this is the wrong way to proceed: it entails a misconception of what traditional descriptions mean to the believer in the context of religious life. When an Orthodox Jew says 'I believe in Torah from Heaven', her primary concern is not to discuss facts or establish history, but to make a statement on an entirely different plane. It reflects her wish to establish a much stronger claim that will regulate her entire life. . . . Does this understanding of the function of religious truth statements mean that she regards the divine origin of Torah as less true than scientific beliefs? No . . . the considerations brought to bear in determining the validity of such religious statements is taken from within the religious framework itself.[81]

The 'religious framework' operates on an 'entirely different plane' to that of 'scientific beliefs'. It comprises its very own language game for which internal rather than external categories bolster belief. The 'theological non sequitur', a rhetorical question that most succinctly lays out Ross's view, appears, ironically, in parentheses: '(does the divinity of the Torah logically depend upon its literary genesis and manner of transmission?)'.[82] In the light of her treatment of the problem of language and her justification of the non-realism of religious truth statements by reference to kabbalistic instrumentalism, it is hardly surprising that Ross no longer grounds her belief in the divinity of the Torah in a literalist understanding of sources:

On a rational plane, I therefore set out to release the doctrine of revelation from the simplistic dictation metaphor by pointing out that God does not speak via vocal cords but rather through the dynamics of history and the developing human understanding triggered in its wake. Acknowledging that the Torah and halakha were born in a broader socio-cultural context, I argued, need not bear any contradiction to religious claims of divine authorship. Given God's options of deputized speech and illocutionary acts, it is perfectly possible to view the Torah as a document that is all human and all divine at one and the same time.[83]

Her acceptance of the implications for religion of the cultural-linguistic turn does not force her to discard entirely her belief in the Torah's divine origins. On the contrary, she reconfigures Jewish theology in a way that enables her to conceive of the Torah in precisely such terms, as the product of Jewish 'expressions' of intimations with the divine.

The notion of cumulative revelation therefore begins to make sense within a kabbalistic hermeneutical system which values the holistic nature of interpretations:

---

[81] Ross, *Expanding the Palace of Torah*, 193–4.
[82] Ibid. 191.   [83] Ross, 'The Implications of the Feminization of Theology', 126.

Those of a more mystic propensity will view them [successive hearings of God's Torah] more abstractly, as a gradual exposure of the metaphysical divine essence on its earthly level. . . . I am contending that unfreezing our concept of revelation—moving away from the simplistic metaphor of God dictating the entire Torah to Moses—does not require a nontraditional theological framework.[84]

Cumulative revelation 'unfreezes' or 'releases' contemporary believers from the obligation to accept in a doctrinal manner the belief that each word of the Written Torah was literally dictated to Moses on Mount Sinai. The fact that this conception of revelation is drawn from kabbalah also strengthens its appeal. It is worth returning to the conclusion of her article 'Religious Belief in a Postmodern Age', quoted in part in the Introduction, to conclude this section:

I do believe that traditionalists confronting the radical implications of contemporary scientific and moral insights, and seeking to incorporate these into their religious way of life without forfeiting its credibility or normative force, will intuitively gravitate towards some of the more promising implications that the postmodern sensibility holds for traditional Jewish belief when informed by a mystic sensibility. The sympathy of so-called 'secularists' for more fluid forms of New Age spirituality and the rise of 'HaBaKookism' (an amalgam of more individualized anti-establishment modes of religiosity gleaned from the writings of Habad, Bratzlav and R. Kook) amongst some segments of religious youth in Israel are testimony to this trend.[85]

It is hard not to read Ross's prediction that an increasing number of contemporary Jews will 'intuitively gravitate' to a kabbalistic 'sensibility' as an autobiographical observation.

Imaging and Imagining: 'Visionary Theology' for the Postmodern Age

A postmodern theology configures an alternative understanding of the relationship between the collective and its canonical texts. It calls upon the community—as an incubator of meaning—to generate scriptural interpretations relevant precisely to the particular context in which the people find themselves. Former efforts to uncover a pure, contextless, essential reading of Scripture are effectively rendered null and void. This is a very conscious effort to subject the notion of 'meaning' to temporal circumstances, bolstering the collective's role in shaping its own canon.

[84] Ross, *Expanding the Palace of Torah*, 198.
[85] Ross, 'Religious Belief in a Postmodern Age', 239.

The doctrine of *torah min hashamayim* therefore remains, for both Shagar and Ross, at the threshold of Jewish belief. Shagar, on the one hand, claims the Torah as 'the Truth', yet acknowledges at the same time that such a concept is merely a human construct.[86] Although the Torah is the 'absolute object', its meaning is in constant flux.[87] Ross, on the other hand, breaks down the distinction between the literal and the metaphorical in her understanding of the relevance of religious truth-claims. Both thinkers retain the divine element of the terminology of *torah min hashamayim* but attribute different meanings to it. They harness its inimitable significance, all the while removing from the traditional understanding of the concept all foundationalist and essentialist connotations.

What remains, then, that allows the Torah to qualify as divine? To a postmodernist, the answer to that question is precisely in the hands of the community. Jews resort to a unique language game when interpreting canonical texts, which follows distinct, carefully crafted rules. The truth-claims they formulate do not necessarily relate to any objective reality. Rather, they apply to a different realm which has a very concrete and significant impact on the lives of all those who, by the language they speak and customs they observe, inhabit the same space. In effect, revelation occurs each time a new generation creates a new layer of meaning by resorting to the same language game.

[86] Shagar, *Broken Vessels* (Heb.), 21.   [87] Ibid. 34.

CONCLUSION

'Visionary Theology'

This book has explored how Ross and Shagar advocate restoring, or 'returning to', theology, following the linguistic-cultural turn and the postmodern critique. It has shown that these tentative responses to postmodernism can at times bring creative, even liberating, insights into the wellspring of Jewish thought. Such attempts at weathering the storm of challenges set by deconstructionism, relativism, and cultural particularism are far from simple, however. They involve major theological reconfigurations designed to reshape traditional concepts in order to make them thrive alongside the postmodern critique. At the same time, they must strive to preserve those principles at the heart of Judaism which validate and indeed inspire faith. Both scholars outline a new methodology for the construction of a compelling Jewish theology in a post-modern age. Their efforts lay the groundwork for what I term a 'visionary theology', the defining feature of which is the supplanting of literalism in language by the imaginative. The idea parallels the phenomenological treatment of the subjective human experience as a separate realm beyond reality. Here, the language used in religious discourse envisions a distinct mystical world and, by use of metaphors, poetically captures the divine.

I qualify this theology as 'visionary' for several reasons. First, because of the attempt it makes to envision God, albeit in the absence of empirical 'evidence', and therefore in a provisional manner. Second, since this new theological path is still developing, it is, to a large extent, tentative and specu-lative—in other words, a mere vision, that is yet to materialize. Finally, the term 'visionary' conveys the significance of the active; it emphasizes the believer's ability to generate the divine in imagination and language. I trust the term will inspire future discussions on a vibrant postmodern theology. For now, it is worth reviewing the vision laid forth in this book. I will then explore some of its practical implications using as an example the theme of interfaith relations.

Culture: Immersion and Community

Postmodernism in its radical form professes reality to be formed of multiple different perspectives. There are only ever particularistic understandings of 'the way things are', based on local perceptions and interpretations and informed therefore by the individual's cultural baggage. This realization renders impossible both the existence of the self as an objective, independent consciousness and the possibility of universalizing truth-claims. It also rejects the idea of an essential or universal 'Truth', rendering the concept subject to perception. Having internalized this facet of the postmodern critique, Ross seeks to establish a non-foundationalist theology that neither rests on mere empiricism nor purports to have access to a source of revealed, ultimate knowledge. To this end, she turns to the notion of intersubjective agreement as the means by which to evaluate religious truth-claims. Shagar, similarly, claims that full immersion in one's own world-view is actually preferable to searching for an objective truth. His approach takes it as a given that all beliefs and opinions are social or cultural constructions and grants on that basis the possibility of a hierarchy of truths. He posits, however, that their true value lies in the role they play in the formation of the individual's identity or 'self-definition'.[1] In other words, they are valuable only insofar as they are one's own. Shagar nonetheless does leave the door open for a 'positive pluralism', on the condition that this does not undermine the believer's faith.

To accept the idea of conflicting revelations as a positive state of affairs requires, as I have demonstrated, a certain degree of familiarity with kabbalah. Attempts to rid religion of absolutism might seem well-intentioned and honourable: they are unlikely to convince, however, as long as kabbalistic erudition remains inaccessible—or even unappealing—to a large proportion of Jews. Still, visionary theology does adequately address the postmodern critique and provides sufficient grounds for holding on to one's beliefs.

Language: Poetics and Imagination

Language is an instrument which generates and perpetuates the values of its corresponding culture. According to postmodern theory influenced by phenomenology, religious language is not descriptive but evocative and creative. The terms a religious group uses in reference to God reveal a great deal about the group itself—how it aspires and appeals to the divine—but nothing at all about God. They engender a new reality within the believer's imagination or, in Ross's terms, enable her to 'reconstruct a credible facsimile of the undifferentiated and infinite Reality beyond . . . at least from our point of view'.[2]

Although the language used to envision this alternative space is necessarily

---

[1] Shagar, *A Time of Freedom* (Heb.), 125–6.
[2] Ross, 'Religious Belief in a Postmodern Age', 235.

metaphorical, it can nonetheless arouse powerful emotions or prompt intense reactions. How successful it is in doing so depends, according to Shagar, on the individual's temporality—a concept that effectively encompasses mindset, physical space, motivation, social environment, and more. Indeed, Shagar expends great effort in demarcating specific conditions for imagining the divine, so as to ensure an acceptable degree of conformity between his students' respective visions. He clearly sees the importance of anchoring their conceptions of God in some common textual sources. How else, effectively, could one ensure that Jews all end up imagining the same God?

In spite of this difficulty, the newfound understanding of religious language is gaining popularity among contemporary Jewish philosophers and researchers. Daniel Rynhold, for example, praised Elliot Wolfson for propounding precisely this idea in his writings: '[Wolfson] emphasizes how the poetic nature of language yields a convergence of the visual and verbal, revealing an essential similarity between revelation and poetry.'[3]

These thinkers often appeal to kabbalah as a model that similarly employs language poetically rather than mimetically (to use Drob's distinction). They find themselves walking a tightrope, rejecting as meaningless all forms of metaphysical truth-claims, while nonetheless affirming an ontological ground for religious language. The conclusions they reach therefore remain speculative, based as they are not on metaphysical truths but on the volatile imagination of cultural collectives. Such discourses end up selectively integrating or rejecting elements of the postmodern critique, precisely on the basis of their compatibility with Jewish thought. One should therefore consider such a theology a response to, rather than a component of, postmodernism.

Revelation: Continuity

The pervasive influence of language and culture in the formation of religious beliefs has important implications for the doctrine of Torah from Heaven and particularly the idea of revelation. Ross, on the one hand, recasts religious language as a Wittgensteinian 'game' in which Jews participate by virtue of the fact that each new generation accepts the Torah upon itself as its primary cultural linguistic filter.[4] The layers of scriptural interpretation which accumulate over time, drawn from the confrontation of the immutable canon with readers' ever-changing temporality but nonetheless maintaining the text's relevance in the believers' lives, testify to a 'cumulative revelation'. Shagar, on the other hand, limits the scope of the language game to the particular methodology of scriptural interpretation used in the context of *lamdanut*. The revelatory experience

---

[3] Rynhold, review of Hughes and Wolfson (eds.), *New Directions in Jewish Philosophy*.
[4] Ross, *Expanding the Palace of Torah*, 198.

occurs, in his opinion, in the very practice of Torah study, where the learner can witness at first hand and perpetuate the covenant which unites God and the Jewish people. Both thinkers ultimately accept the dual notions that the community is the primary *incubator* of meaning and that the Torah is perpetually being 'received' or 'revealed'. They therefore manage to reaffirm the concept of *torah min hashamayim*—albeit by reconfiguring the term significantly —without stripping it of the powerful implications of the idea of divinity it conveys.

Looking ahead, however, this partial and tentative espousal of post-modernism in Jewish theology is bound to raise questions. The thought occurred to Gavin Hyman while discussing this very same phenomenon in a Christian context. Having in recent decades embraced postmodernism in order to make theology possible, he asks whether Christian theologians might not seek in the future to 'out-narrate' and 'overcome' this very same postmodernism in order to reinstate the primacy of Christianity.[5] It is hard not to apply the same logic to Jewish thought. Do Jews embrace postmodern-ism only on the condition that it will eventually give way to a reinvigorated Jewish theology?

Postmodern Jewish Thought as Visionary Theology

The postmodern critique does not cause truth to become relative, nor does it change the way language functions. It has no direct impact on the world but brings about a dramatic change in how society, culture, and humanity are understood. Its aims are simply to uncover how things have always been— that personal opinions have always masqueraded as knowledge; that humans can never approach a subject from a perfectly objective standpoint—and to discuss the theological implications of these facts with honesty and integrity.

The scholarly and social attention the themes discussed in this book have received in recent decades betrays a sense of dissatisfaction with accepted models of Jewish theology and betokens the need for an overhaul of sorts. Whether a visionary theology constitutes an adequate solution to the prob-lem remains to be seen. Some might deem it unrealistic to expect kabbal-istic motifs to take as prominent a role in religious discourse as I suggest. The supplanting of scientific empiricism with mystical imagination may indeed seem difficult to swallow, especially considering the extent to which academic disciplines rely nowadays on empirical evidence. Furthermore, the amalgamation of Jewish thought with postmodernism might seem un-natural and unsettling. All forms of hyphenation between Torah and extrane-

[5] Hyman, *The Predicament of Postmodern Theology*, 29.

ous philosophical currents trigger at first a sense of cognitive dissonance, postmodernism simply being the most recent candidate.

The fact remains that too few alternatives to neo-pragmatism have been put forward to date, as a result of which many observant Jews find it difficult to justify their practices and beliefs in a meaningful manner. A visionary theology does release religion from the burden of proving its own truthfulness or value on empirical grounds. A new way of 'doing' theology might indeed prove liberating. There is plenty of research currently being done on mysticism in university Jewish studies departments, which could indeed stimulate invigorating debate and spawn refreshing paradigms for faith in the twenty-first century.

The Future: Jewish Approaches to Other Religions and Interreligious Dialogue

It will have become obvious by now that any serious religious attempt at wrestling with the cultural-linguistic critique involves a thorough rereading of canonical texts. These texts frame religious beliefs and filter how people relate to the world around them. They have little meaning as such, but hold immense power as soon as they are subject to *interpretation*. The reader ought to be conscious of the responsibilities she carries and the values she wishes to disseminate when interpreting canonical sources. Jonathan Sacks goes so far as to qualify interpretation as 'the single most important fact about a sacred text':

This is what makes fundamentalism—text *without* interpretation—an act of violence against tradition. In fact, fundamentalists and today's atheists share the same approach to texts. They read them directly and literally, ignoring the single most important fact about a sacred text, namely that its meaning is not self-evident. . . . The word, given in love, invites its interpretation in love.[6]

The message or meaning drawn from canonical sources through the act of interpretation may appear to acquire an existence of its own. It may even seem to relate only tenuously to the text from which it developed. I do not suggest that Sacks wholeheartedly embraces the cultural-linguistic turn, yet in this specific extract his hermeneutics certainly resonate to the mind of the postmodern reader. To him, a sacred text is incomplete without its interpretation. And in order to understand the sources correctly, it is necessary for the reader to understand and cultivate the values that her community upholds. Failure to do so would lead her to fall into the trap of literalism, out of which unspeakable violence emerges:

[6] Sacks, *Not in God's Name*, 219; see also id., *The Dignity of Difference*.

This means that we have little choice but to re-examine the theology that leads to violent conflict in the first place. *If we do not do the theological work, we will face a continuation of the terror that has marked our century thus far, for it has no other natural end.*[7]

In order to face both the violence that Derrida attributes to writing—which becomes stagnant as soon as it has been written—and the physical violence which Sacks here describes, we must rise to the challenge and 'do the theological work'. It is up to us to provide compelling theologies to take us through the twenty-first century.

Visionary theology minimizes the popular concern with moral relativism, usually expressed by those who still hold on to metaphysical notions of truth. It distances itself from absolutism as well as from the relativist overtones often apparent among radical postmodernists, but still upholds the idea of ultimate values (reconsidered following the malaise of existentialism and modern science). Its proponents' purpose is to recover from the destruction witnessed under the banner of neo-pragmatism and embrace a new, energizing theological approach. Their pioneering insights carry profound implications for all areas of Jewish thought. The concluding section of this book uses interreligious dialogue as an example to show that a postmodern Jewish theology can bear promising fruit for the future.

There have been engaging and thought-provoking discussions in recent years within the Jewish community focusing on the challenges of postmodernism. Yet strangely enough, as soon as the subject shifts (as it naturally does) to religious truth-claims in other faith communities, many suddenly fall victim to a peculiar type of paralysis. It remains the case, nonetheless, that other religions also consider the Hebrew Scriptures sacred, and read into them a completely different set of values and ideas.[8] How does a postmodern Jewish theology wrestle, then, with alternative notions of revelation and foreign religious narratives?

Chosenness and the Rejection of the Universal

On the theme of chosenness—which looms large over Jewish approaches to other religions (particularly the monotheistic ones) and their respective claims to revelation—different strands exist within traditional sources.[9] The

---

[7] Sacks, *Not in God's Name*, 21 (emphasis in original).

[8] While it really requires its own discussion, I would like to point to the international movement known as 'scriptural reasoning', which has come to embody a reparative, joint theology through group study of Scripture. It subscribes to the idea of multiple and conflicting accounts of revelation and aims to facilitate sharing those accounts in a non-hegemonic discourse.

[9] For a discussion on the concept of chosenness in contemporary Jewish thought (accord-

idea of Noahide laws, derived from Genesis 9: 9 and later and more significantly in *Sanhedrin*, implies that some form of covenant exists between non-
Jews and God.[10] The revelation in Exodus 20, in contrast, occurred in the
presence of Israelites only, never to be re-enacted with other nations. There
have been times in history when Jewish thinkers emphasized exclusivity and
chosenness, and other periods when they preferred to view divine–human
relations in more inclusive and relational terms. Alan Brill actually distinguishes five strands in Jewish attitudes towards external truths: inclusivist,
universalist, pluralist, exclusivist, and ecclesiocentric (centred on halakhah
as the source of truth).[11]

Among modernists, there is a definite sense of discomfort with the concept of chosenness, it being open to distortion and abuse. More recent philosophers, however, have attempted to move beyond Brill's five categories,
usually building on changes in the understanding of the concept of truth and
emphasizing the relational dimension in divine–human interactions. They
do not write off chosenness altogether—the theme being inseparable from
the larger context of Abrahamic monotheism[12]—but actually focus on the
multifarious interpretations it has been subject to throughout history. Some
therefore view it as an injunction to act justly towards one's neighbour, while
others use it as a prism through which to view the misery experienced by
Jews over time as providential, part of the mysterious design of a nonetheless
loving God.[13]

Jonathan Sacks, for example, sharpens the idea of particularity in the
Jewish tradition, arguing that it is a development of, rather than a move
against, universalism. He likens the relationship between God and humanity
to the love of a parent for her children. Within that framework, he argues, the
theme of chosenness does not imply favouritism of any sort:

Anyway, we do not believe that you have to be Jewish to get to Heaven. The great of
the nations of the world, the righteous, the pious, have a share also. In other words,
Judaism is not an exclusive religion. It leaves space for others. Or—and here let
me put it a bit more radically—again, I haven't heard it said before but here it is.
In Judaism—and I don't know if this is true in any other faith—but in Judaism,
God is bigger than religion. If there is only one God, and there are many faiths,
many paths to His presence, God is bigger than religion.[14]

To Sacks, the motif of chosenness is not exclusionary and Judaism does not

ing to David Hartman, Irving Greenberg, and Eugene Borowitz), see Gillman, 'Covenant and
Chosenness in Postmodern Jewish Thought'.

[10] BT *San.* 56a–56b. [11] Brill, *Judaism and Other Religions.*
[12] See Firestone, *Who Are the Real Chosen People?*, 147. [13] Ibid.
[14] Sacks, 'Jewish Identity'.

have an exclusive claim to God's love. He later develops this idea by demonstrating that the 'consistent theme' of Scripture, when approached through the lens of rabbinic Judaism and with an adequate mindset, is actually 'not sibling rivalry—competition for God's love—but rather, understanding that we each have a place in God's universe of justice and love'.[15] Particularly striking is the fact that he derives this idea from the very proof texts for chosenness:

So that is God saying that there is no universal language. There is no one ultimate truth for humanity. From then on there is going to be diversity in culture, in civilisation and so on. And it is at that point when mankind is de-universalised, deconstructed, that God chooses not man in general, not humanity in general, not Adam, not Cain, not Noah, etc. He chooses somebody in particular. He chooses Avraham and Sarah, who do not represent all of humanity, who are just one couple, one family, ultimately one tribe—a bunch of tribes, a nation—who will remain distinctive, singular, particular, an *am segulah*, a particularly cherished people.[16]

In God's appointing of Abraham and Sarah, Sacks reads a conscious decision on behalf of the Almighty to accept the existence of particular collectives as an ideal rather than gather humanity as a whole under one single banner. Each nation thereby acquires a truth of its own and a way of relating to the divine which makes it unique:

That idea, that God speaks to mankind in many different languages, and it is our task to respect those differences while being true to our own heritage, our own language, while making space for people who are different, that I think is the idea of particularity. And I think the world needs it now.[17]

With this pluralistic stance, according to which there are actually many paths to God, also comes a definite shift towards recognizing the uniqueness of each religion. The widespread belief in the early modern period that all religions shared a common core may have inspired the principle of toleration and, later, multiculturalism, yet contemporary experience teaches quite the opposite, that true interreligious understanding must acknowledge the cultural and linguistic barriers which set communities apart from one another. As Stephen Prothero writes:

We pretend these differences are trivial because it makes us feel safer, or more moral. But pretending that the world's religions are the same does not make our world safer. Like all forms of ignorance, it makes our world more dangerous. What we need on this furiously religious planet is a realistic view of where religious rivals

---

[15] Sacks, *Not in God's Name*; see also id., *Dignity of Difference*, 218.
[16] Sacks, 'Jewish Identity'.   [17] Ibid.

clash and where they can cooperate. Approaching this volatile topic from a new angle may be scary. But the world is what it is. And both tolerance and respect are empty virtues until we actually know something about whomever it is we are supposed to be tolerating or respecting.[18]

Many theologians and philosophers today, Jews and non-Jews alike, are coming to share Prothero's assessment of the misplaced idealism of modernity and the dangers inherent in turning a blind eye to the particulars of each religious group. They adopt a more nuanced conception of truth that allows them to speak of God's word, God's world, and God's revelation as univocal and subjective: 'The likeness and nature of every single individual creature of God is unique. There are no two alike. . . . Each of our religious traditions reflects the truth of God and of God's creation. Each scripture is a revelation of the divine message.'[19] This relational or covenantal conception of human–divine relations comes to replace both the exclusivism that derives from a literal understanding of the concept of chosenness and the distorted worldview that emanates from an uninformed, essentialized universalism.

Rejection of Moral Relativism

Sacks draws an important distinction between 'moral' and 'scientific' truths. The former he qualifies as covenantal, the latter as ontological. A moral truth, he explains, does not in fact presume to communicate anything relating to the metaphysical realm or to reality, and therefore can fully engage with cultural idiosyncrasies or alternative truth-claims:

Moral truth is something else. Moral truth is not something that is refuted by experience but it can collapse because one of us gives way. Somebody was expecting us to be there for them but we weren't. We walked away. We said we don't want to know. That is moral faithlessness. That is *sheker*. It means that either we don't mean it now or that we didn't mean it then. But we are not true to our word. In Judaism, there is a particular kind of *emet* which is moral truth, which is covenantal. It is not ontological. It is not a matter of facts. It's a matter of obligations and commitments. And therefore there are those two kinds of truth. They are really not confusing because they are totally and absolutely different from one another. If other religions could conceive their truth covenantally instead of ontologically, then other religions would find it possible to make space for yet other religions.[20]

Sacks's notion of 'moral truth' determines a certain kind of behaviour— 'obligations and commitments'—geared specifically towards the other, be it God or fellow human beings. Its basis is therefore covenantal, not ontologi-

---

[18] Prothero, *God Is Not One*, 4–5.   [19] Firestone, *Who Are the Real Chosen People?*, 149.
[20] Sacks, 'Jewish Identity'.

cal: it does not lay claim to an absolute reality or identify its origins in a revealed truth but rather dictates ethical norms which frame the way a Jew relates to the world around her, including her daily interactions with her non-Jewish counterparts. His is one example of many contemporary attempts to accommodate cultural particularism and epistemological relativism without at the same time succumbing to an all-embracing nihilism.

By reconfiguring our understanding of the relation between God and Israel in general, and of the concept of chosenness in particular, the question of competing truths and relativism loses much of its urgency. Postmodernists have come to accept the fact that particular communities or collectives design and perpetuate, through language and rituals, a unique value system. This observation does not refer to a new phenomenon: it qualifies a state of affairs that has always existed, but which former generations of thinkers failed to recognize. But because postmodernism breaks down the notions of universalism and foundationalism, it is able to see things in a different light. It brings to the forefront the violence that inevitably accompanies absolutism, highlights the subjective and relative nature of the narratives in which we have been locked, and, ultimately, makes us conscious of the vast networks of perspectives, values, and world-views which exist beyond our own. Once we realize that the notions of truth and meaning are subject to a particular and unique context, we can safely abandon the hegemonic quest of universalism and accept the 'otherness' we find in other religions or cultures.

This point perhaps supports some of the contemporary Jewish efforts (by, among others, Goshen-Gottstein, Jospe, and Gellman) to address interfaith relations and dialogue. It proves, on the one hand, that relativism is far less of a problem than it is often made out to be. On the other, as I have demonstrated, postmodernism does not inevitably collapse into moral nihilism. The way Derrida characterized justice as an irrepressible, 'indeconstructible' force shows that there still is room in postmodernism for ethics. By accepting the idea of co-ownership of sacred texts, we gain a greater appreciation of the sophistication and subtlety of the religious narrative of other faith communities, without necessarily giving them equal weight to our own.

I conclude with a plea for a beginning. It is crucial that contemporary theologians learn to accommodate postmodern thinking. Looking ahead, we must learn from and engage with the concerns of the present day, including developments in technology, aesthetics, and semiotics, so that Jewish thought remains relevant.

The visionary theology I propose in this book reconfigures certain key religious concepts. It empowers the community by placing upon its shoulders the responsibility of shaping and preserving its own system of values and beliefs. Following a thorough examination of the function of religious language, inspired to a great extent by Wittgenstein and Ricœur, this theology denies itself the purpose of describing reality. It does not lay claim to any form of truth which transcends the particular perspective of its adherents. Rather, it focuses on their imagination, refracting reality in such a way as to enable them to experience the elements of divinity hidden beneath the surface, so to speak.

I have sought to present an embryonic model of an honest, dynamic theology, one that wrestles with various elements of the heartland of the Jewish tradition—from textual hermeneutics to mysticism—and leads to a re-envisioning and reinvigorating approach to contemporary Jewish theology.

BIBLIOGRAPHY

ADORNO, T. W., *Aesthetic Theory* (London: Continuum, 2004).

ALMOND, I., *The New Orientalists: Postmodern Representations of Islam from Foucault to Baudrillard* (London: Tauris, 2007).

AMMICHT-QUINN, R., *Von Lissabon bis Auschwitz: Zum Paradigmawechsel in der Theodizeefrage* (Freiburg: Herder, 1992).

ARIEL, D., *Kabbalah: The Mystic Quest in Judaism* (Lanham, Md.: Rowman & Littlefield, 2006).

ASSAF, D., *Untold Tales of the Hasidim: Crisis and Discontent in the History of Hasidim*, trans. D. Ordan (Waltham, Mass.: Brandeis University Press, 2010).

BAKHTIN, M., *Speech Genres and Other Late Essays*, trans. V. W. McGee (Austin: University of Texas Press, 1986).

BAREL, E., 'On Patriarchy and the Voices of Women: A Critical Glance at Rav Shagar's Approach to Women's Torah Study' (Heb.), *Akdamut*, 20 (2008), 39–54.

BATNITZKY, L., 'Revelation, Language and Commentary', in M. L. Morgan and P. E. Gordon (eds.), *The Cambridge Companion to Modern Jewish Philosophy* (Cambridge: Cambridge University Press, 2007), 300–23.

BAUDRILLARD, J., *Simulacres et simulation* (Paris: Galilée, 1981).

BEN-PAZI, H., 'The Immense House of Postcards: The Idea of Tradition Following Levinas and Derrida', *Forum Philosophicum*, 1 (2016), 43–71.

—— *Interpretation as an Ethical Act: Levinas' Hermeneutics* [Haparshanut kema'aseh musari: hahermenutikah shel imanuel levinas] (Tel Aviv: Resling, 2012).

BEN-SHLOMO, J., 'Gershom Scholem on Pantheism in the Kabbalah', in P. Mendes-Flohr (ed.), *Gershom Scholem: The Man and His Works* (Jerusalem: Israel Academy for Sciences and Humanities, 1994), 56–71.

BENSON, O., and J. STANGROOM, *Why Truth Matters* (London: Continuum, 2006).

BERGER, Y., and D. SHATZ (eds.), *Judaism, Science and Modern Responsibility* (Lanham, Md.: Rowman & Littlefield, 2006).

BERLEANT, A., 'Leaving Relativism', in Y. Ariel, S. Biderman, and O. Rotem (eds.), *Relativism and Beyond* (Boston: Brill, 1998), 68–88.

BERNSTEIN, R., *Beyond Objectivism and Relativism* (Philadelphia: University of Pennsylvania Press, 1983).

BOURGEOIS, P. L., 'Ricœur and Lyotard in Postmodern Dialogue', in D. M. Kaplan (ed.), *Reading Ricœur* (Albany: State University of New York Press, 2008), 163–82.

BOYARIN, D., *Intertextuality and the Reading of Midrash* (Bloomington: Indiana University Press, 1990).

BOYARIN, D., *Socrates and the Fat Rabbis* (Chicago: University of Chicago Press, 2009).

BRAITERMAN, Z., *(God) After Auschwitz: Tradition and Change in Post-Holocaust Jewish Thought* (Princeton, NJ: Princeton University Press, 2002).

BRANDES, Y., T. GANZEL, and H. DEUTSCH (eds.), *Between God and Man: The Believer and Textual Criticism* [Be'einei elohim ve'adam: ha'adam hama'amin vemeḥkar hamikra] (Jerusalem: Beit Morasha, 2015).

BRILL, A., *Judaism and Other Religions: Models of Understanding* (New York: Palgrave Macmillan, 2010).

—— 'Prof. Tamar Ross Responds to the Comments', *Kavvanah* (24 June 2013).

BROGAARD, B., 'Centred Worlds and the Content of Perception', in S. D. Hales (ed.), *A Companion to Relativism* (Oxford: Wiley-Blackwell, 2011), 53–81.

BURRUS, V., '*Creatio ex Libidine*: Reading Ancient Logos Differently', in Y. Sherwood and K. Hart (eds.), *Derrida and Religion: Other Testaments* (Oxford: Routledge, 2005), 114–56.

CAHANA, B., 'The Internet as Metaphor: Education in the Shadow of Postmodernism' (Heb.), *Tsohar*, 33 (2008), 95–102.

—— 'Where the Wind Blows: Contemporary Religious Thought in Response to Postmodernism: Investigation and Critique' (Heb.), *Akdamut*, 20 (2008), 9–38.

CAPLAN, K., *Orthodoxy in the New Times* [Ortodoksiyah be'olam haḥadash] (Jerusalem: Mercaz Zalman Shazar, 2002).

CAPUTO, J. D., *On Religion: Thinking in Action* (New York: Routledge, 2001).

—— *The Weakness of God: The Theology of the Event* (Bloomington: Indiana University Press, 2006).

CARLSON, T. A., 'Postmetaphysical Theology', in K. J. Vanhoozer (ed.), *The Cambridge Companion to Postmodern Theology* (Cambridge: Cambridge University Press, 2003), 58–75.

'The Condition of Jewish Belief: A Symposium', *Commentary*, 42/2 (Aug. 1966), 71–160; repr. *The Condition of Jewish Belief* (New York: Macmillan, 1966).

COX, J. L., *A Guide to the Phenomenology of Religion: Key Figures, Formative Influences, and Subsequent Debates* (New York: Continuum, 2006).

CUPITT, D., *Above Us Only Sky: The Religion of Ordinary Life* (Salem, Mass.: Polebridge Press, 2008).

—— *Taking Leave of God* (London: SCM Press, 2001).

DERRIDA, J., *Acts of Religion*, ed. G. Anidjar (London: Routledge, 2002).

—— *The Animal That Therefore I Am*, trans. D. Mills, ed. M. L. Mallet (New York: Fordham University Press, 2008).

—— *Dissemination* (London: Continuum, 1981).

—— *The Gift of Death* (Chicago: University of Chicago Press, 1995).

—— *Of Grammatology*, trans. G. C. Spivak (Baltimore: Johns Hopkins University Press, 1974).

—— *On the Name*, trans. D. Wood, J. P. Leavey, and I. McLeod, ed. T. Dutoit (Stanford, Calif.: Stanford University Press, 1995).

—— *Speech and Phenomena and Other Essays on Husserl's Theory of Signs* (Evanston, Ill.: Northwestern University Press, 1973).

—— *Writing and Difference* (London: Routledge, 1978).

DESCARTES, R., *Meditations of First Philosophy* (Whitefish, Mont.: Kessinger, 2004).

DROB, S. L., *Kabbalah and Postmodernism: A Dialogue* (New York: Peter Lang, 2009).

EAGLETON, T., *The Illusions of Postmodernism* (Oxford: Blackwell, 1996).

EARNSHAW, S., and J. DOWSON (eds.), *Postmodern Subjects / Postmodern Texts* (Amsterdam: Rodopi, 1995).

ELDAR, I., review of R. Horen, *Life as Longing: New Readings of the Parables of Rabbi Nahman of Bratslav* (Heb.), *Mekor rishon* (5 Nov. 2010), 7–18.

ELIOR, R., *The Paradoxical Ascent to God: The Kabbalistic Theosophy of Habad Hasidism*, trans. J. M. Green (Albany: State University of New York Press, 1993).

FARBER, A., and R. CORRINGTON, *Semiotics of Religion* (Davis: University of California Press, 1993).

FEINSTEIN, M., *Igerot mosheh: yoreh de'ah* [responsa], 4 vols. (New York: Judaica Press, 1959–81).

FELDMANN KAYE, M., 'The Effects of Globalization on Religious Leadership', lecture delivered at the Jerusalem Centre for Ethics, Mishkenot Sha'ananim, Jerusalem, 11 Sept. 2011.

—— 'Interreligious Dialogue in a Postmodern Age' (Heb.), *De'ot*, 55 (2011), 30–3.

—— 'Playing the Language Game: The Meaning of Religious Language in the Theology of Tamar Ross', in R. Irshai and D. Schwartz (eds.), *A New Spirit in the Palace of Torah: Jubilee Volume in Honour of Professor Tamar Ross on the Occasion of her Eightieth Birthday* [Ruah hadashah mima'al lah] (Ramat Gan: Bar-Ilan University Press, 2018), 21*–53*.

—— 'The Use of Hasidism in Responding to the Challenges of Postmodernism and Technology: The Case of Rav Shagar', in Shlomo Zukier (ed.), *Contemporary Uses and Forms of Hasidut* (Northvale, NJ: Jason Aronson, forthcoming).

—— and C. CORIC, 'Interreligious "Reasoning" with Israelis and Palestinians, Bosniak Serbs and Croats', *Bosnae* (forthcoming).

FINKELMAN, Y., 'A Critique of *Expanding the Palace of Torah: Orthodoxy and Feminism* by Tamar Ross', *Edah Journal*, 4/2 (2004), 1–10.

FIRESTONE, R., *Who Are the Real Chosen People? The Meaning of Chosenness in Judaism, Christianity and Islam* (Woodstock, Vt.: Skylights, 2008).

FISHER, C., 'Jewish Philosophy: Living Language at Its Limits', in H. Tirosh-Samuelson and A. W. Hughes (eds.), *Jewish Philosophy for the Twenty-First Century: Personal Reflections* (Boston: Brill, 2014), 81–100.

FOUCAULT, M., *Aesthetics, Method and Epistemology: Essential Works of Foucault 1954–1984*, ed. J. D. Faubion (New York: The New Press, 1994).

—— *Discourse and Truth: The Problematisation of Parrhesia*, lectures given at the University of California at Berkeley, Oct.–Nov. 1983 (Berkeley: University of California Press, 1983).

FOUCAULT, M., *Ethics: Subjectivity and Truth*, trans. R. Hurley et al., ed. P. Rabinow (New York: The New Press, 1994).

—— *Madness and Civilisation: A History of Insanity in an Age of Reason* (London: Routledge, 1989).

FRIMER, A., 'Guarding the Treasure', review of T. Ross, *Expanding the Palace of Torah, BDD: Journal of Torah and Scholarship*, 18 (2007), Eng. section, 67–106.

FUCHS, I., 'Her Own Voice and Torah Study: Rabbi Shimon Rosenberg and Cultural Feminism' [Kol mishelah velimud torah: harav shimon rosenberg vefeminizem tarbuti], unpublished.

GARB, J., *The Chosen Will Become Herds: Studies in Twentieth-Century Kabbalah* (New Haven: Yale University Press, 2009).

GEERTZ, C., *The Interpretation of Cultures: Selected Essays* (New York: Basic Books, 1973).

GELLMAN, Y., 'Judaism and Buddhism: A Jewish Approach to Godless Religions', in A. Goshen-Gottstein and D. Novak (eds.), *Jewish Theology and World Religions* (Oxford: Littman Library, 2012), 299–316.

—— *This Was from God: A Contemporary Theology of Torah and History* (Brighton, Mass.: Academic Studies Press, 2016).

GILLER, P., 'Kabbalah and Contemporary Judaism', in F. E. Greenspahn (ed.), *Jewish Mysticism and Kabbalah: New Insights and Scholarship* (New York: New York University Press, 2011), 231–8.

GILLESPIE, M. A., *Nihilism before Nietzsche* (Chicago: University of Chicago Press, 1995).

GILLMAN, N., 'Covenant and Chosenness in Postmodern Jewish Thought', in R. Jospe, T. G. Madsen, and S. Ward (eds.), *Covenant and Chosenness in Judaism and Mormonism* (Cranbury, NJ: University of Denver, 2001), 103–25.

—— *Sacred Fragments: Recovering Theology for the Modern Jew* (Philadelphia: Jewish Publication Society, 1991).

GOLDMAN, E., D. STATMAN, and A. SAGI, *Judaism without Illusions* [Yahadut lelo ashlayah] (Jerusalem: Shalom Hartman Institute, 2009).

GOLE, N., 'Contemporary Islamic Movements and New Sources of Religious Tolerance' (Heb.), in S. Fischer and A. B. Seligman (eds.), *The Burden of Tolerance: Religious Traditions and the Challenge of Pluralism* [Ol hasovlanut: mesorot datiyot ve'etgar hapluralizem] (Jerusalem: Van Leer Jerusalem Institute / Kibbutz Hame'uhad, 2007), 29–48.

GOODMAN, L. E., 'Doing Jewish Philosophy in America', in R. Jospe and D. Schwartz (eds.), *Jewish Philosophy: Perspectives and Retrospectives* (Boston: Academic Studies Press, 2012), 33–56.

—— *In Defense of Truth: A Pluralistic Approach* (New York: Humanities Books, 2001).

GOSHEN-GOTTSTEIN, A., 'Towards a Jewish Theology of World Religions: Framing the Issues', in A. Goshen-Gottstein and D. Novak (eds.), *Jewish Theology and World Religions* (Oxford: Littman Library, 2012), 1–37.

GREEN, A., *Tormented Master: The Life and Spiritual Quest of Rabbi Nahman of Bratslav* (Woodstock, Vt.: Jewish Lights Publishing, 1992).

GRIFFIN, D. R., J. B. COBB, M. P. FORD, and P. A. Y. GUNTER (eds.), *Founders of Constructive Postmodern Philosophy: Peirce, James, Bergson, Whitehead and Hartshorne* (Albany: State University of New York Press, 1993).

GURVITZ, D., *Postmodernism: Culture and Literature at the End of the Twentieth Century* [Postmodernizem: tarbut vesifrut besof hame'ah ha'esrim] (Tel Aviv: Dvir, 1998).

GUR-ZEV, I., *Education in the Postmodern Age* [Ḥinukh be'idan hapostmoderni] (Jerusalem: Magnes Press, 1996).

HABERMAS, J., *The Philosophical Discourse of Modernity*, trans. F. Lawrence (Cambridge, Mass.: MIT Press, 1987).

HALBERTAL, M., *Interpretative Revolutions in the Making* [Mahapekhot parshaniyot behithavutan] (Jerusalem: Magnes Press, 1997).

HALIVNI, D. W., *Revelation Restored: Divine Writ and Critical Responses* (Oxford: Oxford University Press, 1998; repr. SCM Press, 2001).

HALLAMISH, M., *An Introduction to Kabbalah*, trans. R. Bar Ilan and O. Wiskind-Elper (Albany: State University of New York Press, 1999).

HANDELMAN, S., *The Slayers of Moses: The Emergence of Rabbinic Interpretation in Modern Literary Theory* (Albany: State University of New York Press, 1982).

HARRIS, J. F., *Analytic Philosophy of Religion* (Dordrecht: Kluwer, 2002).

HARRIS, M., *Faith without Fear: Unresolved Issues in Modern Orthodoxy* (Portland, Oreg.: Vallentine Mitchell, 2015).

HASHKES, H., 'Studying Torah as a Reality Check: The Study of a Midrash', *Journal of Jewish Thought and Philosophy*, 16/2 (2008), 149–93.

—— 'Towards a Jewish Postliberal Theology' (Heb.), *Identities: Journal of Jewish Culture and Identity*, 2 (2012), 121–50.

HAYIM OF VOLOZHIN, *Nefesh haḥayim* (1824).

HEFTER, H., 'Is Belief in Revelation Possible in the Postmodern Age?', *Jerusalem Post Magazine* (21 Jan. 2011).

HEIDEGGER, M., *The Basic Problems of Phenomenology*, trans. A. Hofstadter (Bloomington: Indiana University Press, 1982).

—— *Nietzsche: Nihilism* (New York: Harper & Row, 1982).

—— *The Phenomenology of Religious Life*, trans. M. Fritsch and J. A. Gosetti-Ferencei (Bloomington: Indiana University Press, 2004).

HERMAN, J. R., 'The Contextual Illusion', in K. Patton and B. C. Ray (eds.), *A Magic Still Dwells: Comparative Religion in the Postmodern Age* (Los Angeles: University of California Press, 2000), 92–100.

HICK, J., *Classical and Contemporary Readings in the Philosophy of Religion* (Upper Saddle River, NJ: Prentice Hall, 1990).

HUSS, B., M. PASI, and K. VON STUCKARD (eds.), *Kabbalah and Modernity: Interpretations, Translations and Adaptations* (Leiden: Martinus Nijhoff, 2010).

HUYSSENS, A., *After the Great Divide: Modernism, Mass Culture, Postmodernism* (Bloomington: Indiana University Press, 1986).

HYMAN, G., *The Predicament of Postmodern Theology: Radical Orthodoxy or Nihilist Textualism?* (Louisville, Ky.: Westminster John Knox Press, 2001).

JACOBS, L., *We Have Reason to Believe: Some Aspects of Jewish Thought Examined in Light of Modern Thought* (London: Vallentine Mitchell, 1962).

JAMES, W., *Pragmatism: A New Name for Some Old Ways of Thinking* (Rockville, Md.: Arc Manor, 2008).

JOSPE, R., 'Pluralism out of the Sources of Judaism: Religious Pluralism without Relativism', *Studies in Jewish-Christian Relations*, 2/2 (2008), 92–113.

JOTKOWITZ, A., '"And Now the Child Will Ask": The Post-Modern Theology of Rav Shagar', *Tradition*, 45/2 (2012), 49–66.

KANT, I., *Religion and Rational Theology*, trans. and ed. A. W. Wood and G. di Giovanni (Cambridge: Cambridge University Press, 1996).

KAPLAN, A., *Rabbi Nachman's Wisdom* (Jerusalem: Breslov Research Institute, 1973).

KAUFMAN, T., *In All Your Ways Know Him: The Concept of God and Materialism in Early Hasidism* [Bekhol derakheikha da'ehu: tefisat haelohut veha'avodah begashmiyut bereshit haḥasidut] (Ramat Gan: Bar Ilan University Press, 2009).

KAUFMAN, W. E., *Contemporary Jewish Philosophies* (Detroit: Wayne State University Press, 1992).

KEARNEY, R., *Anatheism: Returning to God after God* (New York: Columbia University Press, 2010).

—— 'Deconstruction, God and the Possible', in Y. Sherwood and K. Hart (eds.), *Derrida and Religion: Other Testaments* (New York: Routledge, 2005), 297–308.

—— *The God Who May Be: The Hermeneutics of Religion* (Bloomington: Indiana University Press, 2001).

KELLNER, M., *Must a Jew Believe Anything?* (London: Littman Library, 1999).

KEPNES, S. (ed.), *Interpreting Judaism in a Postmodern Age* (New York: New York University Press, 1996).

—— review of A. W. Hughes and E. R. Wolfson (eds.), *New Directions in Jewish Philosophy*, H-Judaic (Apr. 2013).

—— *The Text as Thou* (Bloomington: Indiana University Press, 1992).

—— P. OCHS, and R. GIBBS, *Reasoning after Revelation: Dialogues in Postmodern Jewish Philosophy* (Boulder, Colo.: Westview Press, 1998).

KLEIN, E., *Kabbalah of Creation: The Mysticism of Isaac Luria, Founder of Modern Kabbalah* (Berkeley, Calif.: North Atlantic Books, 2005).

KLEMM, D. E., *Meanings in Text and Actions* (Charlottesville: University Press of Virginia, 1993).

—— 'Philosophy and Kerygma: Ricœur as Reader of the Bible', in D. M. Kaplan (ed.), *Reading Ricœur* (Albany: State University of New York Press, 2008), 47–68.

KUGEL, J., 'Two Introductions to Midrash', *Prooftexts*, 3/2 (1983), 131–55.

KULA, A., *Existential or Non-Essential? History, Language, Religious Language and the Nature of Deity* [Havaiya o lo haya? Historiyah vesifrut, safah datit vedemut ha'el] (Jerusalem: Kibbutz Hadati, 2011).

LACAN, J., *Écrits* (Paris: Seuil, 1973).

LAST-STONE, S., 'Tolerance Versus Pluralism in Judaism' (Heb.), in S. Fischer and A. B. Seligman (eds.), *The Burden of Tolerance: Religious Traditions and the Challenge of Pluralism* [Ol hasovlanut: mesorot datiyot ve'etgar haplural-izem] (Jerusalem: Van Leer Jerusalem Institute/Kibbutz Hame'uhad, 2007), 219–36.

LEVINAS, E., *Beyond the Verse: Talmudic Readings and Lectures*, trans. G. D. Mole (London: Athlone Press, 1994).

LEWIS, D. K., *On the Plurality of Worlds* (Oxford: Blackwell, 1986).

LINDBECK, G., *The Nature of Doctrine: Religion and Theology in a Postliberal Age* (Philadelphia: Westminster Press, 1984).

LYOTARD, J.-F., *The Postmodern Condition: A Report on Knowledge*, trans. G. Bennington and B. Massumi (Minneapolis: University of Minnesota Press, 1984).

MAGID, S., *God's Voice from the Void: Old and New Studies in Bratslav Hasidism* (Albany: State University of New York Press, 2002).

—— 'The Settler Nakba and the Rise of Post-Modern Post-Zionist Religious Ideology on the West Bank', *The Tablet* (19 Sept. 2017).

MAHMUTCEHAJIC, R., 'The Bosnian Question' (Heb.), in S. Fischer and A. B. Seligman (eds.), *The Burden of Tolerance: Religious Traditions and the Challenge of Pluralism* [Ol hasovlanut: mesorot datiyot ve'etgar hapluralizem] (Jerusalem: Van Leer Jerusalem Institute/Kibbutz Hame'uhad, 2007), 81–118.

MAIMON, D., 'Tolerance Despite Disagreement in Medieval Egypt: Rabbi Avraham the Son of Maimonides and the Islamic Mystics' (Heb.), in S. Fischer and A. B. Seligman (eds.), *The Burden of Tolerance: Religious Traditions and the Challenge of Pluralism* [Ol hasovlanut: mesorot datiyot ve'etgar hapluralizem] (Jerusalem: Van Leer Jerusalem Institute/Kibbutz Hame'uhad, 2007), 286–301.

MAIMONIDES, *Guide of the Perplexed*, trans. S. Pines (Chicago: Chicago University Press, 1963).

MAKKREEL, R. A., and S. LUFT (eds.), *Neo-Kantianism in Contemporary Philosophy* (Bloomington: Indiana University Press, 2010).

MARGALIT, A., 'On Religious Pluralism', in D. Heyd (ed.), *Toleration: An Elusive Virtue* (Princeton: Princeton University Press, 2001), 147–57.

MARION, J., *On the Ego and on God: Further Cartesian Questions*, trans. C. M. Gschwandtner (New York: Fordham University Press, 2007).

—— *The Visible and the Revealed*, trans. C. M. Gschwandtner et al. (New York: Fordham University Press, 2008).

MARK, Z., *Mysticism and Madness: The Religious Thought of Rabbi Nachman of Bratslav* (Jerusalem: Kogod Library of Jewish Studies, Shalom Hartman Institute, 2009).

MEHLMAN, J. (ed.), *French Freud: Structural Studies in Psychoanalysis* (New Haven, Conn.: Yale University Press, 1972).

MERLEAU-PONTY, M., *Phenomenology of Perception* (New York: Routledge, 2002).

MEVORAKH, Y., 'Secular Belief as Reification of the Infinite' (Heb.), *Mekor rishon* (4 Jan. 2012).

MILL, J. S., *Utilitarianism*, ed. O. Piest (Indianapolis: Bobbs-Merrill, 1957).

MIRON, G., *The Waning of the Emancipation Era: Historical Memory and Images of the Past under the Impact of Fascism. Germany, France, Hungary* [Bestav yemei ha'emantsipatsiyah: zikaron histori vedimui ever taḥat iyum hafashism. germaniyah, tzarfat, hungariyah] (Jerusalem: Zalman Shazar Centre for Jewish History, 2011).

MURDOCH, I., *The Sovereignty of Good* (London: Routledge, 1971).

NAHMAN OF BRATSLAV, *Likutei moharan* [hasidic interpretations of rabbinic texts] (New York, 1966).

NISHITANI, K., *Religion and Nothingness*, trans. J. Van Bragt (Berkeley: University of California Press, 1982).

OCHS, P., *Another Reformation: Postliberal Christianity and the Jews* (Grand Rapids, Mich.: Baker, 2011).

—— *Pragmatism and the Logic of Scripture* (Cambridge: Cambridge University Press, 1998).

—— (ed.), *The Return to Scripture in Judaism and Christianity: Essays in Postcritical Scriptural Interpretation* (New York: Paulist Press, 1993).

O'GRADY, P., *Relativism* (Montreal: McGill-Queens University Press, 2002).

OLTHIUS, J. H. (ed.), *Religion With/Out Religion: The Prayers and Tears of John D. Caputo* (London: Routledge, 2002).

OPHIR, A., 'Postmodernism: A Philosophical Position' (Heb.), in I. Gur-Ze'ev (ed.), *Education in a Postmodern Age* [Ḥinukh be'idan hapostmoderni] (Jerusalem: Alma, 1987), 135–64.

OUAKNIN, M. A., *The Burnt Book: Reading the Talmud* (Princeton, NJ: Princeton University Press, 1995).

PATTON, K., and B. C. RAY (eds.), *A Magic Still Dwells: Comparative Religion in the Postmodern Age* (Los Angeles: University of California Press, 2000).

PEIRCE, C. S., *Peirce on Signs: Writings on Semiotics*, ed. J. Hope (Chapel Hill: University of North Carolina Press, 1991).

PENNER, H., *Mysticism and Religious Traditions* (Oxford: Oxford University Press, 1983).

PHILLIPS, D. Z., 'Religious Beliefs and Language Games', in B. Mitchell (ed.), *The Philosophy of Religion* (London: Oxford University Press, 1971).

PHILLIPS, P. J. J., *The Challenge of Relativism: Its Nature and Limits* (London: Continuum, 2007).

PINNOCK, S. K., *Beyond Theodicy: Jewish and Christian Continental Thinkers Respond to the Holocaust* (Albany: State University of New York Press, 2002).

POPPER, K., *Conjectures and Refutations: The Growth of Scientific Knowledge* (New York: Routledge, 2010).

PROTHERO, S., *God Is Not One: The Eight Rival Religions that Run the World* (London: HarperCollins, 2011).

PUTNAM, H., 'Rorty on Reality and Justification', in Y. Ariel, S. Biderman, and O. Rotem (eds.), *Relativism and Beyond* (Leiden: Brill, 1998), 3–14.

PYPER, H. S., 'Other Eyes: Reading and Not Reading the Hebrew Scriptures/Old Testament with a Little Help from Derrida and Cixous', in Y. Sherwood and K. Hart (eds.), *Derrida and Religion: Other Testaments* (New York: Routledge, 2005), 159–74.

RAVITZKY, A., 'The Question of Tolerance in the Jewish Religious Tradition', in Y. Elman and J. S. Gurock (eds.), *Hazon Nahum: Studies in Jewish Law, Thought and History Presented to Dr. Norman Lamm on the Occasion of His Seventieth Birthday* (New York: Yeshiva University Press, 1997), 386–400.

RICŒUR, P., *The Rule of Metaphor: The Creation of Meaning in Language*, trans. R. Czerny, K. McLaughlin, and J. Costello (London: Routledge, 2003).

—— and D. IHDE, *The Conflict of Interpretations: Essays in Hermeneutics* (Evanston, Ill.: Northwestern University Press, 1974).

RORTY, R., *Consequences of Pragmatism: Essays 1972–1980* (Minneapolis: University of Minnesota Press, 1982).

—— *An Ethics for Today: Finding Common Ground between Philosophy and Religion* (New York: Columbia University Press, 2011).

RORTY, R., *Philosophy as Cultural Politics* (Cambridge: Cambridge University Press, 2007).

—— *Philosophy and the Mirror of Nature* (Princeton, NJ: Princeton University Press, 1980).

—— 'Remarks on Deconstruction and Pragmatism', in S. Critchley and C. Mouffe (eds.), *Deconstruction and Pragmatism* (New York: Routledge, 1997), 13–19.

—— *The Rorty Reader*, ed. C. J. Voparil and R. J. Bernstein (Oxford: Wiley-Blackwell, 2010).

—— G. VATTIMO, and S. ZABALA, *The Future of Religion* (New York: Columbia University Press, 2005).

ROSEN, S., 'Nietzsche's Double Rhetoric: Which Nihilism?', in J. Metzger (ed.), *Nietzsche, Nihilism, and the Philosophy of the Future* (London: Continuum, 2009), 9–19.

ROSENAK, A., *Halakhah as an Agent of Change: Critical Studies in the Philosophy of Halakhah* [Hahalakhah kemeḥolelet shinui: iyunim bikorti'im bephilosophiah shel halakhah] (Jerusalem: Magnes Press, 2009).

—— '"Pre-Postmodern": Four Jewish Nationalist Thinkers of the Last Century', trans. J. Linsider, *Common Knowledge*, 18/2 (2012), 292–311.

ROSENBERG, S., 'Revelation', in A. A. Cohen and P. R. Mendes-Flohr (eds.), *Contemporary Jewish Religious Thought: Essays on Critical Concepts, Movements and Beliefs* (New York: The Free Press, 1988), 813–17.

—— *Torah and Science in New Jewish Thought* [Torah umada behagut yehudit haḥadashah] (Jerusalem: Magnes Press, 1999).

ROSS, T., 'The Cognitive Value of Religious Truth Statements: Rabbi A. I. Kook and Postmodernism', in Y. Elman and J. S. Gurock (eds.), *Hazon Nahum: Studies in Jewish Law, Thought and History Presented to Dr. Norman Lamm on the Occasion of His Seventieth Birthday* (New York: Yeshiva University Press, 1997), 479–528; repr. in H. Tirosh-Samuelson and A. W. Hughes (eds.), *Tamar Ross: Constructing Faith* (Leiden: Brill, 2016), 41–85.

—— *Expanding the Palace of Torah: Orthodoxy and Feminism* (New Haven: Brandeis University Press, 2004).

—— 'Guarding the Treasure and Guarding the Tongue: Response to A. Frimer's Review of *Expanding the Palace of Torah: Orthodoxy and Feminism*', *BDD: Journal of Torah and Scholarship*, 19 (2008), 93–124.

—— 'The Implications of the Feminization of Theology: Deconstructing Sacred Texts as an Educational Issue', in Z. Gross, L. Davies, and Al-K. Diab (eds.), *Gender, Religion, and Education in a Chaotic Postmodern World* (Dordrecht: Springer, 2013), 125–36.

—— 'Overcoming the Epistemological Barrier', in H. Tirosh-Samuelson and A. W. Hughes (eds.), *Jewish Philosophy for the Twenty-First Century: Personal Reflections* (Boston: Brill, 2014), 372–89.

—— 'A Premature Enthusiasm? Several Comments on "Where is the Wind Blowing? Contemporary Religious Thought Confronts Postmodernism—A Survey and Critique" by Baruch Kahana' (Heb.), *Akdamut*, 21 (2008), 178–83.

—— 'Reflections on the Possibilities of Interfaith Communication in Our Day', *Edah Journal*, 1/1 (2000), 1–6.

—— 'Religious Belief in a Postmodern Age', in A. Sagi and D. Schwartz (eds.), *Faith: Jewish Perspectives* (Boston: Academic Studies Press, 2013), 188–240.

—— 'Response to Yoel Finkelman, "A Critique of *Expanding the Palace of Torah*"', *Edah Journal*, 4/2 (2004), 11–25.

—— *Two Commentaries on the Teaching of Tsimtsum: R. Hayim of Volozhin and R. Shneur Zalman* [Shenei peirushim letorat hatsimtsum: rabi shneiur zalman miliyadi] (Jerusalem: Hebrew University of Jerusalem, 1981), 153–69.

ROTH, M., 'Judaism in the Straits of Modernity and Postmodernity' (Heb.), in S. Rosenberg, A. Berholtz, and B. Ish-Shalom (eds.), *In the Ways of Peace: Aspects of Jewish Thought* [Bedarkhei shalom: iyunim behagut yehudit] (Jerusalem: Beit Morasha, 2007), 33–54.

RYNHOLD, D., review of A. W. Hughes and E. R. Wolfson (eds.), *New Directions in Jewish Philosophy*, *Journal of Modern Jewish Studies*, 11 (2012), 430.

SACKS, J., *Crisis and Covenant: Jewish Thought after the Holocaust* (Manchester: Manchester University Press, 1992).

—— *The Dignity of Difference* (London: Bloomsbury, 2001).

—— *The Great Partnership: Science, Religion and the Search for Meaning* (New York: Schocken, 2011).

—— 'Jewish Identity: The Concept of a Chosen People', *Faith Lectures* (8 May 2001), Office of Rabbi Sacks at <rabbisacks.org>.

—— 'The Messianic Idea Today', *Faith Lectures* (6 June 2001), Office of Rabbi Sacks at <rabbisacks.org>.

—— 'Nostalgia for the Numinous', review of T. Eagleton, *Culture and the Death of God*, *Jewish Review of Books*, 18 (2014).

—— *Not in God's Name: Confronting Religious Violence* (London: Hodder & Stoughton, 2015).

—— 'Revelation: Torah from Heaven', *Faith Lectures* (23 Feb. 2001), Office of Rabbi Sacks at <rabbisacks.org>.

—— *Universalizing Particularity*, ed. H. Tirosh-Samuelson and A. Hughes (Boston: Brill, 2013).

SAGI, A., *The Open Canon: On the Meaning of Halakhic Discourse* (London: Continuum, 2007).

—— 'Toward a Jewish Philosophy', in H. Tirosh-Samuelson and A. W. Hughes (eds.), *Jewish Philosophy for the Twenty-First Century: Personal Reflections* (Boston: Brill, 2014), 391–409.

SAGI, A., *Tradition vs. Traditionalism: Contemporary Perspectives in Jewish Thought*, trans. B. Stein (Amsterdam: Rodopi, 2008).

——Z. SAGI, D. SCHWARTZ, and Y. STERN (eds.), *Judaism Inside and Out: Dialogue between Worlds* [Yahadut panim veḥutz: diyalog ben olamot] (Jerusalem: Magnes Press, 1999).

SAUSSURE, F. DE, *Course in General Linguistics*, trans. W. Baskin (Glasgow: Fontana/Collins, 1974).

SERI-LEVI, G., review of G. Zivan, *Religion without Illusions: Facing a Postmodern World* (Heb.), *Hatsofeh* (7 Apr. 2006).

SHAGAR [SHIMON GERSHON ROSENBERG], *Broken Vessels: Torah and Religious Zionism in a Postmodern Environment* [Kelim shevurim: torah vetsiyonut-datit besevivah postmodernit: derashot lemo'adei zemanenu], ed. O. Tzurieli (Efrat: Institute for the Writings of Rav Shagar, 2004).

—— *Chance and Providence: Discourses on the Inner Meaning of Purim*, trans. N. Moses, ed. O. Tzurieli (Jerusalem: Toby Press, 2010).

—— *Faith Shattered and Restored*, trans. E. Leshem, ed. Z. Maor (Jerusalem: Maggid, 2017).

—— 'Father God, Mother Land' (Heb.), *Hatsofeh* (2001), 9–13; (2004), 149–58.

—— 'A Group of Friends with Yarmulkes Go to the Pub' (Heb.), *Hatsofeh* (2003), 10.

—— *In the Shadow of Faith: Discourses and Articles for the Festival of Tabernacles* [Betzel ha'emunah: derashot vema'amarim lehag sukot], ed. Z. Maor (Efrat: Institute for the Writings of Rav Shagar, 2011).

—— 'The Land is a Body', *Mekor rishon* (29 Jan. 2010), 22–3.

—— *Loving You Unto Death* [Ahevukh ad mavet], ed. N. Samet (Efrat: Machon Binah Le'itim, 2004).

—— *Man to Woman, a Jew to His Land* [Ish le'ishah, yehudi le'artso] (2004).

—— 'My Faith' [Emunati], unpublished (2004).

—— 'New Age and Kabbalah' (Heb.), *Kelim shevurim*, 2 (forthcoming).

—— *On His Torah He Meditates: The Study of Talmud as a Quest for God* [Betorato yehegeh: limud gemara kevakashat elokim], ed. Z. Maor (Efrat: Institute for the Writings of Rav Shagar, 2010).

—— *The Remnant of Faith: Postmodern Teachings on Jewish Festivals* [She'erit ha'emunah: derashot postmoderniyot lemo'adei yisra'el], ed. Y. Mevorah and E. Abramovitz (Efrat: Institute for the Writings of Rav Shagar, 2014).

—— 'Similar Qualities of Postmodern Religious Identity: Four Different Voices on the Theme of Change' (Heb.), *De'ot*, 29 (2007), 4–8.

—— *Tablets and Broken Tablets: Jewish Thought in the Age of Postmodernism* [Luḥot veshivrei luḥot], ed. Dov Eichenwald and Amichai Berholtz (Efrat: Institute for the Writings of Rav Shagar, 2013).

—— *Thy Face I Shall Seek: Discourses of Harav Shagar Delivered at Yeshivat Hakotel in 1991* [Paneikha avakesh: derashot shene'emru beyeshivat hakotel], ed. U. Fuchs and M. Werdiger (Efrat: Institute for the Writings of Rav Shagar, 2007).

—— *A Time of Freedom: Discourses for Pesach* [Zeman shel ḥerut: derashot leḥag hapesaḥ], ed. Y. Mevorah (Efrat: Institute for the Writings of Rav Shagar, 2011).

—— *We Walk in Fervour: Selected Works* [Nehelakh beragesh: mivḥar ma'amarim], ed. Z. Maor and S. Deutsch (Efrat: Institute for the Writings of Rav Shagar, 2008).

—— and Y. DREYFUS, *Beloved Friends: Wedding Homilies* [Re'im ha'ahuvim: derashot ḥatunah] (Efrat: Institute for the Writings of Rav Shagar, 2008).

SHAPIRO, M., *Changing the Immutable: How Orthodox Judaism Rewrites Its History* (Oxford: Littman Library, 2015).

—— *The Limits of Orthodox Theology: Maimonides' Thirteen Principles Reappraised* (Oxford: Littman Library, 2004).

SHATZ, D., 'Rav Kook and Modern Orthodoxy: The Ambiguity of Openness', in M. Z. Sokol (ed.), *Engaging Modernity: Rabbinic Leaders and the Challenge of the Twentieth Century* (Northvale, NJ: Jason Aronson, 1997), 91–115.

SHAY, E., 'Research in Jewish Thought and the Postmodern Discourse' (Heb.), *Tsohar*, 33 (2008), 51–7.

SHELEG, Y., 'How Do You Like Your Halakha?', *Haaretz* (27 Sept. 2006).

SHNERB, N., 'A Parable of a Wise Man Who Despairs of Reason' (Heb.), review of Shagar, *Broken Vessels*. At http://old.kipasruga.com/upload/users_files/1061. PDF, visited 23 May 2018.

SHNEUR ZALMAN, *Ma'amarei admor hazaken*, 27 vols. (Brooklyn, NY: Kehot Publication Society, n.d.).

—— *Tanya: likutei amarim* (Brooklyn, NY: Kehot Publication Society, 2014).

SHOKEK, S., *Kabbalah and the Art of Being: The Smithsonian Lectures* (London: Routledge, 2001).

SILMAN, Y., *The Voice is Heard at Sinai: Once or Ongoing?* [Kol gadol velo yasaf: torat yisra'el ben shelemut lehishtalemut] (Jerusalem: Magnes Press, 1999).

SOLOMON, N., *Torah from Heaven: The Reconstruction of Faith* (Oxford: Littman Library, 2012).

SOLOMON, R. C., *From Rationalism to Existentialism: The Existentialists and Their Nineteenth-Century Backgrounds* (Lanham, Md.: Rowman & Littlefield, 2001).

STAAL, F., 'Beyond Relativism', in Y. Ariel, S. Biderman, and O. Rotem (eds.), *Relativism and Beyond* (Boston: Brill, 1998), 37–66.

STEINBOCK, A. J., *Phenomenology and Mysticism: The Verticality of Religious Experience* (Bloomington: Indiana University Press, 2007).

STERN, N., *Post-Orthodoxy: An Anthropological Analysis of the Theological and Sociological Boundaries of Contemporary Orthodox Judaism* (New York: State University of New York at Binghamton, 2008).

TAYLOR, M. C., *Erring: A Postmodern A/theology* (Chicago: University of Chicago Press, 1984).

TIROSH-SAMUELSON, H., 'The Preciousness of Being Human: Jewish Philosophy and the Challenge of Technology', in H. Tirosh-Samuelson and A. W. Hughes (eds.), *Jewish Philosophy for the Twenty-First Century: Personal Reflections* (Boston: Brill, 2014), 428–57.

TZUR, A., 'The Deconstruction of Holiness: Preface to the Thought of Rav Shagar' (Heb.), *Akdamut*, 21 (2008), 110–39.

UEBEL, T. E., *Overcoming Logical Positivism from Within* (Atlanta, Ga.: Rodopi, 1992).

URIAN, D., 'Baalei Teshuvah: Returnees to the Religious Fold in Israeli Theatre', in D. Urian and E. Karsh (eds.), *In Search of Identity: Jewish Aspects in Israeli Culture* (London: Frank Cass, 1999), 230–52.

WALLACE, M., 'Ricœur, Rorty and the Question of Revelation', in D. Klemm and W. Schweiker (eds.), *Meanings in Text and Actions* (Charlottesville: University Press of Virginia, 1993), 275–91.

WITTGENSTEIN, L., *Lectures and Conversations on Aesthetics, Psychology and Religious Belief*, ed. C. Barrett (Oxford: Blackwell, 1970).

—— *Philosophical Investigations*, trans. G. E. M. Anscombe (Oxford: Blackwell, 1953).

WOLFSON, E., 'From Sealed Book to Open Text: Time, Memory and Narrativity in Kabbalistic Hermeneutics', in S. Kepnes (ed.), *Interpreting Judaism in a Postmodern Age* (New York: New York University Press, 1996), 145–80.

—— 'Skepticism and Keeping Faith', in H. Tirosh-Samuelson and A. W. Hughes (eds.), *Jewish Philosophy for the Twenty-First Century: Personal Reflections* (Boston: Brill, 2014), 481–515.

WURZBURGER, W. S., 'Rav Soloveitchik as a Posek of Postmodern Orthodoxy', in M. Z. Sokol (ed.), *Engaging Modernity: Rabbinic Leaders and the Challenge of the Twentieth Century* (Northvale, NJ: Jason Aronson, 1997), 119–36.

WYSCHOGROD, E., 'Hasidism, Hellenism, Holocaust', in S. Kepnes (ed.), *Interpreting Judaism in a Postmodern Age* (New York: New York University Press, 1996), 301–20.

—— *Saints and Postmodernism: Revisioning Moral Philosophy* (Chicago: University of Chicago Press, 1990).

ZIVAN, G., *Religion without Illusions: Facing a Postmodern World* [Dat lelo ashelayah; nokhah olam postmoderni] (Jerusalem: Kibbutz Hame'uhad/Shalom Hartman Institute, 2005).

ŽIŽEK, S., *Enjoy Your Symptom! Jacques Lacan in Hollywood and Out*, 2nd edn. (New York: Routledge, 2001).

—— *Looking Awry: An Introduction to Jacques Lacan through Popular Culture* (Cambridge, Mass.: MIT Press, 1991), 21–47.

—— *On Belief* (New York: Routledge, 2001).

—— *The Parallax View* (Cambridge, Mass,: MIT Press, 2006).

—— *The Sublime Object of Ideology* (London: Verso, 1989).

ZOHAR, Z., 'Something Dreadful in the City of Damascus' (Heb.), in S. Fischer and A. B. Seligman (eds.), *The Burden of Tolerance: Religious Traditions and the Challenge of Pluralism* [Ol hasovlanut: mesorot datiyot ve'etgar hapluralizem] (Jerusalem: Van Leer Jerusalem Institute / Kibbutz Hame'uhad, 2007), 302–29.

INDEX

Printed and bound by CPI Group (UK) Ltd, Croydon, CR0 4YY

13/04/2025

14656583-0005